W9-CLA-699

# Keep On Pushing

## Black Power Music
## From Blues to Hip-Hop

**Denise Sullivan**

Lawrence Hill Books

Library of Congress Cataloging-in-Publication Data

Sullivan, Denise.
  Keep on pushing : Black power music from blues to hip-hop / Denise Sullivan.
    p. cm.
  Includes bibliographical references and index.
  ISBN 978-1-55652-817-0
  1. African Americans—Music—History and criticism. 2. Black power—United
States. 3. Blacks—Music—History and criticism. I. Title.
  ML3556.S94 2011
  781.64089'96073—dc22
                                    2011013914

All lyrics reprinted by permission of Len Chandler, Buffy Sainte-Marie, Richie Havens, Phranc, Michael Franti, Janis Ian, Penelope Houston, and Debora Iyall.

Cover design: TG Design
Cover photographs left to right: Ornette Coleman, 1980s; James Brown, 1960s; Nina Simone, late 1960s; and Flavor Flav and Chuck D of Public Enemy all used with credit to Photofest. Crowd supporting Black Panthers ca. 1960s–70s © Flip Schulke/Corbis.
Interior design: PerfecType, Nashville, TN

© 2011 by Denise Sullivan
All rights reserved
Published by Lawrence Hill Books
An imprint of Chicago Review Press, Incorporated
814 North Franklin Street
Chicago, Illinois 60610
ISBN: 978-1-55652-817-0
Printed in the United States of America
5 4 3 2 1

# Keep On Pushing

To all the freedom singers: past, present, and, especially, future

# Contents

# Intro

Not long before she died in 2008, the singer Odetta was asked if there were a song she'd like to be remembered by. "Yes," she said, then from her depths rose the notes of the lamentation "Sometimes I Feel Like a Motherless Child." Outlining the song's genius, she noted, "Not all the time, but *sometimes*, I feel like a motherless child."

Odetta had spent a lifetime devoted to singing and to the study of the songs of her African American heritage. Following my own research in preparation for writing this book, it's Odetta's remarks on the songs of slavery—and why they are also the songs of freedom and liberation—that I found to be the most valuable in conveying the essence of music's potential to unleash power. She said,

> You're walking down life's road, society's foot is on your throat. Every which way you turn you can't get out from under that foot. And you reach a fork in the road and you can either lie down and die, or insist upon your own individual life. Those people who made up the songs were the ones who insisted upon life and living, who reaffirmed themselves. They didn't just fall down into the cracks or the holes. I think that was an incredible example for me and I learned from that.[1]

Odetta's words speak directly to the question of power—who's got it and who does not—and its fundamental relationship at the intersection of music and political and social movements. That Odetta was an African American and a woman giving her fierce voice to the concept of power is no coincidence. That she first took a stand in the pre-civil-rights era of the fifties is purely inspirational; that she kept up the momentum for fifty years is miraculous. She was a champion of life, and she sang as if she'd die for her people.

Born on New Year's Eve in Birmingham, Alabama, Odetta was just nineteen when she was introduced to the music of Lead Belly. He immediately became her favorite singer after she heard his music on the coffeehouse and cafe scene just starting to brew in San Francisco in 1949, the year he died. The old songs were still very much alive to her, waiting to be put to use for a new purpose, and she set about learning Lead Belly's slave songs, work songs, prison songs, and freedom songs, trusting in her bones that these musical depictions of human strength and suffering would still need to be sung one hundred years or more from when she was born. Picking up the guitar and letting her hair go natural, Odetta claimed her power. "Folk music straightened my back and kinked my hair," she said, and it did so just in time for a new style of music coming on. It was a little more forceful, a little more demanding, and it spoke to the new generation, with its mind set on freedom.

Long before civil rights, Black Power, and women's liberation were designated the most powerful people movements in the twentieth century, Odetta was among those visionary souls who dared to sing a dream of freedom. Her story, like those of the musicians you will read about here, creates a bridge from the old world to the new, from the time when black folks and women were supposed to know their so-called places to the era of broader freedoms and equality in the ongoing fight for justice. Like prayers, the songs were free for the singing, and Odetta was free to sing them, though as an earthbound woman, it wasn't always going to be easy—the look on her face often revealed more than the songs did. The civil rights movement with which she was aligned has been well documented; plenty has also been written on the connection between the gospel and soul music that immediately followed in the new era of black pride and consciousness. Less documented is the collective exploration of cultural heritage and identity, the pride, power, and political changes identity creates, and music's key role in those explorations and changes. To put it another way: among political and social historians it is widely accepted that the Black Power movement was the model for women's liberation, gay liberation, and other minority and cultural liberation movements that followed, winning rights for Native, Latino, and Asian Americans, and seniors, children, and the handicapped, among other people. And just as Black Power had its roots in the freedom movements that preceded it, the music that accompanied Black Power was rooted in earlier movements, though the way it grew is trickier to delineate. The soundtrack to Black Power was created by all kinds of soul-powered people: activists, orators, and poets, as well as musicians of all types, from classical to rock. The soundtrack's route from there to here is circuitous, with unexpected twists, standstills, violence, surprise breakthroughs, and glass ceilings. It also includes white and Native people, as did the Freedom Rides organized by the Congress of Racial Equality (CORE) and the Student Nonviolent Coordinating Committee (SNCC) in the sixties and John Brown's and Harriet Tubman's abolitionist efforts one hundred years earlier. Indeed, there were inspirational moments along freedom's road in the sixties—good reasons to celebrate and occasional victory songs to be sung. But the soundtrack to liberation dared to question the new freedoms and the quality of life "freedom" brought in the face of liberty's inconsistencies and its costs, especially in a time of war: "What's Going On?" "Who Will Survive America?" and "Compared to What?" And though the movement may have been extinguished, its soundtrack will not be vanquished—though like the movement, there were some serious attempts made to silence it.

Undeniably, considering how it motivated young people and documented the times, music's intersection with political and social events in the sixties has not been matched since. The period was a clear demonstration of how anger at injustice and a desire for change could galvanize large groups of people for a cause, just as sure as the music could. The songs of black liberation are about pulling together as a people in the name of survival. The songs ask listeners to join together and do something. The songs stir the soul in the place where the universal chords of sisterhood and brotherhood ring. Liberation music is music as a necessary companion, a friend who entertains, tells stories, and soothes pain—in a time of rising tension, war, and senseless violence.

Though some music from the sixties sounds dated and clearly belongs to the psychedelic era, the music rooted in black liberation is unbound by time. It is always relevant, any time or any place in the world where people are broke and hungry and in need of relief. Empowering music—the old songs and the new—felt essential in the run-up to the 2008 election of Barack Obama, the first black president of the United States. It remains essential now—in a time of war, economic disaster, health crises, and ecological emergency. The lyrics offer incendiary rage and righteousness, while in the music are ineffable sounds of every deep emotion, from despair to elation. The songs are perfect accompaniments for people in search of their constitutional rights to freedom, equality, and the ever-elusive liberty and justice, not just for some but for all. The songs of black freedom carry us from sleep to awakening, from hopelessness to faith, from bravado to true courage, from chaos to peace, sometimes all within the same song. Like a traditional ballad of mixed origins that gets handed down and rearranged over time, parts of the story you are about to read will ring through while other parts will evaporate quickly, lost in the mist that fogs the unique lenses through which we see our own histories. In the words of W. E. B. Du Bois, "I pray you then receive my little book in all charity, studying my words with me, forgiving my mistake and foible for the sake of faith and passion that is in me, and seeking the grain of truth hidden there."[2]

Some of the songs and singers you will read about are familiar and legendary, while others have largely gone unheard; some were deemed by government and law enforcement so strong as to be dangerous—a threat to national security. But in stark contrast to the words and actions of oppression, singing is an act of life and liberation. As we sing along, these songs invite us to tap into an energy reserve that is accessible to all, if only we choose to plug into it. It's about power: who's got it, who needs it, how to get it, and what to do with it once it's got. And it's what Odetta was singing about all along.

# 1

# Freedom Now

**W**ho ever heard of angry revolutionists all harmonizing 'We Shall Overcome . . . Suum Day' . . . Who ever heard of angry revolutionists swinging their bare feet together with their oppressor in lily pad park pools, with gospels and guitars and 'I Have a Dream' speeches? And the black masses in America were—and still are—having a nightmare," was Malcolm X's take on music and freedom movement: what's singing got to do with it?[1]

Ever since 1961, when Dr. Martin Luther King Jr. and the Southern Christian Leadership Conference (SCLC) took their voting rights and desegregation campaign to Albany, Georgia, singing had been an important tool in the nonviolent fight. At turns disarming and disturbing, verses and choruses coexisted with the slogans and prayers that drove the marches. The freedom movement—as in Freedom Summer, the freedom rides, and the slogan "Freedom Now"—were inextricably linked to song.

Young freedom mover Len Chandler had time for both Dr. King and Malcolm X, who history has shown were more in agreement than poles apart. Like his heroes, Chandler had a gift for words, and he used it to write songs on the spot—on a march, in jail, or while recovering from wounds inflicted on him on the bloody roads of Selma and Montgomery. A contemporary of Bob Dylan, Joan Baez, and Richie Havens, Chandler's story serves as a guide to the songwriter's experience during the unique era when songs contributed to propelling a mass movement. Chandler started out by borrowing high-flying gospel melodies and setting them to lyrical themes that stung, writing music specifically for movement; eventually he came to write originals. And though he didn't set out to be a freedom singer, or to find trouble, whether as a boy growing up in Akron, Ohio, or a young man in the Birmingham jail, both singing and trouble had a way of finding him. "My mother was someone who said, 'Just don't take any shit,'" Chandler says. And so he learned to fight back with songs, joining the men and women from the North and South—the singers and the unsung who reached out and brought others along with a song—walking the line for freedom and singing their way to consciousness in a new era of politicization.

"More than any other person, Malcolm X was responsible for the growing consciousness and the new militancy of black people," writes activist, musician, photographer, and author Julius Lester, and there was no doubt that from Memphis to Detroit, from Harlem to Watts, a new Afrocentric consciousness was rising.[2] The words of blues and jazz poets were mixing it up with the sermons of preachers, the melodies of Calypso singers, and voices from Africa. The ballads of the British Isles that had melded into gospel and slave songs were getting written over with R&B emotion and jazz courage. From this mix, a powerful new strain of popular music emerged. The bold sounds spoke to rebellion—there was an anger, an urgency, and a stridency in the notes, with a little bebop and Little Richard thrown into the mix. The beautiful chaos of horn charts collided with the comfort of church music; these new combinations were the early rumblings that helped to rearrange the polite "moon in June" status quo. The sheer force of the notes coming from the new breed of singer and player got folks listening. They began to recognize themselves and their own strength wrapped within each song's intensity. Like Billie Holiday's anti-lynching statement "Strange Fruit" from a previous era, the new songs were fearless at unmasking the ugly and shameful truths about society in the land of the free—truths that people could no longer let go unspoken and unheard, not with the scenes they faced in Mississippi and Alabama and the nightmare unfolding in Vietnam. And yet as the year turned from 1959 to 1960, the naming of this powerful new movement was still a few years away: Amiri Baraka was still known as LeRoi Jones, and Stokely Carmichael, a new arrival at Howard University, was just becoming acquainted with student organizing committees. No plans had been laid for a Black Arts Movement or the Mississippi Freedom Summer. Certainly there was not an organized movement to claim Black Power. But there were songs—and they were starting to be sung.

## Old Folks, New Folks

Around the same time, the major musical currents shaping contemporary jazz, folk, and rock were beginning to converge in a powerful new strain of freedom music. The songs and stories of some of its groundbreaking players— some known and some less so—serve as beacons to illuminate the era.

Out in California Odetta had been bashing out Lead Belly songs. Following a brief period in which she was being groomed to be the next Marian Anderson—"Because I was a big, black young lady"—Odetta decided she had no desire to be "another somebody." She joined the cast of *Finian's Rainbow,* a popular musical that takes a satirical look at southern bigotry. She discovered the bohemian life in San Francisco while on tour with the company show. "We'd finish our play, we'd go to the joint, and people were sitting around playing guitars and singing songs and it felt like home."

When Odetta was six years old, her mother moved them from Alabama to California. "The first wound that I received was on a train going to Los Angeles. A conductor comes back and tells the train we colored people had to get out of the car and go somewhere else. That one was the first wound. That's when I got the message that what I was and what I was from was not worth anything. The wound caused the fear, the hate . . . and the music has healed me." She also credits the music for shaping her identity. "We were not taught about ourselves. When I started in the years of folk music it was a discovery. What is called a natural today used to be called an Odetta."[3]

Though the classical music she'd been raised on had been "a nice exercise . . . it had nothing to do with my life." Tired of singing the songs of white people for white people, she embarked on a personal discovery of folk music. She uncovered Lead Belly's Library of Congress recordings compiled by musicologists John and Alan Lomax. "It helped me see myself, instead of waiting for someone to look at me and say I'm OK. The folk songs, the anger, the venom, the hatred of myself and everybody and everything else . . .

I could get my rocks off within those work songs and things without having to say I hate you and I hate me . . . As a matter of fact it was that area of the work songs and prison songs that helped heal me a great deal." She sang Lead Belly's "Cotton Fields" and "Rock Island Line" among other traditional folk and blues songs at the Tin Angel in San Francisco with guitarist Larry Mohr. Following the release of *Odetta Sings Ballads and Blues* in 1956, her versions of these songs created a foundation for the folk and gospel sound at the dawn of the civil rights movement.

It is hard to imagine potent political material with an emphasis on black pride developing without Odetta's influence, just as it is difficult to imagine civil rights music without the contributions of Bob Dylan, on whom she was a key influence.

"The first thing that turned me on to folk music was Odetta," Dylan once said. "I heard a record of hers in a record store, back when you could listen to records right there in the store. That was in '58 or something like that. Right then and there I went out and traded my electric guitar and amplifier for an acoustical guitar, a flat-top Gibson."[4] He learned Odetta's versions of "Mule Skinner Blues," "Jack o' Diamonds," " 'Buked and Scorned," and "Water Boy," along with her arrangements of Lead Belly's "Take This Hammer" and "Alabama Bound." Woody Guthrie and Ramblin' Jack Elliott were also in Dylan's orbit of influence as he began to expand the boundaries of folk music with his original contributions.

Against a backdrop of racial division and community organizing, a great revival in American folk and traditional music—played by black and white, young and old—was now underway, despite the US government's intention to shut it down. The House Un-American Activities Committee (HUAC) had spent the 1950s investigating the political lives of suspected Communists, especially artists and others of influence in society. Many key artists were blacklisted and were kept from performing. In 1955, the committee caught up with folk music scion Pete Seeger; he didn't appear on network television again until the mid-sixties. Seeger had been under surveillance since at least the mid-forties by the FBI and the CIA, as had actor, orator, singer, and black rights and anti-imperialist advocate Paul Robeson. Robeson's passport was revoked so that he should not influence his growing international audience on matters race- and labor-related.

Lead Belly had his own unfortunate brushes with authority. Having served his time and hoping to relaunch his life, Huddie Ledbetter—as he'd been born—moved north, though his associations with blacklisted folksingers Seeger and Guthrie aligned him with left-wing causes, leaving him out in the cold. He tried heading west, hoping to make it in Hollywood, but again the doors he knocked on were largely closed. "The artist in Lead Belly was a hungry man," says Seeger. "Hungry to see himself in the best of clothes, on the best street, in the best car, the best world. He knew he could help his folks everywhere to keep up their fight and their faith."[5] Despite his apolitical stature, Lead Belly's voice sang out like a musical bellwether in the years leading up to the civil rights era. "There is some quality in Lead Belly that just goes to the soul of me. I can't really say what it is," said Odetta. "I suppose if we could put words to those areas of response, those areas that hold for us such significant feeling, we would say the words, then dissect them, and then we'd mess that up, too. So I can appreciate the fact that there is no way for me to really describe everything that I feel when I listen to Lead Belly."[6]

## The New Sound in Jazz

Right round the time Odetta threw down the hot comb and picked up the guitar, alto saxman Ornette Coleman was saying with his horn what words could not describe. Fusing blues and jazz to African forms, he began the work that would prepare the way for his albums *Something Else!!!! The Shape of Jazz to Come* and *Change of the Century*, expressions of the new sound in jazz. His experiments were dubbed free jazz, and its angular horn squonks and unorthodox rhythms easily fit with the stirrings of pride and power bubbling beneath the surface of the fight for civil rights. Coleman's music wasn't easy; his transposed notes and unorthodox harmonies voiced frustration, despair, elation, beauty, and tears, as well as sheer rage. He avoided ideology, but his music unleashed an energy that could be heard by those tuned into its message. And like liberation itself, his experiments in avant-garde and free jazz were met with resistance by the establishment. Recalling the poverty and racism of his Forth Worth, Texas, upbringing, Coleman was inspired to join the fight in which his jazz forebears Charlie Parker, Dizzy Gillespie, and Thelonious Monk had landed their own blows to racism. They had also been victimized by it. On a break from his set at Birdland in 1959, Miles Davis escorted a white woman to her taxicab. While enjoying a cigarette before his next set, he was asked to "move along" by the beat cop. After refusing the officer's request, he was beaten, arrested, and hospitalized, and his cabaret license was revoked.

Surviving harassment, crossing color lines, resisting authority, forging new areas of sound with the invention of bebop, and moving jazz from nightclub entertainment into realms of high art was the work of these past masters and key players in jazz's liberation. As with Coleman, the jazz forerunners had left their impression on musician and playwright Archie Shepp, who from an early age was inspired by the possibilities jazz offered a young black man. "As a younger man, being exposed to modern music—black music—was really quite important to me, in the forming of my identity, in the forming of my goals," he says. Shepp's music-loving family—his father was a blues fan and his grandfather a banjo player—moved from Florida to Philadelphia in the early 1940s. Shepp also played the banjo, but the sound of Jimmy McGriff's alto sax floating through the neighborhood inspired him to switch instruments. "Even giving the blues all its due, people like Parker and Gillespie, Monk, actually provided younger black people with another image of themselves. They were really role models for me; they gave me somewhere to go."

## The Freedom Suites

Two albums credited for fusing the politics of black liberation with the new sound are Sonny Rollins's *Freedom Suite*—the first experiment—and Max Roach's *Freedom Now*—the fulfillment of the form. *Freedom Suite*, the 1958 album on which saxophonist Rollins was accompanied by bassist Oscar Pettiford and drummer Max Roach, was the first to take a giant step toward political-musical fusion. Its first track, "The Freedom Suite," was an original piece by Rollins, partially composed of standards and characterized by changing tempos and variations on improvised themes. The nearly twenty-minute song was the first jazz instrumental to claim social issues as its inspiration. "America is deeply rooted in Negro culture, its colloquialisms, its humor, its music. How ironic that the Negro who more than any other people can claim America's culture as his own is being persecuted and repressed. That the Negro who has exemplified the humanities in his very existence is being rewarded with inhumanity," proclaimed Rollins in the album's original sleeve notes.

Roach's album, which followed in 1960, its complete title *We Insist! Max Roach's Freedom Now Suite*, was larger in scope. The work was conceived as a performance piece to coincide with the centennial of the Emancipation Proclamation, and freedom was its through line, right down to the cover art featuring three African American men at a lunch counter with a white waiter on standby. The intense project, with lyrics by Oscar Brown Jr. and vocals by Abbey Lincoln, captured the sound of exploitation, degradation, and, ultimately, freedom. The album made a radical statement—politically as well as sonically—and is a cornerstone recording in the history of contemporary black liberation music. Making a link between the oppression of blacks throughout the world, Roach and other politically motivated American artists like Harry Belafonte and Nina Simone were seeking to parallel the civil rights movement in the United States with the unfolding liberation of Kenya, Ghana, Congo, and Algeria. The year 1960 was dubbed the Year of Africa, and independence from France, Britain, and Belgium signaled hope that human rights, dignity, and economic health would be restored throughout the continent.

In South Africa, apartheid was still many years away from resolution, and music played a significant role in the struggle. Merging regional music and church music, South African musicians had established a tradition of freedom singing in the forties; the movement gained momentum as singers took their music and their cause to world stages.

Inspired by the political works of singer-activist Paul Robeson, Belafonte reached out to foster a cross-cultural alliance with South African artists like singer Miriam Makeba and trumpeter and composer Hugh Masekela. On the Greenwich Village music scene, Belafonte had familiarized himself with traditional folk songs. In 1956 he had released *Calypso*, which later sold millions. By no means an easy-listening experience, calypso is a potent form of anti-imperialist expression, a fact that is often concealed by its breezy steel drum sounds. The actor and singer who popularized "Day-O (The Banana Boat Song)" would, like fellow calypso artists Maya Angelou and Louis Farrakhan, successfully cross to another stage. Belafonte's entertainment career was ultimately eclipsed by his humanitarian efforts. He financed civil rights movement activities, helped organize the March on Washington, and was a confidant of Dr. King. Belafonte supported the work of world-class players like Masekela and Makeba, introducing the South African musicians to his American audiences. The musicians in turn introduced him to the breadth and depth of Africa's music. As a member of the Jazz Epistles featuring Dollar Brand (also known as Abdullah Ibrahaim), Masekela traveled the globe, leaving South Africa shortly after the Sharpeville massacre in 1960.

Mama Africa, as Makeba was known, also toured the world. In 1960, as she attempted to return to Africa for her mother's funeral, she found her passport had been revoked. It was during this period of exile that Makeba and Nina Simone struck up a friendship that would last their lifetimes.

———

Just as the groundbreakers before them had, Coleman and Shepp encountered obstacles and extreme reactions as their work hovered in the outer reaches of so-called acceptable musical society. But the music was finding an audience with the tuned-in, hip, intellectual crowd, and people who could hear and appreciate free jazz as the new art form that it was—the musical equivalent to abstract expressionism and the Beat movement. As a horn player, Shepp grew up searching for John Coltrane in Philadelphia, though instead he found Cecil Taylor in New York City. After studying theater at Goddard College, he arrived on the scene at the end of 1959 when a chance meeting on the street with avant-garde pianist Taylor landed him his first professional recording date and a stint with Taylor's band.

"Cecil opened up a number of doors for me intellectually—made me understand that music is an intelligent pursuit, not one that's dominated by people that couldn't do anything else," Shepp says. "He dropped that on me quite clearly since he was so much more brilliant academically than people I knew who thought they were pretty smart!"

Inspired by "the new thing," John Coltrane explored the new languages and landscapes being forged by Coleman, Eric Dolphy, Cecil Taylor and Archie Shepp, Pharoah Sanders and Sun Ra, and others experimenting with breaking free of old codes, though the new thing wasn't entirely popular with his existing audience.

"The established jazz people called John Coltrane anti-jazz and hated the fact that the musicians were experimental and trying to change forms," explains John Sinclair, a writer, poet, and music fanatic who soaked in the new jazz sounds. As a freelance contributor to the jazz journal *Downbeat* and music editor and columnist at the *Fifth Estate*, Detroit's underground paper, "I was among about four people in America who had a good opinion of it and started to write about it. There was another white guy and the black guys A. B. Spellman and LeRoi Jones [Amiri Baraka].

"The jazz cats were all here first, at great risk to themselves and their career and with no possible benefit that you could have as jazz artists," says Sinclair.

"This recent music is significant of more 'radical' changes and reevaluations of social and emotional attitudes toward the general environment," wrote Amiri Baraka of Coleman, Taylor, Coltrane, and the explosion in jazz. "But I cannot think that the music itself is a more radical, or any more illogical extension of the kinetic philosophy that has informed Negro music since its inception in America. Negro music is always radical in the context of formal American culture," Baraka said in *Blues People*, his classic book on black sounds.[7] Making more overtly political music and linking up the music directly with politics seemed to be the path toward achieving greater liberty. From the sustenance hymns of slaves, to bop, and now in avant-garde, African American musical output kicked against the pricks, and the effort yielded varying degrees of freedom as well as suffering.

Starting in the mid-fifties, jazz players served as cultural ambassadors and public relations tools as part of a US government program to export American culture overseas at the height of the Cold War. Confronting the inevitable questions on US race relations and desegregation, the presence of bandleaders Duke Ellington, Louis Armstrong, and Dizzy Gillespie outside of the United States essentially backfired when everyone was forced to admit that the jazz musicians, some of America's greatest cultural exports, weren't exactly handled like national treasures at home, a point reinforced by the early 1960s reports of racial hatred on southern soil. The bandleaders were forthright about their experiences, and the music did the rest of the talking, whether traditional, bebop, or avant-garde. The very invention of jazz was liberation, and playing it was a statement, a creative expression of something entirely new. Not only did jazz serve as a device to throw off the European classical tradition on which it was partially based, it became a showcase for African melodic roots and its contributing influence on the music of the

American south. It was beboppers who noted the connection first, finding kinship between their highly disciplined form and that of the ancients. While performing with a traditional dancer, a cast of Afro-Cuban drummers, and Max Roach at an African cultural event, "Charlie Parker and I found the connections between Afro-Cuban and African music and discovered the identity of our music with theirs," writes Gillespie. "The music proclaimed our identity. It made every statement we wanted to make."[8]

Post-bop modern jazz was associated with other modes of expression, such as painting and poetry, and other regional music, specifically that of India and the Far East. The study of religion and philosophy became a part of jazz discovery. Distancing themselves from Western religious practice and seeking sanctuary from racism, jazz artists found the road to enlightenment by developing an interest in Islam or converting to one of its branches.

## The Black Muslims

For some seekers, the Black Muslims and the charismatic Minister Malcolm X served as an introduction to the Islamic faith independent of the religion's central teachings. On the surface, Malcolm X was like jazz to Dr. King's traditional gospel: his sound reached the day shift, the night shift, the overnight shift, and the shiftless in its urgency. Malcolm X's truths and rhythms struck chords closer to the sounds of everyday people and of the streets and prison from which he came. It was closer to the sound of revolution, and it did not intend to wait politely like the words and music of the righteous Dr. King and his gospel and folk queens, Mahalia Jackson and Joan Baez. You did not have to be a black separatist or a Black Muslim to appreciate the commitment Malcolm X made to the cause of human rights.

Originally founded in 1930, the Nation of Islam (NOI) gained ground in the 1950s under the leadership of Elijah Muhammad and Malcolm X. The NOI preached that blacks were the original human beings and that whites were "devils." Islam was "the black man's religion," and Christianity was "the white man's faith that had been taught to blacks in order to keep them subservient and exploitable." Under the name the Charmer, NOI's modern-day representative Louis Farrakhan recorded a calypso single, "A White Man's Heaven Is a Black Man's Hell."

Malcolm X would later make the observation that jazz was an area where black artists were given true liberation. "It's the only area on the American scene where the black man has been free to create," he said.[9] Archie Shepp explains it this way: "It is antiwar; it is opposed to Vietnam; it is for Cuba, it is for the liberation of all people. That is the nature of jazz. Why is it so? Because jazz is a music itself born out of oppression, born out of the enslavement of my people."[10]

"They were the first ones really to say that," says John Sinclair, "that white people were doing what they were doing because they meant to—it wasn't a mistake. They understood that their salvation was only going to come from themselves." As a resident of Detroit in tune with the racial tension in the North and in the South, Sinclair says he observed the climate change from integrationist to separatist thinking. Judged on the basis of his skin, the Black Muslims would've recognized Sinclair as a white devil, but he was drawn toward their side of black equality, by any means necessary.

Among other musicians attracted to the Black Muslim's message was R&B bandleader Johnny Otis and his discovery, the blues singer Etta James. "Hearing the white man called the devil didn't bother me at all. Calling *anybody* the devil gave me a chuckle," writes James, who is African American and white, in her autobiography.[11] James was the child of a young, wayward mother and an absent father whom James never knew but claimed was pool shark Minnesota Fats. Her success as a singer for the pioneering rock 'n' blues label Chess Records of Chicago transformed her from a child in the Los Angeles ghetto to an R&B star. Initially James, who struggled with addiction, joined the Black Muslims as a way to get clean. As Jamesetta X, she attended Temple 15 in Atlanta, where Louis Farrakhan was minister: "I became an honorable Elijah Muhammad Muslim . . . No more slave name." She believes that her enthusiasm for the NOI was what compelled one of her admirers, the boxer Cassius Clay, toward exploring and becoming directly involved with the faith. However, in James's case the faith didn't stick; she left it after calling herself a Muslim for ten years. "Looking back, I see it as something of a fad for me—it was the radical, the 'in' thing to do—but at the time I took it seriously." However the community's messages on pride and self-determination stayed with her, especially in difficult times. "If I didn't fall off the wagon so easily and frequently, Islam might've helped me avoid all sorts of problems."

James's early mentor Johnny Otis was especially influenced by Malcolm X's liberation rhetoric. As the son of Greek immigrants, Otis lived his life if not passing then certainly living more comfortably among blacks, participating in the struggle and becoming adept at his own political and spiritual speechifying: "Whites can exalt about 'bombs bursting in air,' but if a Black man or woman so much as suggests kickin' some ass to get free, the right wing bristles, and the liberals are pained," he writes.[12] Otis discovered, produced, and nurtured gigantic talents; he recorded the foundational rock 'n' roll song "Hound Dog" by Big Mama Thornton and worked with rock pioneer Hank Ballard and soul singer Jackie Wilson. On the road, Otis saw the rigors of racism. He participated in organizing discussions and boycotts and ultimately parlayed his frontline musical experience and strong point of view into broadcasting his political beliefs. He contributed to community welfare by becoming a preacher himself. Though Otis admired Dr. King, "I guess my role model was more Malcolm X," he says.

## Where Folk Meets Jazz, Poetry, Politics, and Africa

Her political involvement stirring, Nina Simone was among the artists who congregated at the Village Gate, the club at the heart of the Greenwich Village jazz scene. "Politics was mixed in so much with what went on at the Gate, I remember it now as two sides of one coin, politics and jazz," she writes in her memoir.[13] As an artist who would come to defy all standard classification, Nina Simone's album *Little Girl Blue*, alternately known as *Jazz as Played in an Exclusive Side Street Club*, was simply one of those late 1950s recordings that every American household seemed to own, sold largely on the strength of her Billie Holiday–inspired take of "I Loves You, Porgy" from the popular musical *Porgy and Bess*. "She was put in a jazz category but she very strongly said she was not a jazz artist," says Al Schackman. Deeply involved in the movement himself, Schackman was a player with Harry Belafonte and a practitioner of Sufism; he was also Simone's sole collaborator, musical director, and guitarist. A Greenwich Village regular himself—"They used to call me Sparks. I think I was one of the first electric guitar players on the scene"—Schackman says of Simone, "If you wanted to classify her, she said she was a folk artist." But Simone's folk was not coffeehouse strumming; rather, it was folk as in the people's music. She felt folk was more inclusive and indicative of the breadth of her work, plus she resented the jazz tag, feeling ghettoized and hemmed in by the label.

Simone's coming to black consciousness had been coaxed along by friends already committed to the movement for equality: writers James Baldwin, Lorraine Hansberry, and LeRoi Jones; the comedians Dick Gregory and Bill Cosby; and jazz poet Langston Hughes. Chronicling the New Negro Movement of the 1920s and 1930s, Hughes was a leading figure in the Harlem Renaissance. Originally a midwesterner with a family history that includes mixed-race people and abolitionists, Hughes wrote about lives in a vernacular that was familiar and authentic. He incorporated the sound of music into his prose and poems: "Take Harlem's heartbeat, Make it a drumbeat, Put it on a record, Let it whirl." His style was a breakthrough in modern literature and its lyricism translated into the development of blacker voices in music, too. Simone, Len Chandler, and Richie Havens are just three of many artists who say they were profoundly influenced by Hughes's jazz-inspired work. His ability to distill truth and outrage while maintaining an uncommon faith in humankind had a profound impact on the voices of the freedom movement.

As a teenaged library clerk in Akron, Len Chandler discovered Hughes. "My job was to shelve and I got really good at it, really fast. . . . I would hide and read and in the last hour, I'd be a blinding streak and get everything done. One of the things I found was *Shakespeare in Harlem*. He became a big favorite of mine and I read everything he did." Chandler says he fell into the pictures of Picasso and the words of John Steinbeck in the comfort of his middle-class childhood. "My father played in the Tuskegee Air Force Army Band, behind Lena Horne," he explains, so clearly talent ran in the family. As for his stepmother, "She contributed a lot to who I am and what I'm about. She made possible every opportunity a child in Akron could enjoy, culturally, educationally, sports. . . . I went to summer camps, I learned to swim and ride horses," he says. He attended the Cleveland opera; as an usher, he watched orchestras and legendary composers and players like Vladimir Horowitz. "From the time I was about fourteen, I saw everything that happened in that town and when I say everything I mean everything." Chandler left Akron on a classical music scholarship to Columbia University in New York; he too arrived in Greenwich Village.

Richie Havens didn't have to travel as far to find himself at the center of the action there. A budding poet, painter, and doo-wop singer from Bedford-Stuyvesant, it never occurred to him to visit the Village till some kids on the block called him a beatnik. Deciding to investigate for himself, he was turned on to the new folk sound there by the song "Get Together" by Dino Valenti.

Love is but a song we sing, fear's the way we die.

"He wrote it in 1958," Havens says. "We were awakening by these songs." As a young songwriter, Fred Neil's "Tear Down the Walls" moved Havens similarly.

The music's in the air, where every man is free.

"In 1959? I'm going, wow. Almost nobody was asking those kinds of things or projecting them," he says. "We'd sit at a table with our little books and Allen Ginsberg would say, what's in those books? Get up there and read them! That's how it began for me." After his baptism into folk tradition in a Village coffeehouse by Ginsberg, Havens began to blend his Bed-Stuy doo-wop poetics with his developing style of percussive acoustic guitar.

With the Village doing its job on its new arrivals, Nina Simone included, it was inevitable there would be a defining moment, one that gave Simone direction, away from jazz and into the area that would and helped shape her into the singularly potent, impossible-to-pigeonhole international artist she was becoming. "Babatunde Olatunji took us to Africa for a big international festival, to Nigeria. That was really the beginning of her African traditions," explains Schackman. Babatunde "Michael" Olatunji had come to America in 1950 on a scholarship from Lagos, Nigeria. On his way to becoming a master drummer, the activist and educator studied public policy at New York University and founded the Olatunji Center For African Culture in Harlem and fell in with the jazz crowd, specifically John Coltrane. Olatunji jammed with Max Roach on *We Insist! Max Roach's Freedom Now Suite*. Olatunji's 1960 album, *Drums of Passion*, was a watershed recording. Not only did it introduce the American masses to African music (it sold upward of five million copies), its release coincided exactly with the sit-in at the North Carolina lunch-counter that marked the beginning of student involvement in the nonviolent desegregation campaign. Olatunji had attended Morehouse University in

Atlanta; he rode in the front of buses there before his New York arrival and was acquainted with the movement toward nonviolent desegregation. He was a profound influence and fixture on the rapidly expanding civil rights scene.

Between his music studies uptown at Columbia, Len Chandler worked a day job at a downtown center for children in need; the boys there led him to the singing sessions at Washington Square Park. Folk wasn't exactly Len's bag, but he knew the songs of Woody Guthrie, Lead Belly, and Big Bill Broonzy well enough to get by and soon was getting paid to play. "Hugh Romney— Wavy Gravy—took me down to Orchard Street in New York and put me in a costume. I had a chambray work shirt, some real nice black boots and a little bandana handkerchief around my neck and that became my folk costume," he says. Securing gigs at all the folk clubs, he held a regular spot at the Gaslight, one of the Village's most desirable venues, notable for its history of beat poetry readings and its prestige bookings of folksingers. Following a performance there, Chandler was tapped for contract with a Detroit television show, performing two songs a night. He took the gig, using it as an opportunity to expand his traditional folk repertoire. When he returned to New York thirteen weeks later, "everyone had on the same black jeans and chambray shirt," he says. The golden age of Greenwich Village had begun; the scene's most famous son, Bob Dylan, arrived there in January of 1961.

"When Dylan came to town, he wasn't writing much, he wasn't writing anything, really," Chandler remembers. "We'd drink coffee and look through the daily newspapers left behind on the counter to see if there was any song material in any of it," Dylan writes in his book *Chronicles* of himself and Chandler. "I hadn't yet begun writing streams of songs like I would, but Len was and everything around us looked absurd—there was a certain consciousness of madness at work."[14] Dylan's self-directed studies of history, current events, traditional music, and the rebellion songs of Ireland's Clancy Brothers and Tommy Makem were parts of a longer equation; his Greenwich Village relocation and relationship with a politically aware young woman, Suze Rotolo, further flesh out the portrait of a musician as a young man, just one of many folksingers on the new beat.

"The first song I ever heard of Dylan's was 'Hey ho, hey Lead Belly, I just want to sing your name' . . . stuff like that," says Chandler. In December 1961, Chandler wrote his first song. "I was playing up in Saratoga Springs,

New York. On the front page of the newspaper, the two pulp newspapers, the *Daily News* and the *Post*, they had similar pictures. There had been a terrible school bus accident in Greeley, Colorado, and I wrote about that. What was so heavy about it was everyone had seen that photo and it was really shocking . . . women standing like that [hands to face], kids messed up on the ground, and so I wrote . . . about that and played it as my last song of the set that night." The audience was devastated, to the point of being struck silent by Chandler's performance of his freshly composed original song. "I left the stage and went into the dressing room, took off my shirt . . . wiped myself off, put on a new shirt, put my guitar away and then applause started. People were hammering the tables and stomping, screaming and I thought . . . this is *something*."

Alongside the folk standards on Bob Dylan's 1962 debut album were two original songs: "Song to Woody" (inspired by Guthrie's "1913 Massacre") and "Talkin' New York" fit neatly into his set of otherwise traditional arrangements and blues. Dylan borrowed Chandler's melody for another of his own songs, the early civil rights era eulogy "The Death of Emmett Till," about a fourteen-year-old African American boy from Chicago who was brutally murdered on a visit to Money, Mississippi, in 1955 because he spoke to a white woman.

"[Chandler] played me this one and he said, 'Don't those chords sound nice' and I said, 'They sure do,' so I stole it. I stole the whole thing," laughed Dylan during Cynthia Gooding's radio show in 1962. "Len didn't seem to mind," he wrote later in *Chronicles: Volume One*. In the spirit of folk's tradition of love and theft, borrowing and sharing was standard practice among folksingers, especially within the close circle of Greenwich Village friends.

Dylan first began intently studying the Civil War while attending a well-appointed high school in Hibbing, Minnesota. "The age I was living in didn't resemble this age, but yet it did in some mysterious and traditional way," he writes. "Back there, America was put on the cross, died and was resurrected. There was nothing synthetic about it. The godawful truth of that would be the all-encompassing template of everything I would write."[15] Dylan's material developed into pointed statements on injustice; as he deepened his queries into the human condition and the causes that drive people toward or away from certain actions, he made the transformation from folk imitator to innovator. "It was what was happening around him, right at the moment," says Chandler.

Beyond the insular yet international island of Manhattan, there were other simultaneous movements and interpretations of freedom. James Marshall Hendrix of Seattle was just out of the army, living in Nashville. Before it became known almost exclusively for its country scene, Music City was a stop on the so-called Chitlin Circuit, the clubs dotting the south where African Americans worked without hassle in the era of segregation. Hendrix was part of the high-level R&B scene there, sharpening his tools as a sideman. "Every Sunday we used to go downtown to watch the race riots. We'd take a picnic basket because they wouldn't serve us in the restaurant," he said.[16] He was arrested with his musician friend Billy Cox during a lunch counter demonstration there in 1962. In Detroit, a hotbed for freethinking and musical innovation, for musician and entrepreneur Berry Gordy Jr. black unity was a way to financial freedom. Tired of earning pennies on the dollar for his compositions for R&B singer Jackie Wilson, he formed the labels Tamla and Motown in 1959 and began to bank on the dividends of building an all-black business empire. He built rosters consisting almost entirely of kids from around the way. As it turned out, Tamla's first national hit, "Money (That's What I Want)" sung by Barrett Strong, was as prophetic as it was strong: "Well now give me money (that's what I want) . . . I wanna be free."

In part, the birth of rock 'n' roll in the 1950s had successfully launched an integration campaign; as a demonstration of unification between black and white, the merging of "hillbilly" and "race music" was a wild success. However, it wasn't long before the inevitable conservative backlash campaign to denounce the musical miscegenation started. As the 1960s began, rock's originators were largely shunted aside for a whitewashed version of music founded largely on black creative inspiration; white remakes of black records. In the record business existed a system of unfortunate and unfair business practice—something that Gordy had initially tried to offset, though would later be accused of practicing himself—that persisted until the music business's general decline in the early twenty-first century. Disputes over money matters between artist and label, black and white, businessmen and artists would haunt the record business for at least fifty years. Nina Simone was among those ripped off royally upon the release of her now-classic 1958 album *Little Girl Blue*. When she measured the album's popularity against her earnings from it, she became aware fairly quickly that she'd been done wrong. In her lifetime she never collected what she was due for the album's enduring success through the years. Hers is one of many stories that demonstrate the necessity of financial equality, education, and empowerment for recording artists from lower-income backgrounds. In particular need of representation was the young talent pool emerging from black America that Gordy helped initiate. Eventually a network of musician and professional associations developed to support eclectic artists from divergent socio-economic backgrounds, but economic justice remains an issue for recording artists.

Artistically, the new voices of freedom and equality found a West Coast advocate in Ed Pearl. There were few places to hear the new music outside of Greenwich Village, but when Pearl, owner of the Los Angeles club the Ash Grove, attended the first annual Newport Folk Festival in Rhode Island in 1959, his entrée to the East Coast folk establishment led directly to the introduction of folk and traditional music to the West Coast. "I met Alan Lomax, the New Lost City Ramblers . . . people had started hearing good things about the Ash Grove, so I had all these good people doing the booking. I still hadn't yet had the great traditional singers, but then Bess [Lomax] Hawes brought in Lightnin' Hopkins. Slow but sure, word got around and I started to hire Big Joe Williams. I introduced Lightnin' to Brownie [McGhee] and Sonny [Terry]."

The list of legends who would went west and filled Pearl's club with music starts with Maybelle Carter, Roscoe Holcomb, Robert Pete Williams, Sleepy John Estes, Howlin' Wolf, Willie Dixon, Muddy Waters, Bukka White, Lightnin' Hopkins, Mance Lipscomb, and Doc Watson. It continues with Mississippis—John Hurt and Fred MacDowell—and includes the three Bigs: Joe Turner, Joe Williams, and Willie Mae "Big Mama" Thornton. There were hundreds more. Pearl suggests these bookings affected the young folk as much as Woody Guthrie shaped Bob Dylan singing his way out of Minnesota and Greenwich Village, much as Beatlemania would eventually launch a thousand rock bands and encourage boys to grow their hair long. The folk and blues revival's black/white, young/old, traditional/contemporary, and country/urban music contrasts were a direct link to the "justice and equality for all" politics of the civil rights movement and the nation's rapidly growing social consciousness led by its youth. "At the Folklore Center I'd seen posters of folk shows at the Ash Grove and I used to dream about playing there," writes Dylan.[17]

In Memphis, high school student Booker T. Jones quietly integrated his quartet, the M.G.'s, who were cooking up the basis for the sound of Stax Records. As Soulsville U.S.A., Stax became synonymous with a deeper kind of southern music that mixed gospel and rock 'n' roll and defined the sound of soulfulness for most of the sixties. Meanwhile in New York, making his recorded debut at the age of twenty as a harmonica player on a Belafonte album, Bob Dylan's Columbia Records debut *Bob Dylan* was a collection of mostly traditional songs. *The Freewheelin' Bob Dylan* established him as a writer with more than old folk renditions on his mind. Dylan was well on his way toward changing the way the masses and his fellow artists related to political matters mixed with folk music. When she met Dylan, Joan Baez was folk music's reigning queen at age nineteen. Inspired by Odetta and Pete Seeger, Baez made her debut on the Cambridge folk scene holding down a spot at Club 47. She appeared at the Newport Folk Festival in 1959, and invited Dylan to perform there in 1963. Baez practiced civil disobedience as a student and studied pacifism and the nonviolence teachings of Dr. King. She was enfolded into the civil rights movement not only as an entertainer but as a living example of its core values, singing to workers in Mississippi while she continued to study and teach nonviolence in her home state of California.

Like Baez, Len Chandler had walked with Dr. King in Alabama and Mississippi; he had taken the Freedom Rides for interstate bus desegregation and sung for voting rights. Chandler, Baez, and Dylan came together at the historic March on Washington For Jobs and Freedom on August 28, 1963. Chandler led Baez and Dylan in a sing-along version of "Keep Your Eyes on the Prize," customizing the lyrics to the song also known as "Gospel Plough," for the historic occasion. The march coincided with the centennial year of the Emancipation Proclamation and will be forever remembered for Dr. King's "I Have a Dream" speech. Belafonte organized the singers that day, pulling in Odetta, Marian Anderson, the Freedom Singers, and Peter, Paul and Mary. Olatunji was in attendance, as was Dizzy Gillespie. Gospel queen Mahalia Jackson of New Orleans was also there that day; she often sang on the most important occasions at which Dr. King spoke, the pair working in tandem, her voice a kind of hallelujah chorus, of a piece with his testimonies. The singing at the mass gatherings not only provided entertainment, it served as a way for audiences to participate in the event. Music's ability to reach the place in the heart that words alone simply cannot access made it essential to the spoken presentations and to keeping the human spirit awake. If the justice and morality at the basis of Dr. King's message couldn't reach its intended audience, perhaps some familiar words from a gospel song could get the job done. "Jesus died to set me free, nailed to that cross on Calvary," sang Jackson that day, from "'Buked and Scorned," Dr. King's last-minute special request. The gospel classic circulated in the sixties in a secular folk arrangement; it was performed by Odetta and was rearranged as a blues song by Lightnin' Hopkins, who cautioned, "You're going to need somebody on your bond." As sung by Jackson, "'Buked and Scorned" was offered not only as a balm and a prayer, but as an indictment of America.

## America Is Singing

Though as a bluesman Hopkins and others like him had sung songs of black strength and white scorn, the blues weren't represented at the March, even though in his satirical campaign for president, Dizzy Gillespie said if elected he'd rename the White House the Blues House. The blues were the original cries of freedom, yet there were other forms of freedom song and singers conspicuous by their absence on that day. Where were the fathers of rock and soul, the free jazz players and the young gospel voices who called freedom's name with their horns and impassioned pleas of Good Golly! Good God! and Have Mercy! They too had sung for liberation, pioneering breaks in the color barrier, traveling through towns where their presence was less than welcome, entering through the back door when it meant the difference between violence and keeping the peace. They had all been testifying through songs in their own ways.

The jazzmen had used their technical mastery and were taking jazz to the next level—sonically and spiritually improvising, though some like Thelonious Monk were skeptical about joining up; he once told Freedom Singer Bernice Johnson, "You are gonna get yourselves killed walkin' out here in these streets in front of these crazy white people, your local crazy white people who've got guns." But even he'd thrown his trademark hat into the freedom effort, lending his financial and artistic support. A week before the March on Washington he played a fundraiser for the Negro American Labor Council, which escorted busloads of workers to the March.[18]

Like Monk, gospel turned pop great Sam Cooke watched the event at home on TV that day, where the March and its music made an indelible impact on him and the direction political song would take.

The story goes that Cooke was so inspired by Bob Dylan's performance of "Blowin' in the Wind," he decided he should write his own protest song.

> I was born by the river in a little tent
> And just like the river, I've been running ever since
> It's been a long time coming but I know a change is gonna come

Opening with the sweetness—birth in a little tent, perhaps referring to the singer's own beginnings in Clarksdale, Mississippi—the song recounts with a bitter tone the imagery of a runaway slave, *running ever since*, before it turns toward the one thing that can't be taken away from a person, the sanctuary of the spirit or the soul: Deep in my heart, I do believe, *I know a change is gonna come*.

"A Change Is Gonna Come" rose to become one of the movement's most important anthems; Cooke's song served as a new template for the message songs that would be sung by black artists. At the time of its immediate release it wasn't embraced as a hit, but Cooke and his management pushed for a second release of it and when they got it, the song made the Top 10 on the R&B charts and by early 1965 had cracked the Top 40 charts, transforming the shape of R&B to come. Though Cooke would not live to see the success of his song, he hit a vein for his contemporaries—Curtis Mayfield, James Brown, Aretha Franklin, Wilson Pickett, and Solomon Burke among them—to go on and mine further. The new strain of secular music from the soul conveyed plainly the gut feelings about getting left back and left behind. It was messier and more complicated than the reverential tones of "We Shall Overcome," but the new direct musical communication had an emotional component and power to it. Not only did it evoke empathy and tears from listeners, but it also summoned them to dance while its singers tore it up to the breaking point. Telling the stories of struggle and performing and participating on community action lines was one thing, but transferring the energy of the struggle and delivering it personally, taking the racial crisis in progress and turning it into a human problem rather than a political one, was the new sound's genius. Many of the new music's messengers had come from gospel tradition; they knew of handclapping, exhortations, and exclamations and audience participation. And yet, this was very clearly nighttime music, its concerns often earthly and bodily, but with an unbreakable spirit. This was soul music and it was about to explode.

———————

Though not all were in agreement on how the movement should move forward, the musical followers of the Black Muslims and Malcolm X, SNCC, and the SCLC and Dr. King were united in a mass chorus to move. Student leader Julian Bond built on Langston Hughes's response to Walt Whitman, hearing pride and the power in the all the degrees, shades, and sounds of blackness. Bond wrote:

> I too, hear America singing
> But from where I stand
> I can only hear Little Richard
> And Fats Domino.
> But sometimes,
> I hear Ray Charles
> Drowning in his own tears
> or Bird
> Relaxing at Camarillo
> Or Horace Silver doodling,
> Then I don't mind standing
>     a little longer.

Neither jazz, nor folk, nor poetry, nor rock 'n' roll could single-handedly render a people free, but they all helped set the course on the path to pride and contributed to the necessary development of an almighty body politic. America was singing, and her people were calling her out.

# Everybody Knows About
# Mississippi . . . Goddam!

ollowing the murder of NAACP field secretary Medgar Evers in front
of his home in Jackson, Mississippi, in June 1963 and the bombing that
killed four girls—Addie Mae Collins, Cynthia Wesley, Denise McNair, and
Carole Robertson—in the basement of the 16th Street Baptist Church in
Birmingham, Alabama, that September, Nina Simone thought it would be
a good idea to pick up a gun. "Then Andy, my husband at the time, said to
me—he said to me, 'Nina, you can't kill anyone. You are a musician. Do
what you do,'" Simone recalls.[1] That's when she put down the words and
music to "Mississippi Goddam," her indictment of southern racism.

> Alabama's got me so upset
> Tennessee's made me lose my rest
> And everybody knows about Mississippi—Goddam!

"I shut myself up in a room and that song happened," she said. From that
moment forward, Simone became committed to writing and performing
material that would jolt people awake or into action; "Mississippi Goddam" remains one of her most enduring pieces of work, delivered like a
satirical show tune by a woman on fire. In the summer of 1963, the time
of the March on Washington and mobilizing tragedies in Alabama and Mississippi, Simone felt the pull to choose a side. She had been introduced

to the Student Nonviolent Coordinating Committee (SNCC) leader Stokely Carmichael by her friend Miriam Makeba in 1962. Carmichael called Nina "the true singer of the civil rights movement." Simone wrote, "During the '60s I was told every SNCC group played Nina Simone recordings. They played my music because they knew where I was coming from, my message was the same as theirs. They were inspired by it."[2] But it was Simone's introduction to the Nation of Islam and the speeches of Malcolm X that served as her inspiration as she began thinking on matters of separatism versus integration, violence versus nonviolence. She came to believe in anti-oppression achieved through revolution—a complete dismantling of the existing power structure with the intention of forming a new society. "And this change," she writes, "had to start with my own people, with black revolution."[3]

"Mississippi Goddam" was published in *Broadside*, a mimeographed newsletter founded by activists Sis Cunningham and Gordon Freisen in New York in 1962 for the express purpose of delivering the news via topical song. *Broadside* revived the centuries-old tradition of disseminating information on sheets of paper at the street level. New works by the Greenwich Village neighborhood musicians, with their socially and politically charged lyrics deemed too controversial for mainstream play, was exactly the kind of material *Broadside* was fit to print. Simone, Pete Seeger, and Phil Ochs all contributed, as did Dylan as Blind Boy Grunt, thirteen-year-old Janis Ian as Blind Girl Grunt, and Native Americans Buffy Sainte-Marie and Peter La Farge. Len Chandler's songs, among many, many more, were published by *Broadside*. "I was doing things like when those four little girls got blown up in the church, I wrote a song," says Chandler.

> I've got to go downtown, go downtown today,
> Put my body on the line, meet the picket signs and
>     the wife's coming to take me away.
> I don't want no trouble with the bossman,
>     I don't want no trouble with you,
> But it's been so long, things have been so wrong and
>     I know what I've got to do

"I'd make five hundred photocopies and pass them out in front of a demonstration and sing it. That's when I got hooked up with Cordell Reagon," he says. "*Broadside* invited me to come south for a conference of singers and songwriters in the Freedom movement." Akron's Len Chandler, Greenwich Village folksinger, was shipping out to rural Georgia.

Albany, Georgia, was home to a fierce early desegregation campaign run by Dr. King in 1961. It was also home to the Freedom Singers, the group formed by SNCC field secretary Cordell Reagon at the suggestion of Pete Seeger to help promote the cause of nonviolent teachings and to raise money for SNCC on the road. As a student leader, Reagon was a veteran of multiple sit-ins and voter registration drives when he recruited another student leader and singer, Bernice Johnson, along with Charles Neblett and Rutha Harris, for his quartet; he and Bernice Johnson married in 1963. Their stages were picket lines, folk clubs, and the March on Washington. The vocal quartet traveled throughout the country, singing in elementary schools, universities, and especially jail cells, where they sat alongside fellow student demonstrators who dared to raise their voices against Jim Crow. As student activists, they had participated firsthand in desegregation efforts organized by SNCC and the NAACP; in Albany they were joined by Martin Luther King Jr. and the membership of the Southern Christian Leadership Conference (SCLC) when the town had served as a test site for larger, more visible actions in Birmingham and Selma.

In 1963 the Freedom Singers traveled to Los Angeles for an unprecedented six-week run at the folk club the Ash Grove on a fund-raising and awareness campaign. "The Freedom Singers were among the most important fulfillments of the Ash Grove vision that I had," explains the club's owner, Ed Pearl. "They were young at the time . . . and they were singing songs that came from the actual lives and struggles of the civil rights movement. It was their culture . . . their music. All these younger people in the audience had already turned on to Lightnin' Hopkins and Bill Monroe and respected southern culture from a distance . . . But here were young people involved in a nationwide cause. Some of the Freedom Rider buses used the Ash Grove to pick up people to go to the South. It was an important lesson to a younger generation of people," says Pearl. Booking performers like Bessie Jones and the Georgia Sea Islanders—who preserved their plantation history, Gullah heritage, and stories of slave ancestry—Pearl provided a stage for voices from the South and allowed Western listeners a step into otherwise unheard tradition. He then leavened that tradition by drawing young listeners and players to his club; the sights, sounds, and ideas presented there further contributed to the creation of a forward-thinking youth culture weaned on folk music.

"Strange Fruit," the anti-lynching song that Abel Meeropol wrote from his poem and Billie Holiday made famous, was the high bar that young Bob Dylan reached for with his own compositions. His "Oxford Town" concerns the case of James Meredith, the first African American student to be admitted to the University of Mississippi; "Masters of War" takes aim at the military-industrial complex. And "Blowin' in the Wind" is, well, "Blowin' in the Wind."

"The very first time Dylan heard anyone playing one of his songs—the very first time—he was sitting on my fire escape," remembers Chandler. "Our two next-door neighbors, two girls, Renee and Sally, had a *Broadside* magazine and they were playing 'Blowin' in the Wind.'" The song, perhaps Dylan's most famous and enduring, is set to the tune of "No More Auction Block for Me," a slave-era song that had previously been performed by Odetta and Paul Robeson. The album also contained "A Hard Rain's A-Gonna Fall," a litany of injustice and other atrocities called on to be washed away, featuring another borrowed melody, "Lord Randall," European in origin. "But I tell you what," says Chandler, "When I heard 'A Hard Rain's A-Gonna Fall,' I started playing it. I played it on a twelve-string with open tuning. The open tuning is a real wild tuning that is C-G-C-G-C-E. When three Cs are happening, two Gs, and one E, but when it's a twelve-string, that's a lot of Cs. It really rings. When I played it on the twelve-string, it was really a moving thing." Chandler's own recording break was still another four years away, while the freedom movement marched on and the coffeehouse sound developed into the folk rock we know today.

## Spirituals, Radicals, and Radical Spirituals

Freedom Singer Bernice Johnson Reagon explains how African American choral music combined with the youth energy in the freedom movement. "I heard 'Keep Your Eyes on the Prize' in church, but I didn't *understand* it till I was in jail the first time," she says.[4] "There's nothing to hearing a spiritual without understanding that it's a radical statement. It's as radical a statement as you can find." She suggests the essential relationship between the traditional African American songbook and freedom, and how the old spirituals, rearranged to fit the times, were a natural basis for the Freedom Singers' repertoire as well as for the movement. "When we sing, we announce our existence," she says. The songs born from slavery—whether sung in abolitionist times or in the modern Freedom era—were concerned with liberation from bondage, absolute equality, and a resolve to push forward. Whether that freedom comes on earth or in heaven is less relevant than the way the songs forge a connection to a shared cultural heritage and history of oppression.

Johnson Reagon suggests that singing spirituals is essential to connecting to one's African American heritage. "The part of your being that is tampered with when you run sound through your body is a part of you that our culture thinks should be developed and cultivated, that you should be familiar with, that you should be able to get to as often as possible. And if it is not developed, you are underdeveloped as a human being. If you go through your life and you don't meet this part of yourself, somehow, the culture has failed you."

Though he wasn't raised on gospel, Len Chandler says while he was down south, he'd find himself "in the zone," lifted by the power of a centuries-old tradition of collective singing to freedom. Describing what he calls his "bougie" childhood church in Akron he says, "If the piano player who could play that stuff really started to swing things, the minister would say no, no, no. We were singing Bach. He wanted us singing anthems. The congregation *could* sing like that—'Amazing Grace'—but they didn't want us doing that. Their vision of upwardly mobile was, 'I'm going to college, I'm middle class, we don't want you doing that.'" Similar to Odetta's studying Marian Anderson and conventional opera, Chandler says studying the vocals of Enrico Caruso and George London didn't serve him as a folky freedom singer. "I lost what could've been a major part of my tool kit," he says. During his time in the South, singing and attending meetings and rallies with Cordell Reagon throughout Georgia, Tennessee, Alabama, and Arkansas, Chandler further acquainted himself with the style of traditional and gospel song that is bound to southern black culture. He heard how gospel songs like "99 and a Half Won't Do," as led by Carlton Reese of the Birmingham Mass Choir, could be flipped to speak to issues of desegregation during the Freedom Summer voter registration drives of 1964, gaining momentum and intensity alongside the movement. *"Five, ten, fifteen, twenty, twenty won't do, twenty five thirty, thirty won't do thirty-five, forty, forty won't do*—running all the way to 100—*because 99 and a half won't do,"* sings Chandler. "I was listening to people singing with all that southern soul. With my little esoteric, poetic references and metaphors and stuff, I thought, my shit is gonna fall flat as a pancake!" Through a process of imitation and unlearning what he knew about singing, Chandler found his own voice—clear and strong, and delivered it with a poet's grace and a beatnik's wink.

---

Nina Simone was in the process of finding a root to her music too, with its direct connections to a churchy southern childhood. Born Eunice Kathleen Waymon, the daughter of a Methodist minister mother and an odd-jobbing father from Tryon, North Carolina, Simone officially started her musical life at four, when she was encouraged to sing and play piano with her mother's African Methodist Episcopal (AME) church choir. Clearly she showed promise, and her teachers and townspeople took a collection for Eunice's schooling. Attending summer session at the Juilliard School and continuing private lessons, she applied to the Curtis Institute of Music in Philadelphia. She was denied admission and believed it was an act of racism. Seeking work as an accompanist, she found a following in an Atlantic City piano bar and, thinking the job would shame her family, renamed herself Nina Simone.

Though the civil rights struggle encapsulated Simone's core ideals of anti-oppression, anti-imperialism, personal dignity, and human rights, Simone began to part ways with the civil rights movement in America and align herself with more radical voices. Deeply moved by injustices to black and so-called third world people, Simone looked more to the words of Malcolm X for solace. "Truth is on the side of the oppressed today," he stated.[5] The singer was not alone in her passion to explore the other options to Dr. King's desegregation plan. Following his famous rap taunt, to float like a butterfly, sting like a bee, and whup Sonny Liston, Cassius Clay, the new heavyweight champion of the world, went public with his conversion to Islam and name change to Muhammad Ali. Inspired by the Black Muslims in the early sixties, Ali's politicization was controversial for its embrace of black separatism.

Simone threw her lot in with the international liberation cause, becoming an emphatic supporter of the freedom movement sweeping the states of Africa. She sought to bring the continent's distinct rhythms, as well its unique regional styles—hairdos, jewelry, and fabrics—to her stage. As she further discovered the politics of liberation, her personal position grew more and more militant. "She didn't want to do benefits. She was not nonviolent," says her guitarist Al Schackman. "A lot of people in the movement for a long time thought she wasn't interested in the movement. She was so much bigger than just that. I remember a time at some kind of a civil rights function, cocktail party thing, I was standing with her and somebody came up to her and said, 'Nina, how come you're not interested in civil rights?' She looked at them and she was screaming, 'Civil rights? I don't have to be interested in civil rights. I am civil rights.'"

In her songs, Simone covered the globe, from New Orleans and "House of the Rising Sun" to Nigeria with Olatunji and "Zungo." France was represented by Jacques Brel's "Ne Me Quitte Pas," and she transmuted "Black Is the Color of My True Love's Hair," a ballad likely of Scottish origin first discovered in the hills of Appalachia. Within Simone's repertory an active listener could discover distinct and shared origins of indigenous music—you could get a sense that the Celtic Ballads and American blues and jazz shared a reliance on blue or long notes, the flatted fifths, thirds, and sevenths to set moods of melancholy. Her commitment to dynamic and emotional song interpretation is the quality that Richie Havens says freed him to sing, especially the songs of others, in whatever mode he saw fit. Simone and Havens became friends and in 1963 they toured together. They were on the road, driving to the next gig and listening to the car radio, when they heard President Kennedy had been shot. "It was one of the saddest days of my life and of course the tour was over. From that moment on there was a new depth in everything I sang or interpreted," says Havens.[6] He credits Simone and writer and activist James Baldwin for contributing directly to the development of his own brand of socially conscious work. By virtue of his fierce style of acoustic guitar strumming, Havens would get lumped into a folk or folk-rock bag too, though like Simone, his music would grow to defy boundaries.

By the mid-sixties, Simone was at work deepening her repertoire, moving fluidly from Duke Ellington to Jimmy Webb, from traditional folk to the contemporary songs of Greenwich Village. In the early 1960s, a hardcore Simone fan, Eric Burdon of the British beat group the Animals, paid tribute to his idol's work when he cut his own version of "House of the Rising Sun;" later he took on the Simone original, "Don't Let Me Be Misunderstood," the first cut on her 1964 album, *Broadway-Blues-Ballads* which had introduced her more thoroughly to young European rock audiences. Schackman tells a story of a night backstage at the Village Gate, when he believes Simone and Burdon met for the first time. "One time, Art D'Lugoff, the owner of the Village Gate, brought an artist back to see Nina and he said he was like her biggest fan . . . He told her what a fan he was and that she had inspired him . . . and she attacked him for stealing her song . . . this white guy had stolen 'her song.' I'll never forget that. He was scared half out of his mind."

Burdon remembers it differently: "So you're the honky motherfucker who stole my song and got a hit out of it," she said to him. "Hey, listen, if you will admit that the work song in your set this evening probably belongs to the bones of some poor unfortunate buried in an unmarked grave in Angola State Penitentiary—then I'll admit that your rendition inspired us to record the song," he shot back. Simone didn't seem to mind that Burdon's point was hardly a fair analogy, though she couldn't deny that some of her tunes were borrowed. The meeting marked the beginning of a long professional friendship: on one hand Burdon and his group the Animals stole from Simone's tradition, while on another, they'd introduced Simone to a generation of English and European rock fans who anticipated her arrival abroad—a prospect she looked forward to fulfilling.[7]

Other songwriters Simone came to favor were Bob Dylan and Richie Havens and later George Harrison and the Australian Gibb Brothers of the Bee Gees. "If she did a piece of music, she would change it completely, not even thinking about it," says Schackman. "She wouldn't be concerned necessarily of where it came from or whom it came from. It's only what it meant to her. Indeed some of her most evocative versions emerged that way, as when she did Dylan's 'The Times They Are A-Changin.' . . . She was very aware of the meaning and the spirit inside of that song." Among Schackman's favorite Dylan interpretations is Simone's recording of "Ballad of Hollis Brown," the story of a starving farmer who kills himself and his family out of desperation. "It's an amazing piece of work," he says.

As Schackman and Simone strummed their way through "Hollis Brown," Dylan was taking his own new roads, on the verge of making his historic electric appearance at the Newport Folk Festival, notorious for upsetting the old-guard folk brigade. "Everybody's freaking out," says Len Chandler, who also performed there that year. "I didn't. I liked it. I thought it was great! I wanted to do some of that." However, Chandler continued to work in traditional folk, acoustic mode. He performed his own songs on what he calls "so-called protest night," though he was surprised to find the folkies in the audience weren't ready for his strong antiwar stance. "I broke a string and while I was fixing the string, I said something about how I wished we could do something that would stop people doing the jive things they're doing in our name in Vietnam and Laos and got booed." The chilly reception at Newport from some uptight members of the folkie set wasn't about to send Chandler changing his onstage point of view, nor the content of his songs as he made preparations for the recording of *To Be A Man* at Columbia Studios in New York.

---

On the jazz side, Archie Shepp followed his Cecil Taylor gig with the formation of his own quintet, the New York Contemporary Five, which featured Don Cherry of Ornette Coleman's quartet. Following a string of Danish tour dates in 1963, Shepp started hanging out religiously at the John Coltrane and The Thelonious Monk gigs every weekend at the Five Spot. Coltrane was a legend to him, "ever since the time I started to play the sax I became interested in starting to play the notes above high F." Eventually Shepp introduced himself to Coltrane, who became another teacher. "When I finally got my own recording contract with Impulse, it was because he put in a word for me," Shepp says. The 1964 session yielded *Four for Trane*. Though the album consists largely of reimagined Coltrane tunes, it was played in a tone that was developing into something uniquely Archie Shepp.[8]

Shepp recalls the time when John Coltrane invited him to the 1965 recording session for *Ascension*; it was a turning point for Coltrane, who had moved into improvising with a large band, as well as for Shepp. "I didn't really quite know what his concept was," Shepp says, though the juxtaposition of Coltrane's composition with the improvisations of the musicians sitting in was certainly a breakthrough in music. "I didn't quite understand what I was doing, I suppose that's what John wanted—that there should be complete freedom of expression. Structured cacophony," he says. "There was something about Coltrane which was very disturbing to critics and writers at that time . . . Even though he never spoke about politics that I knew of, he legitimized this term free jazz, which in a sense I think was an attempt to make not only a musical but a social statement. New York was a hotbed of social organizations from the Communists to the Trotskyites. Anyone who went there at that point was bound to be politicized or radicalized and I was no different," says Shepp.[9] As a follower of Malcolm X, Shepp perhaps heard the common threads in Coltrane's and Malcolm's work, concerned as they were with human potential. "Neither was ever content with a static description of reality," writes Frank Kofsky in *Black Nationalism and the Revolution in Music*. "Both continually brought their most treasured concepts, assumptions, and definitions under relentless scrutiny."[10]

## The Great Folk Scare

Back in the Village, Richie Havens was also beginning to write original material that tangled with politics, from the war in Vietnam to the war at home. "Handsome Johnny" was his collaboration with his friend Lou Gossett Jr., another Village folkie.

> He who rides with the Klan,
> He is a devil and not a man

wrote Havens in "The Klan." "All music is folk music," says Havens, echoing the sentiments of Nina Simone. But folk music was about to change. The younger generation of politically motivated black acoustic guitar pickers, like Julius Lester and Jackie Washington, were waiting on the slow train to the recording studio like Havens and Chandler. Josh White was bouncing back from the blackout that kept him off the airwaves. So were Lead Belly, Pete Seeger, and Paul Robeson. Country bluesmen Mississippi John Hurt, Skip James, and Son House in their retirement age were in the midst of rediscovery by record labels and young audiences. But the acoustic guitar was on its way out of fashion, and African American acoustic players seemed to be moving steadily toward extinction. Chandler persisted in keeping folk alive.

In 1964 he recorded "Going to Get My Baby Out of Jail" with Bernice Johnson, and started to sing his own compositions, songs like "To Be a Man" and "Keep On Keeping On." Chandler delivered them in a warm tenor and a passion that connected directly to the listener.

> There's a mountain in the bottom of that sea we flounder in;
> If we find that mountaintop, we wouldn't need to swim,
> If we'd found that mountain sooner,
> > just think where we could have been . . .
> So I guess I've gotta . . . keep on keepin' on

Chandler says of his new songs, "They liked 'em. Some little old lady with glaucoma came up to me and said, 'Son, you gonna sing that "Keep on Keeping On" song again? I liked that.' Cordell told me, you'd better call up your wife and tell her you're not comin' home, because you're coming with me. I said, 'Where we going?' and he said, 'Arkansas.'"

Bridging the gap between East and West folk and the North/South division was Ed Pearl, who had booked the Ash Grove with popular folk acts of the starched, striped shirt and slacks variety in the early sixties. "The kids were immediately attracted to the guitar," he says. This was the period of the Great Folk Scare, when a whitewashed version of the music entered the mainstream—culminating with the network TV show *Hootenanny* and its homogenized, square vision of folk. Instead of showcasing the young folksingers cropping up from Greenwich Village and Cambridge to the West Coast like wild mountain thyme, *Hootenanny* presented everyone *but* the hardcore troubadours like Dylan, Baez, and Len Chandler. They and others boycotted *Hootenanny* in solidarity with Pete Seeger, who was officially in the middle of his blacklisting as a result of refusing to testify before HUAC. Folk's blackout on the airwaves, the red scare, and the coming of the Beatles in a big way in 1964 threatened to put folk out of business. Pearl saw the writing on the wall. "By '63 I decided to go traditional pretty much . . . I wanted John Hurt and Skip James, Doc Watson, Earl Scruggs, Bill Monroe," he says. A new period of cultural exchange and political awakening of southern ways began at Pearl's outpost in Los Angeles. The story of the Ash Grove echoes the journey of the traditional music of the American South to the North and the West; it's an example of where the music entered the popular culture in the early sixties and contributed to launching the folk revival and the creation of folk rock and its protest-oriented repertoire, music that transformed the culture and defined the sixties. The Ash Grove's own dramatic story of survival as an outpost for freethinking also serves as a shadow history of America and the stories of migration, immigration, and the race and class integration issues that bear on progress and the politics of change. Sometimes just hanging around a multicultural, multiracial, political, and artistic environment like the Ash Grove could set a young musician on course, though there were times it seemed the environment was cursed, as there was perpetually a campaign afoot to shut it down and the air of violence shrouded the otherwise harmonious mix.

"People say how did you learn music, I said this was how I learned music . . . by being in the Ash Grove with Ed, at the bar, at my chair," says Ry Cooder, who started showing up at the club when he was twenty.[11] At twenty-two, Taj Mahal, already learned in blues, jazz, and African music, gravitated to the Ash Grove upon his arrival to the West Coast from the Club 47 scene in Cambridge. "I hung out there so much that I eventually moved in," he writes in his memoir, *Autobiography of a Bluesman*. "The musical and political tone was set by Ed. It was very progressive, positive toward all people. There was lots of grassroots politics and grassroots music going on at the Ash Grove [and] at the center of it, real music from all over the place."[12] Together Mahal and Cooder formed the Rising Sons, among the first bands to incorporate traditional instruments into a rock 'n' country–blues mix. One of the first interracial folk rock bands (a few years later, the interracial Paul Butterfield Blues Band and Love with Arthur Lee both signed to Elektra), they contracted to Columbia. Their record went unreleased for nearly thirty years, though today's Americana springs from their bold hybridization of traditional and contemporary sound. Throughout their long respective careers as solo artists, both Mahal and Cooder have used American traditional music and global instrumentation to introduce listeners to indigenous music from Cuba, Africa, and India.

Pearl had successfully created an atmosphere and core audience for a seamless mix that reached across stylistic and racial lines, "a concentration of the greats of white country and black blues . . . I never made any money on the Ash Grove," says Pearl. "I wanted to charge $1. The most I ever charged was $3," a fair price in 1963. Pearl had also been presenting what he calls "semi-political shows," such as Bob Dylan and Joan Baez, Steve Allen and Lenny Bruce, the Freedom Singers and "an antinuclear thing." He and his wife, Kate, went up to Berkeley for the first march against the Vietnam War in 1965. "I went to the Peace and Freedom meeting and nobody knew what they were doing and so by the third day, they asked me to be the head of the L.A. registration drive for the Peace and Freedom Party. So I devoted a lot of time to that," he says. At that time, Pearl opened the Ash Grove doors wider to politicos and their causes of all stripes, granting the community a space to gather for meetings and presentations. The Ash Grove's further politicization converged with the time in the culture that marked the free speech, antiwar, and the about-to-break minority culture movements merging into one. Nowhere was that confluence of connections made more manifest than by the appearance on the folk scene of an incredibly gifted, female, Native American, topical singer-songwriter named Buffy Sainte-Marie.

## "The Red Indian Folksinger"

Born on a Cree Indian reservation in Saskatchewan, Canada, and raised by a white family in Maine and Massachusetts, Buffy Sainte-Marie knew what it felt like to be disconnected from her cultural heritage. "My mom's family was very proud to be in quotes, part Indian . . . I grew up learning that her family was what they said was part Mic-Mac. But what she said to me was that they didn't know anything about it and maybe when I grew up I could find out." The local mailman, Leonard Bayrd of the Narragansett tribe, served as her early connection to Native American culture. "I even have pictures of his trading post. He was a huge influence on me because he and his wife were very kind to me. They didn't sit around and give me Indian lessons, or anything, but on the other hand they didn't chase me away. He used to make beautiful bead work and feather bonnets and all kinds of cultural items—he was so talented—and I was an artsy girl, so I was very much attracted to the craftwork that they did and to their kindness. That's where I really learned about Native American kindness and hospitality for the first time." A natural born seeker, Sainte-Marie gravitated to religion and philosophy classes as a student in the newly established Four Colleges program at the University of Massachusetts, which allowed her to take advantage of courses at the area's four universities. With the intention of carrying on her studies in India, she stopped by Greenwich Village first, checking out the scene there and checking into the YWCA with the cheap guitar on which she'd begun to write her own songs. She became a regular at Gerdes Folk City, where she met Bob Dylan, who in turn sent her to see Sam Hood at the Gaslight. With the help of a good review from Robert Shelton in the *New York Times*, Buffy Sainte-Marie was on her way.

Establishing herself as a player with a deep connection to tradition and yet completely unique, Sainte-Marie was devoted to delivering a new kind truth in her songs. She began to develop lyrics around her antiwar stance, incorporating race and gender matters into the mix. It hadn't occurred to her to politicize; it was just how the songs flowed. Among her followers was fellow Canadian singer-songwriter Joni Mitchell.

"There weren't many woman writing songs at the time . . . Buffy was building a repertoire. Her songs were intelligent, well crafted, and she was a stunning performer," says Mitchell.[13] Sainte-Marie in turn recorded Mitchell's "The Circle Game" and made a point of talking her up in folk circles. "Man, I carried her tape around in my purse for a long time," she says, and eventually she handed it off to the manager who would go on to play an important role in Mitchell's career. The story illustrates how the inside business of music often gets done and how women helped each other long before their own movement was organized. "When I went to Greenwich Village I had never met a businessman. I had never met a lawyer. So I was really, really screwed by the first record company who said, 'Oh you don't have a lawyer? Here, you can use ours,' which is clearly a conflict of interest. The fact that I didn't know about business—socially I was really green—affected not only my business but also my sense of being a loner. I didn't go to where they were drinking after the shows. And that's where you were supposed to do your social networking. So all of those things . . . kinda kept me . . . unique. It wasn't intentional, it's just kinda the way it turned out," says Sainte-Marie.

Buffy wasn't entirely isolated as a Native on the scene. There was Patrick Sky, who was half Creek and with whom she collaborated, and Peter La Farge, a cowboy singer of reportedly Narragansett descent, who had made some noise with his song "The Ballad of Ira Hayes," the story of the Pima Indian who helped raise the flag at Iwo Jima.

> Down the ditches for a thousand years,
>> the water grew Ira's peoples' crops,
> 'Till the white man stole the water rights, and
>> the sparklin' water stopped
> Now Ira's folks were hungry, and their land grew crops of weeds.
> When war came, Ira volunteered, and forgot the white man's greed.

In the spirit of a Woody Guthrie song, "Ira Hayes" concerned the post-war hardship story of the Indian solider famously photographed at Mount Suribachi erecting the flag at Iwo Jima. Post-traumatic stress and alcoholism contributed to Hayes's inability to adapt to a comfortable civilian life, and he died an alcoholic death on the rez. La Farge's song about Hayes moved Johnny Cash enough to record it, along with five more La Farge songs, for the Cash album *Bitter Tears*, devoted to Native concerns. As for La Farge's own story, it is said he was raised by Tewas on the Hopi reservation in New Mexico; when he was nine he was adopted by Pulitzer Prize–winning novelist Oliver La Farge (who wrote *Laughing Boy*, about the plight of the Navajos). As a boy Peter loved the rodeo and by the time he was sixteen he was riding and singing on the circuit where he made connections to traveling singers Cisco Houston and Josh White, both important figures of inspiration to the musicians on the Village folk scene. La Farge recorded five albums of his own for the Folkways label, all paying concern to Native issues. He organized FAIR (the Federation of American Indian Rights), and was subject to countless FBI investigations. But by 1965 at the age of thirty-four, the Native storyteller was gone, a victim of an undisclosed illness or a possible suicide; official accounts record it as a stroke. Though La Farge's actual heritage remains blurry, to this day he is credited with contributing to the creation of a powerful platform for Indian rights through song.

In 1964, Sainte-Marie left the Village to attend a powwow in Saskatchewan. Her relationship to Native music had deepened, and she incorporated its vocal inflections and rhythm-driven elements into her own work, debuting that year with *It's My Way!* for prestigious folk label Vanguard Records. Sainte-Marie is pictured on the cover wielding a bow; she had become an expert at using the hunting weapon as a musical instrument. She plays the traditional song "Cripple Creek" as a solo mouth bow track (years later, Canadians The Band would emulate the sound on their own song "Up on Cripple Creek"). The album opens with "Now That the Buffalo's Gone," a plea for the story of the Native to be heard. The young singer-songwriter composed two songs that became folk and rock standards: "Universal Soldier" and "Cod'ine." A proto-feminist anthem, "Babe in Arms," and a song about familial sexual abuse, titled on the album as "The I****t Song," were bold strokes at the time. The album was a sensation. When Donovan recorded "Universal Soldier" in Sainte-Marie's arrangement in 1965, its message that war is a matter of individual choice resounded. "He's the universal soldier and he's the one to blame" rang true, and Sainte-Marie found herself with a hit. Youth in the North understood the connection between their brothers and sisters in the South and those serving overseas in Vietnam and wanted to do something about it, whether that was participating in Freedom Summer of '64 or the Berkeley rallies in '65. An "Indian girl" greatly affected the worldwide movement toward people's liberation as "Universal Soldier" went on to become an even bigger hit, sung in multiple languages by artists around the globe.

## Keep on Pushing

Another young songwriter who knew the power of an anthem and made the freedom movement sing was Curtis Mayfield of Chicago. Just seventeen and straight out of the Cabrini-Green housing projects when he hit it big with "Your Precious Love," recorded by his vocal group the Impressions, Mayfield was a highly conscious, conscientious, and musically gifted individual. By the early sixties he had already sustained the departure of his childhood gospel choir buddy, Jerry Butler, from the group and was leading Samuel Goodens and Fred Cash on his own as he became a formidable writer of inspirational R&B hits. The Impressions captured the ephemeral spirit of gospel's lift and married it to Mayfield's layered melodies with a message. In 1964 Mayfield came up with the Black-Powered "Keep On Pushing." Its sentiment and language borrowed from a gospel groove and easily adapted to the civil rights cause: "Hallelujah, hallelujah, keep on pushing." "Keep on Pushing" was in

perfect synch with Dr. King and the march forward; it has been characterized as one of the movement's unofficial anthems. "Move up a little higher,"
"I've got my strength," "Keep on pushing," all phrases from the song, also
borrowed from gospel's language and its inspirational intent. These were elements that never strayed far from Mayfield's consciousness, and combined
with the melodious strains to which he set his words, he could disguise the
tougher sentiments by weaving them into the complex harmonies, while
never losing the threads. As time went on, Mayfield became more direct
lyrically, but these early works were foundational to setting soul music in
its new direction while they also passed in the mainstream. The Impressions album *Keep on Pushing* was a Top 10 hit, making its impression on the
masses and on two major twentieth-century Bobs. Robert Nesta Marley had
begun performing with his vocal group, the Wailers, in Kingston, Jamaica, as
if they were their country's answer to the Impressions. "Amen" and "I Made
a Mistake" from *Keep on Pushing* were an important part of their early repertoire. In 1965, Dylan featured a picture of *Keep on Pushing* on the cover
of one of his own albums, *Bringing It All Back Home*. That same year, the
Impressions hit again with "People Get Ready," a song Mayfield was first
inspired to get busy on following the March on Washington, and the song
for which he would become best known. "When humans from all walks of
life can experience a piece of music and feel the same way—that's soul," he
once said.[14] That certainly seems to be the case with "People Get Ready,"
which fifty years later would still be being performed by diverse artists, from
lightweight to the heaviest.

"Keep on Pushing," "People Get Ready," and Sam Cooke's "A Change Is
Gonna Come" are a few examples of powerful message songs that crossed
over to enjoy mighty success beyond the movement. But the otherwise varied
menu of music the freedom movement generated in the late 1950s and early
'60s found little representation on the airwaves save for on one unique, rene-
gade radio program, broadcasting with an unusually strong signal off the coast
of Cuba. Allegedly provided to him by Fidel Castro, former NAACP field
secretary Robert F. Williams broadcast *Radio Free Dixie* from coast to coast
from 1961 to 1965, giving a voice and a soundtrack to the unfolding story of
black liberation. As one of the few outlets on the airwaves for liberation songs
in all their colors and shapes, the show Williams and his wife Mabel created

was a patchwork of poetry, song, and instrumentals combined with their own commentary. Williams believed he was breeding a "new psychological concept of propaganda—the type of music people could feel and would motivate them."[15] The sounds of the free jazzmen, the bold race-centered statements of Nina Simone, relevant old Lead Belly tunes like the "Bourgeois Blues," and the gospel-powered songs of Sam Cooke all found a home on *Radio Free Dixie*, the place where black liberation also found its broadcast voice. During the race riots in 1964 and the Watts riots of 1965, Williams used his platform to back up the action with commentary and rallying cries from afar: "Freedom, Freedom, Freedom Now!"[16]

Stateside, the airwaves had also come alive. Broadcasting from San Francisco, New York, St. Louis, and anywhere else he could find work, the Magnificent Montague was waging a one-man antisegregation campaign. Using his airtime to testify, he dropped key movement phrases such as "Now is the time" and "I ain't gonna let nothing turn me around," punctuating the mic breaks between his black-positive sets that featured Simone and Mahalia Jackson and soul-centered segues of Mayfield, Cooke, Solomon Burke, and Ray Charles. "Play Ray Charles or Solomon Burke or Sam Cooke or Curtis Mayfield from those particular years—I swear they sound different, more soulful," remembers Montague.[17] With the fervor of a preacher, Montague would deliver the old DJ's plea for call-ins as a way to spark discussions on inequality and activism. "Call me now and say you're gonna walk that walk and talk that talk, and if the line is busy get on that other line, get on that telephone to Heaven and call on the Lord."[18] Eventually his catchphrase, "Burn Baby, Burn!"—conceived to describe a record that was burning up the turntable—caught fire when it became the rallying cry during the Watts rebellion of 1965.

## In the Heat of the Summer: Riots and Antiwar Rallies, 1965

The riot in Watts was said to have been sparked by a confrontation between a white officer and a black driver following a failed field sobriety test. According to observers it was just another case of alleged racial profiling and harassment by law enforcement. Lasting over seven days in August 1965, it left thousands injured, even more arrested, and over thirty persons dead. Watts was the largest riot that Los Angeles had seen to date. The LAPD has been beset with allegations of racial injustice and brutality for decades, and nearly fifty years later, Watts has still not fully recovered from its segregation, lack of services, and poor relations between residents and the law—the elements that commonly contribute to urban uprising everywhere.

"In the Heat of the Summer" by Phil Ochs is sometimes mistakenly believed to be about Watts, but it was the Harlem Riot of 1964 that the songwriter actually used as a jumping-off point. Ochs used his observer's eye and the language of activism to tie up the cause of persistent urban rioting in the song's key lines that resonated nationwide in the high season of urban rioting.

> Oh where oh where were the white silver tongues who forgot to listen to the warnings
> . . . we had to make somebody listen in the heat of the summer

Another *Broadside* alumni, Ochs had traded in the idea of being a cub reporter to become a star of topical song; his reputation as a performer informed by political and social news of the world was just about unrivaled. After debuting in 1964 with *All the News That's Fit to Sing*, a well-received set of tunes taken from the headlines, he followed up with "In the Heat of the Summer" on his 1965 album *I Ain't Marching Anymore*. It was later recorded by songster and activist Judy Collins for her *Fifth Album*.

It was such a time of pervasive rebellion that even songs not intended as political could have political connotations and ramifications. Martha and the Vandellas' Motown hit "Dancing in the Street" was perceived in some quarters as a reference to civil unrest. "They're dancin' in Chicago, down in New Orleans. Don't forget the Motor City," Reeves sang out strong. The call to "dance in the streets" was interpreted by watchdogs, observers, and student organizers as a sly reference to an organized, traffic-stopping effort toward social change, if not just a convenient coincidence. Certainly the song and others like it were a product of the times and another example of how a vibrant culture worked to effect empowerment and ultimately change.

More pointed perhaps was a song like Buffy Sainte-Marie's "Universal Soldier," and a new wave of songs that addressed the growing antiwar sentiment that by mid-1964, aided by groups like SNCC and Students for a Democratic Society (SDS), was fomenting on college campuses. Peace was turning into its own movement and by the time draft cards were burning in Berkeley in 1965, the protests were drawing more and more supporters. Not only were the students in opposition to a draft that made them and their peers of low-income status most vulnerable, they believed that a perceived threat of the spread of communism was not good enough reason to launch invasions; that depleting spending resources better used at home was unjust; and that the United States' assertion of power for power's sake was wrong and its legality questionable. These were the ideas that mattered to the students who stood in opposition to the war and to young songwriters like Sainte-Marie. She says the idea for "Universal Soldier" came to her as a result of coming face-to-face with the war's casualties while stranded overnight at the San Francisco Airport. "A bunch of soldiers came through wheeling guys on gurneys and stretchers and wheelchairs . . . just all blown apart. I got to thinking about who's responsible for war . . . and that includes the girls, you know? And in a way, yeah, recruits and soldiers are as responsible as anybody else." Sitting in the airport, she says, "I got to thinking about the people who are career military officers and spend years in college getting advanced degrees in making war, learning how to make war better . . . which made no sense to me. By the time I was flying, I was thinking, yeah but wait a minute, who is it that actually makes the decision to turn one army against another? Ah . . . it's the politicians. . . . By the time it was time for me to go on stage that night I said, who is it who votes for the politicians?"

Also considering the paradoxical notion that we "Kill for Peace" were the Fugs. Comprising poets Ed Sanders and Tuli Kupferberg and the folk musicians who accompanied them, the Fugs stayed on the margins of musical success with their abrasive, satirical rock. Most active from 1965 through 1969, the Fugs were entrenched on the Village scene as artists and activists, though their over-the-top, sometimes crass presentation was too much for the mainstream. Nevertheless, their connection to literature, poetry, and politics and the way they merged it with music grant them status as underground rock giants of the political music genre who also drew attention from the FBI (the investigation was unfounded). Their 1966 self-titled album, with liner notes by Allen Ginsberg, includes the still-relevant satire "Kill for Peace."

The point at which politics met poetry was also crucial for jazz player Archie Shepp. "I began to see the potential for poetry on records when I was in college," he says. "I became deeply involved, engaged politically. We put out pamphlets and made speeches in the streets. We were playing parties and dances to raise money for our political efforts."[19] By and by, the two forces merged in his solo work. "Malcolm, Malcolm-Semper Malcolm" from Shepp's 1965 album *Fire Music* offered a taste of where he was coming from, the spoken tones echoing the mood of gravity and grief contained in the composition.

Songs are not always poems and poems aren't always songs, but the era of freethinking and expression was now under way in earnest, and various arts and disciplines found fresh modes. Poetry could play off contemporary music, echoing the way Langston Hughes had set his poems to the rhythms of jazz in previous decades, and song forms could rely on the cadences of poetry and the poetry of the blues from days gone by. Certainly it could be said that Sainte-Marie's "Universal Soldier" was in line with a traditional rhyming verse and refrain structure, as well as a message of strong social and political intent, especially when delivered by the writer herself. When it was rendered by British folksinger Donovan in gentler wispy folk style, "Universal Soldier" translated into a pop song with wide commercial appeal, palatable to the general listening audience; that it contained a powerful antiwar statement made the song that much more exceptional, a song with inspirational and motivating force.

"A song like 'Until It's Time for You to Go' is just a song written by a girl in love," explains Sainte-Marie, referring to her other hit record from the period and further distinguishing categories of songs that sprung from her personal life. "They're totally different ways of approaching music." Along with Sainte-Marie's emergence from Greenwich Village onto the world stage and the simultaneous success of her songs from each camp came misperceptions of her and her work. "I have a picture that shows Elvis Presley's single of my song 'Until It's Time for You to Go' and it's saying, 'But do you know who really wrote it? It's the red Indian folksinger!'"

Sainte-Marie was not portrayed by the media as a gifted, multidimensional songwriter and scholar; rather, she was written off as a novelty and a curiosity, her political voice amped down while her softer side was brought forward. She admits that her own greenness and discomfort with the business side of music contributed to some of the ill-perceived coverage; she also believes some of it was based on ignorance of cultural diversity. Perhaps if she had a team of professionals backing her up, she could have better swum with the sharks. "I had graduated with a degree in Oriental philosophy and I also had a degree in teaching," she says. But like other artists without the financial resources or business acumen to compete in a record business dominated by white men, Sainte-Marie's earning potential and message were thwarted, while others who were promoted prospered.

Len Chandler's first sign of success was tainted by lack of professional support as well as by general ignorance: "Beans in My Ears" was the closest he'd come to launching a career when his record was banned by the Board of Health. "Apparently there had been a 33 percent rise in foreign objects inserted into children's ears that year as reported by the *New York Times*," he says. "That's when I thought, you really *can* change people's behavior with songs. You can make them put beans in their ears."

From there, Chandler would put his voice to work full time as an on-the-spot, topical political singer. Swept up by the momentum of the movement, with new purpose he turned out songs on the action down south, sometimes adding verse after verse after verse. He rewrote the Kentucky miners song "Which Side Are You On?" (sung to the melody of "Jack-a-Roe").

> Come all you Northern liberals,
>     take a Klansman out to lunch.
> But when you dine instead of whine
> You should serve nonviolent punch
> (Let me tell you now)
> Which side are you on, which side are you on?

He offers up another sample couplet, one that still makes him smile.

> Come all you bourgeois black men, with all your excess fat.
> A few days on the picket line will sure get rid of that

Did he catch any heat for any of the lines?
"Oh yeah!" he laughs, as he sings with glee,

> Come all you bourgeois college girls,
>     pronounce your final G's,
> But don't forget your grandma,

she's still scrubbing on her knees
(Won't you tell me now)
Which side are you on, which side are you on?

"I'd write a song like that and then I'd be singing it in a mass meeting that night. People would be playing and singing for forty-five minutes, until you just wore out," says Chandler. Singing as a group gave people who started as strangers a chance to bond; in communion with each other, they were bound to a common purpose, and singing together was energizing, soul nourishing; it fed their spirits and gave them strength to go forward together as one. Group harmony had provided some of the same functions around campfires and in churches, at sporting events and in bar rooms through the ages, though in the fight for nonviolence, singing was especially used as a tool to disarm. Fannie Lou Hamer understood the power of singing out; she was among those who sang with Len at the meetings and on the lines. A homemaker in her forties, Hamer joined the students of SNCC and became a representative of the Mississippi Freedom Democratic Party (MFDP), addressing the 1964 Democratic Convention with a moving testimony seeking voting rights at the polls and representation for her state's black population among the convention delegates. The party's bid to be seated at the convention was not validated— a result that further politicized the Freedom Party and, according to SNCC leader John Lewis, was a turning point in the civil rights movement. "Those who chose to stay were ready now to play by a different set of rules, their own rules," he writes in his memoir.[20] But her party's presence and Hamer's speech from the floor were powerful enough for President Johnson to attempt to pull the plug on the televised proceedings by calling an emergency press conference of his own. The campaign was nevertheless victorious in affecting the passing of the Voting Rights Act of 1965 (which made discriminatory voting practices against the law). Proclaiming the black citizenry to be "sick and tired of being sick and tired," Hamer had sung her way to a new level of freedom, rousing crowds with her righteous renditions of "Go Tell It on the Mountain" and "This Little Light of Mine," her designated theme song.

Following the publication of his original melody and words to "Father's Grave (For Cordell Reagon)" in *Broadside* in 1964, Chandler wrote songs at every available opportunity, pausing to compose as he walked on marches, working out rhymes. He wrote during the confrontational delayed march in the name of voter rights from Selma to Montgomery in 1965. "The old guys were calling cadence, left, left, left, right, left. I started saying 'Right, right, right' We've been left out, left back, left behind. We want to be on the right foot now." He wrote "Murder on the Road in Alabama" after coming upon a woman shot to death along Highway 80. Calling out Alabama's notorious segregationist governor George Wallace for the state of disaster, Chandler distilled images of the terrorism waged on protesters. "I had the song the next day," he says.

> There's a man behind the guns
> Kills for hate, for fear, for fun,
> And George Wallace is top gun of Alabama

Following the cold-blooded killing of the NAACP's field secretary Evers by a white supremacist in 1963 and the period of ever-intensifying racial hostility in the South, writers got more and more direct with their songs of southern hate. "The Ballad of Medgar Evers" is an a cappella spiritual by the Freedom Singers (a different group than Cordell Reagon's); Dylan had covered the event with "Only a Pawn in Their Game"; Ochs came in with "Too Many Martyrs"; and of course there was Nina Simone's "Mississippi Goddam." Chandler didn't weigh in on the Evers event topically, though one of his songs of southern disharmony was mistaken by *New York Times* critic Robert Shelton as a tribute to Evers. "Shelton said, I 'galvanized a crowd of 11,000 with his obvious response to Medgar Evers.' That was news to me!" says Chandler. Rather, the crowd was responding to "Turn Around Miss Liberty," which married original melody with poetic image.

> Turn around turn around Miss Liberty, turn around I say
> And touch your torch to this cotton curtain
> and shine your light our way

Chandler had begun to take inspiration from beyond old folk melodies and newspaper headlines to develop his own new song style. The new songs were designed "so you could come to it with your own head and hear your own message," he says. Judy Collins recorded "Turn Around Miss Liberty" "but that dude from the record company [Jac Holzman] didn't put it on her album." However, Chandler's woodshedding did yield a song that would be handed down in the folk tradition. He and Beat poet Bob Kaufman used a children's rhyme with slave period origins and turned it into "Green Green Rocky Road," later popularized by Dave Van Ronk. "Bob was borderline tone deaf and I couldn't make head or tail of the melody he was trying to get across to me," recalls Van Ronk. "But Len Chandler was there, a very well-trained, highly trained musician . . . and he deciphered the melody from Bob's uh . . . mooing. Had it not been for Len, there's was no way I would've been able to do that . . . It's become so embedded in my repertory now that I suppose if I have a theme song, that's it."[21] Chandler never recorded it; he was too busy circulating, with the movement and with fellow writers. "I met the poet David Henderson . . . we became friends and he told me Langston Hughes was doing a book of poetry and that I should get my stuff together and he would give it to him," Chandler says.

Months passed, but Len heard nothing from Hughes, nor about his potential solo recording career, which despite his popularity on the club scene was at an impasse. "I was the one that was closing the show all the time, I'm talking about all the time. A lot of people were getting recorded around me and nobody was touching me . . . I wasn't getting a nibble." Finally he'd had enough. "I just made an appointment and went in to see John Hammond," he says. The heavyweight Columbia Records executive was known to be musician friendly; he'd formed liaisons with great artists such as Billie Holiday and Babatunde Olatunji and had brought Aretha Franklin, Pete Seeger, and Dylan, among others, to the label. "I sang him two songs and he gave me a contract that day," says Chandler. "He said that he welcomed the opportunity to record me like he would have liked to have recorded Lead Belly in his prime." It was not a comparison that set well or bode well for Chandler: Though sure enough Lead Belly had specialized in the traditional as well as the topical, the powerful, self-taught southern musician, famous for his booming twelve-string blues and prison time, had little in common with Chandler's classically trained New York via Akron approach to folk singing. "OK, so, he had no idea what to do with me, or around me, or anything," he says. But Chandler had impressed the legendary record man and he was going to get his shot, though it wasn't long before he could see the writing on the wall.

In 1966 heavier fighting in Vietnam was escalating and even vets at home had begun to speak out against the war. Staff Sergeant Barry Sadler scored a #1 hit with a song that celebrated the military, "The Ballad of the Green

Berets.'" "John Hammond saw me in a hallway and said, 'Why don't you write a reply to that,' and so I did: 'Things are in a jam down in Vietnam (get gone), People down there don't dig Uncle Sam (get gone), Rule by the people just can't be wrong (get gone) and the people down there are the Vietcong and you're wrong Sam, scram, why don't you get gone,'" Chandler recalls. "He responded with 'ha ha ha ha ha,' and walked away . . . I thought it was a good song! It was a good response to that stupid Green Beret song."

Recording commenced on Chandler's Columbia Records debut. He had enlisted two of the best session men in the business, Bruce Langhorne and Bill Lee—a guitarist and bassist who knew their way around the folk ranks, having played sessions with everyone from Odetta to Dylan.[22] Though his answer to Sergeant Sadler's song didn't end up in the mix, his edginess was intact on "Missionary Stew #2" and "Feet First Baby," inspired by colonialism and its history of violence. "Bellevue," about the psychiatric unit at New York's public hospital, also had bite. Overall, *To Be a Man* is a collection of mostly contemplative acoustic tracks—songs like "Taking Me Away from You Train" and "Nancy Rose"—that merge the life of the protest singer with the love of his wife at the time. Similarly soft-spoken is "Keep on Keepin' On." "I felt very good when the Reverend Martin Luther King used the phrase 'keep on keepin' on' in one of his speeches in Atlanta; he had learned it from his secretary who saw the song in *Broadside* and liked it," wrote Chandler in the liner notes. Though the singer-songwriter had done his part to fashion a carefully conceived and executed piece, upon release of the album in 1967 it didn't feel like the label held up their end of the deal to support the recording. "It was like no push, nothing," says Chandler.

In Atlanta he heard his song "Minding My Mind" on the radio but was told by locals that they couldn't buy the record in town. Chandler didn't question the poor policy of not backing up airplay with proper distribution; he would come to recognize it as record company shorthand for lack of commitment to a project and knew his days at Columbia weren't long. There was a limit to how much direct protest music could be recorded with high-level corporate support; maybe it wasn't so much what Chandler was saying as what he was doing, backing up his music with activism. "There was only so much of that they wanted to take . . . I'm thinking of Sonia Sanchez," he says, speaking of the poet and educator who got her start in the Black Arts Movement. "In one of her books, she talked about representatives of the government, it might've been FBI, coming to her saying, look, if you lay off being an instigator, rabble rouser, making people less patriotic, your voice will be a hundredfold enhanced. However if you don't, you'll be silenced."[23]

"Basically, she told them to screw off . . . They really told us, you make a deal. Cut this out and you can have all this. My friend Cordell, they really muscled Cordell big-time, to try to get him to inform or to change his road. When I say muscle big-time, I'm talking about harassment, following, steaming-open stuff, really direct intimidation."[24] For his association with the freedom movement and his songs of protest, Chandler dealt with harassment and the invasion of surveillance in its various guises, usually in the form of home visits by government informants masquerading as insiders and friends of the movement. Counter-intelligence was largely succeeding at penetrating the civil rights and antiwar movements, while acts of violence and politically motivated murders escalated. Malcolm X was assassinated on February 21, 1965, shot multiple times at the podium of the Audubon Ballroom, where he was about to address the Organization of Afro-American Unity. Thousands flocked to Harlem over a three-day period to view his body before the burial; Chandler and his fellow Freedom workers were among the mourners.

"My house in New York was as Tokyo was to the Vietnam War—people would come back for rest and relaxation after being down in Mississippi and in the South. One of the girls who was staying with me, Alma from Louisiana, and I had gone to Malcolm's funeral and some guy had picked her up there and attached himself to her. He was very handsome and very articulate—very smooth. He followed her home and started dating her, staying with her and stuff." And just like that, a stranger had inveigled himself into the small circle of friends who congregated at Chandler's place.

"So he started showing me these newspaper articles and told me how he had defended his home in the South and that he'd been run out for having guns and standing up to white folks and all this stuff. Basically, it was an extended entrée into what kind of guns do I have to protect my home? Just transparent," he says. Fully aware that all eyes were on him, Chandler didn't tolerate being played for a fool and kindly directed all moles to the nearest exit.

Now thirty-two years old with some work and life experience to look back on, Chandler could easily have recognized his own dilemma in writer James Baldwin's declaration of what it meant to be a man.

> It comes as a great shock to discover that the country which is your birthplace and to which you owe your life and your identity has not, in its whole system of reality, evolved any place for you. The disaffection, the demoralization, and the gap between one person and another, only on the basis of the color of their skins, begins there and accelerates throughout a whole lifetime. So that presently you realize that you are thirty and you are having a terrible time managing to trust your countrymen. By the time you are thirty, you've been through a certain kind of mill.[25]

The watershed marches from Selma to Montgomery had occurred in March; the work begun in the South by SNCC, the Freedom Riders, the SCLC, Dr. King, and their supporters forged on; and the northern riots continued to blow. The movement had reached a crossroads. Making the north/south commute at regular intervals, Chandler found a fit for his biting satire when he met Lew Irwin in Lowndes County, Alabama, where the pair worked together on a documentary. Working for white landowners, the majority black population of Lowndes County had about as much freedom as their ancestors did before 1865; one hundred years later, local authorities were among the hold-outs in observing new federal Civil Rights Act and Voting Rights Acts. Stokely Carmichael—SNCC's new leader following the departure of John Lewis—took the opportunity to do there what the SNCC organizers had done with the Mississippi Freedom Democratic Party: organize, educate, and get residents directly involved in their local government.

"So I went to Lowndes County, Alabama," says Chandler. "Lew Irwin got me a hotel room. He'd do the shooting with the cameraperson, would describe to me what the hassle was about and then say, 'I need a minute and thirty seconds on that.' And then I would go in the toilet because that's the only place that was totally quiet, come back out, and he'd take his Nagra and I would play it into the Nagra, then he would describe more."

As a result of the activism in town, the Lowndes County Freedom Organization (LCFO) formed as an independent party to run candidates to represent their interests in opposition to the roster of the white supremacist

Alabama Democratic Party. They chose as their emblem a black panther. Chandler wrote a song for them while on the job there.

> Black sheep in the country, black sheep in the town
> Black sheep doesn't have half a chance
> With so many wolves around
> You got to walk with the black panther,
> That's all that you gotta do,
> Cause when you're walking with a big black cat,
> No wolves are gonna bother you

Chandler did not heed the admonitions to quiet down and never adjusted his position to accommodate; rather, he pitched in and sang out louder against oppression wherever it lived, especially in its stealthiest guise. "Right in the middle of when I was 'the angry young black man,'" he says, he was invited to write a jingle for a beer commercial. "I had just seen some documentary where the TV is showing people doing heroin sales on the corner, people shooting up, and I was thinking if the TV can photograph them, why can't the police arrest them? What is that? The other thing was, there was a commercial—an advertisement for diamonds with no money down. They're seducing you to buy diamonds and you can't even pay for them? Diamonds no money down? That's crazy. And then there're all the liquor commercials. So I get invited to do this beer commercial and they say, 'We'd like you to do two songs. We'd like one ballad and one up-tempo, OK?' And I said, 'You'll be able to make your judgment on the basis of this one song.'" He sang:

> Swing up the glass one more time—bourbon, brandy or wine
> It will blackout your brain, it will deaden your pain
> But the subject is willing, one more mercy killing:
> Euthanasia
> If the pain just gets too much to bear
> If you haven't one hope and don't care
> If you're a stranger in town, sit down, I'll buy one more round:
> Euthanasia

Back home in New York, Chandler's phone rang late one night. "I get this call at 12:30 or one o'clock in the morning. He said, 'Len Chandler? This is

Langston Hughes and I said, 'Yeah right, and this is James Baldwin.' I almost hung up on him." Inquiring whether he'd received his telegram, Chandler said no, and Hughes wired it again.

TO: LEN CHANDLER

NEW YORK CITY

BY PHONE I FIND NOBODY HOME AT YOUR HOUSE SO I AM SENDING THIS WIRE TO SAY HEY HOORAY AND GOODMORNING BECAUSE I'VE JUST READ YOUR POEMS AND PROSE AND SONGS YOU SENT ME MONTHS AGO BUT I'VE BEEN IN AFRICA TWICE SINCE THEN AND DID NOT HAVE A CHANCE TO LOOK AT THEM QUIETLY BEFORE NOW. SO HEY, HOORAY, AND GOOD MORNING BECAUSE THEY WONDERFUL.

LANGSTON HUGHES[26]

Hughes would be dead within the year, but the boogie-woogie rhythm of his deferred dream would still beat in the hearts of his children—Len Chandler, Richie Havens, and Nina Simone—and in their songs and in the songs of those they influenced that much stronger. As the continuing incidents of violence in the South and the urban riots and racial inequities in the North could not be quelled, by the fall of 1966 a new morning was breaking on the freedom movement. Attitudes were changing—and in addition to themes of protest and pride, revolution and rebellion were the new rhythms waiting to be captured by a song.

# The Rhythm of the Rebel:
# The Sound of Black Power

In June of 1966, James Meredith walked a one-man March Against Fear from Memphis to Jackson. He was shot down. Singer J. B. Lenoir wrote a blues song about the incident:

> June the sixth, nineteen sixty six
> They shot James Meredith down just like a dog
> I wonder what are you going to do now Mr. President?
> I don't believe you're gonna do nothing at all

Meredith's 1962 bid to become the first black student admitted to the University of Mississippi forced the intervention of the White House, turning the nation's eyes to civil rights issues. Working independently of the support of the larger civil rights movement, Meredith's 1966 effort was an attempt to call attention to the unrelenting white on black violence launched as a consequence of increased civil rights. It also served as flashpoint: as the different factions in the movement rallied for Meredith, his shooting also made way for the new strain of activism. Even Dr. King with his unstinting devotion to nonviolence knew his freedom fighters were tiring, that he was at risk of losing his nonviolent forces.

"When Mr. Meredith was gunned down during his march, I dropped everything to visit him in his hospital room," remembered James Brown. "I was greatly affected by that visit and afterward, I intensified the pledge I had made to myself. . . . It was no longer going to be enough to change the music of a generation—I had to try to change people's way of thinking as well." The soul singer was becoming more conscious of wanting to inject more political content into his shows, and showing up for Meredith was his way of flexing some political muscle with his celebrity status. "I was going to put it to good use and apply it for the good of my people."[1]

Meredith's shooting also had a profound effect on the Student Nonviolent Coordinating Committee (SNCC), which had been undergoing its own reorganization surrounding the upheavals at the 1964 Democratic Convention and in Watts. Stokely Carmichael was among those who no longer saw nonviolence as a way to bring about social change. As a leader of SNCC, now an all-black organization, Carmichael had been committed to nonviolent tactics and had walked its front lines. Now after years engaged in a nonviolent struggle that begat horrific violence, he was moving away from the principle he had espoused. Developing a black consciousness, teaching self-reliance, and coalescing Black Power became revolutionary tools in the fight for liberation.

How could black lives and rights continue to go unprotected by federal and local law enforcement while the crimes perpetrated by Southern whites went unpunished? "We were angry and tired, tired, tired. Tired of folks being brutalized or killed with impunity. Tired of the indifference and complicity of the nation. Tired of mealymouthed politicians. Tired too especially of half-baked, knee-jerk ideas from our side. Particularly of these wretched, pointless marches, appealing to whom? Accomplishing what?" writes Carmichael in his autobiography. He recollected the drive to the hospital to visit Meredith. "What we felt in that car was an all-encompassing anger and frustration, as much with movement futility as with the racist violence."[2] Civil rights workers gathered to finish the march in Meredith's name, and as they passed through Greenwood, Mississippi, Carmichael used the opportunity to deliver a speech that marked a new direction in the movement. Carmichael spoke in a musical cadence, a mixture of the grand tradition of Trinidadian oration that was his birthright and the plain language of the people. It didn't take much for Carmichael to win over the folks he'd become acquainted with during his voter registration drives. They were tired, too.

"What do we want?

"Black Power!"

These were the first utterances of the chant that would make sensational headlines and become the call and response marching song of the Black Power movement. Though CORE endorsed Carmichael, the highest-level representatives of civil rights organizations, including Dr. King, the SCLC, and the NAACP, felt it was necessary to distance themselves from him as he denounced integration and moved SNCC toward an all-black agenda while employing a more revolutionary strategy. He delivered the sound of Black Power on campuses across the country and addressed students at the University of California at Berkeley on October 29, 1966, saying, "We are on the move for our liberation. We're tired of trying to prove things to white people."

Just two weeks before Carmichael's arrival in the Bay Area, two young men who met on the Soul Students Advisory Council at Merritt College in nearby Oakland had armed themselves with knowledge from Mao's *Little Red Book*, Frantz Fanon's *The Wretched of the Earth*, and a copy of Bob Dylan's *Highway 61 Revisited*. Borrowing the logo and name from the Lowndes voting party and inspired by the Southern Negro community defense leagues who'd armed themselves against attacks by law enforcement, they dubbed themselves the Black Panther Party for Self-Defense. Their mission was to protect their immediate community from police violence and to serve it with survival programs to meet its food and medical needs—breakfasts for children, grocery giveaways, and free sickle-cell anemia testing were all part of the plan. The group's cofounders, Huey Newton and Bobby Seale, wished to distinguish themselves from the mainline civil rights movement and issued a statement about taking control of their community's institutions. They advocated free health care for black and all oppressed people, an end to wars of aggression, and the immediate release of all political prisoners. They warned that failure to meet these demands would bring revolution.

Huey Newton believed that if the dilemma of black oppression could be told in a song, it was "Ballad of a Thin Man." Bob Dylan's poetic rant at "Mr. Jones" summed it up perfectly. "Huey P. Newton made me recognize the lyrics. Not only the lyrics of the record, but what the lyrics meant in the record. What the lyrics meant in the history of racism that has perpetuated itself in this world," Seale wrote in his 1967 book *Seize the Time*.

Reporting on racism and social injustice in song was of course Dylan's stock-in-trade during the civil rights era; his point of view was shared by a broad spectrum of his fellow artists. While Newton had his particular interpretation of "Ballad of a Thin Man," Mr. Jones could serve as a stand-in for any lie, even the lie one tells oneself, before it's disrupted by another view. Increasingly, singers had begun to interpret Dylan's songs across racial, gender, and even language lines. So while there were critics who perceived Dylan's "Just Like a Woman" (also from 1966) as negative and one-dimensional, Richie Havens heard it as "Bob Dylan . . . talking about . . . a complex woman . . . the whole of that woman." That same year, sixteen-year-old Stevie Wonder had a hit on "Blowin' in the Wind" and followed its success with the melancholy mood of "A Place in the Sun," which offers its own poetic impulses and allusions to the rivers of Langston Hughes:

> Like a branch on a tree, I keep reaching to be free,
>    moving on, moving on.

The Staple Singers cut Dylan's "A Hard Rain's A-Gonna Fall," adding it to their repertoire of timely statement songs like Buffalo Springfield's "For What It's Worth," and their own direct civil rights statement, "Why (Am I Treated So Bad)?" from their folk gospel album *Freedom Highway*. In this same period the Rolling Stones were enjoying a hit with "The Last Time," a traditional gospel popularized by the Staples in the 1950s, while Dylan was moving further from singing for field workers and marchers and deeper into poetical, philosophical matters, allowing for more open interpretations of his songs.

Among Dylan's central concerns remained a persistent investigation into one of the biggest questions in the black and white world: if there is such a thing as a force for good, how come it has such a damn hard time triumphing over evil? "Ballad of a Thin Man" was neither the first nor the last time a Dylan song rang out to a Black Panther. In a 1968 letter to California governor Ronald Reagan, Black Panther Minister of Information Eldridge Cleaver, composing in prison, referred to Dylan's "empty-handed beggar," adding "except that his hand is not empty anymore. He's got a gun in that hand."

Huey Newton's elaborate take on "Ballad of a Thin Man" identifies Dylan's "geek" as poor blacks and his "freak" as the white who passes by, watching ghetto life as if it's a show. According to Newton, the freak scene described in "Ballad of a Thin Man" is hell on Earth and white privilege is being called upon to confront its responsibility in creating the conditions; he finally understands when the geek "hands [him] a bone." "This song Bobby Dylan was singing became a very big part of that whole publishing operation of the Black Panther paper. And in the background, while we were putting this paper out, this record came up . . . many times we would play that record," writes Seale. "Brother Stokely Carmichael also liked that record. This record became so related to us, even to the brothers who had held down most of the security for the set."[3]

Carmichael's short tenure with the Panthers began following Newton's incarceration for allegedly killing a police officer. Seeking outside support for their Free Huey campaign and finding none from the mainline movement, the Panthers appealed for a merger with SNCC, tapping Jim Forman, H. Rap Brown, and Carmichael for positions in the party. Carmichael became Honorary Prime Minister (the "honorary" to designate the position was appointed).[4] Also parting ways with the old guard civil rights scene was Carmichael's friend Nina Simone, who fell in with the new direction in vanguard politics. She was enthusiastic about the Black Panthers and the call for Black Power. In keeping with the consciousness-raising agenda, she moved from topical to more personal matters in her songwriting: "Four Women" grew from conversations she'd had with black women about hair, skin tone, and body image. Freedom would soon come as women of all races continued to gain ground in their own liberation efforts, but it hadn't come yet. Simone was a leader in matters of turning the personal into the political with her song of black female individuality; she also led by donning her own "freedom cap," her term for wearing her hair natural.

"When 'Four Women' was released in 1966 some black radio stations banned DJs from playing it because they said it 'insulted' black women. That was a stupid thing to do but I wasn't surprised. The song told a truth that many people in the USA—especially black men—weren't ready to acknowledge at that time."[5] Simone's own truth was anger, and it was as if she were foretelling the dissent between the races and the sexes within the movement; her performances became wake-up calls as her songwriting grew more direct and her between-song dialogue unflinching. The gifted artist embraced using her talent to effect change. "What we were looking for then was to shake people out of their complacency," says collaborator Al Schackman. The reactions they received were striking, ranging from critical praise for her boldness to walk-outs from audiences unprepared for Simone's powerful new freedom voice.

Carmichael and the Panthers understood that in order to achieve black freedom—black independence, Black Power—the people needed to be ready, so a violent rhetoric was put into service of the cause. "We must retaliate! We must retaliate!" was the cry in the South in response to the violent resistance of whites to increased civil rights for blacks. Nonviolence was all right as a tactic, but it was by no means the only way to end racism in the form of segregation and police brutality. Like Malcolm X, who had declared that human rights and dignity would be won by any means necessary, Black Power suggested that development of a black consciousness and a commitment to community self-reliance was crucial to gaining freedom from oppression.

Newton and Seale conceived the Ten Point Program as a means to educate the black community about its history, and about its rights as outlined by the Constitution of the United States. Bolstered by the Free Speech movement and antiwar demonstrations taking place on the University of California at Berkeley campus, the pair reached out to students there and on smaller local campuses, as well as to the residents of their immediate Oakland neighborhood communities. They didn't have too much trouble finding interest among folks who'd been beaten down by circumstances—or by the local police. Robert F. Williams in North Carolina and the Deacons of Defense in Louisiana, who both advocated self-defense against the police brutality and white hostility waged on their community, had also inspired the forming Panthers.

It was in the spirit of the times that you might hear Lightnin' Hopkins sing of taking revenge on an abusive plantation owner in "Tom Moore's Farm."

> Ain't but the one thing, I done wrong
> Moved my family down to Mr. Tom Moore's farm.

Mance Lipscomb also sang a version of the Moore Brothers blues. The song, with its add-on verses, passed between the Texas players who cataloged the ongoing abuses on the farm. "But they didn't nobody tell Tom Moore I put it out," said Lipscomb. "He say, Lightnin' Hopkins from Houston, if I see that bastard I'm gon' kill him . . . So I kept that song hid, maybe 30 years."[6]

Though not all involved in the movements were in agreement on matters of Black Nationalism or integration, violence or nonviolence, it was generally agreed that the old ways weren't working and the time had finally come for a radical change.

"Robert F. Williams was one of my heroes. I read *Muhammad Speaks* and *The Inner City Voice*. There weren't many sources for the things I was interested in, so I followed them all. By the time the Panthers came into being, I was coming from there already," says John Sinclair. Sinclair was born into a working class family in Flint, Michigan. His mother was a teacher, known for her interests in "beat poetry and activism," and his father was a factory engineer.[7] Sinclair's own interest in the arts and activism led him to poetry, the formation of an artists' collective, and the accidental management of a rock 'n' roll group. But his charges were not just any band: the MC5's blend of grit-rock was inspired just as much by Chuck Berry as it was by free jazz. Wayne Kramer, Fred Smith, Dennis Thompson, and Rob Tyner were still in high school when they started knocking around in local bands, roughshod musical outfits typical of young groups in the post-Beatles/Stones era, who played blues and R&B-based cover songs. With the addition of Michael Davis they became the MC5. Cranking out covers and grinding originals, the band became central to the underground scene blossoming in their midst. Wayne Kramer says as a young songwriter, a mix of influences, from the high bar Chuck Berry set for rock 'n' roll guitarists to the new sounds of avant-garde jazz coming from Sun Ra, Cecil Taylor, Albert Ayler, John Coltrane, and Archie Shepp, helped him and the MC5 make their unique contribution to rock. "To hear this whole generation of jazz musicians who were breaking the boundaries in the world of jazz opened the door for me and it showed me how to start breaking the boundaries in the world of rock," says Kramer. "If I took my best Chuck Berry solo, you know the highest velocity I could play at, and moved it to the next level, I would be going into the kinds of things that Albert was trying to do with his saxophone or that Pharoah Sanders was trying to do—to move into a more pure, sonic dimension. And the rhythm section—being tied to just one rhythm and start to incorporate polyrhythms and subdivisions and move out of the Western concepts of rhythm and outside of the concepts of Western harmony. Those were the things we were trying to do in the MC5."

Having established himself in town as among the avant-garde's biggest champions, Sinclair was known to the MC5's members as a local writer who primarily followed underground jazz; on one occasion the Five had collectively fired off a letter to the editor in response to one of his "anti-rock" columns. Undaunted in his efforts to preach the intellectual, cultural, and spiritual virtues of free jazz as well as the black liberation cause to the psychedelicized masses, Sinclair found his efforts held little sway with the generation raised on rock 'n' roll—until he found a band of his own to use as a tool for his propaganda.

"I'd been a blues fan and R&B fanatic when I was a youth," says Sinclair. "I'd never heard jazz and then I got turned on and I was listening to Sonny Rollins, Miles Davis, John Coltrane, and Jackie McLean, and I really liked that. I started listening to Coltrane as he got farther and farther out and then Cecil Taylor, Ornette Coleman, and the revolution in jazz . . . Archie Shepp, Sun Ra," he says, pointing to the players known as pioneers of the new, free style, with a touch of blue. Shepp adds, "It was the kind of music that evolved out of the experience of the 1960s—the civil rights movement, the Muslims, the Panthers. There were certain social and political events that were going on concomitantly with the coming of age of John Coltrane, the arrival of Ornette Coleman in New York and people like Cecil Taylor who'd been there for a long time."[8] So too the MC5 grew from this unique period of social, political, and musical upheaval, and created a sound that reverberated through their city with resonances throughout the countercultural movement.

## Beyond Vietnam

On April 4, 1967, Dr. King could no longer remain silent about the escalating violence in Vietnam and delivered his "Beyond Vietnam: A Time to Break the Silence" to clergy and concerned laity at the Riverside Church in New York City, despite being advised against it. Indeed part of King's speech suggested that further silence would be a betrayal of his moral code. He spoke of moving beyond "the prophesying of smooth patriotism to the high grounds of a firm dissent based upon the mandates of conscience and the readings of history."[9]

He outlined seven reasons why the movements for peace and civil rights were naturally connected. He pointed to the promise of the poverty programs enacted in the early 1960s. "Then came the build-up in Vietnam and I watched the program broken and eviscerated as if it were some idle political plaything of a society gone mad on war and I knew America would never invest the necessary funds or energies in rehabilitation of its poor so long as adventures like Vietnam continued to draw men and skills and money like some demonic destructive suction tube," he said. Noting that the draft took black and poor folks to combat in higher proportions, Dr. King also spoke to the inherent difficulty of defending nonviolence as a means to change when government-sanctioned violence overseas raged. He was, after all, a recipient of the Nobel Peace Prize. As a religious leader with a calling to serve humankind, he spoke of the brotherhood of man and his commitment to all people, including the Vietnamese. "They must see Americans as strange liberators," he said. Following the speech, King was denounced by the media, his relationship with President Johnson was destroyed, and polls showed even the American public had turned against him.

Meanwhile, in America's urban centers conditions continued to deteriorate; come summer, the obstacles in freedom's path would be documented in song and observed by singers, just as sure as those outraged by the obstacles in freedom's path would display their outrage. "In June the riots started again, in Tampa, Cincinnati, and Buffalo . . . I played the Newport Jazz Festival in July and got back to Mount Vernon to hear that thirty-six rioters had been killed in Detroit," writes Nina Simone.[10] She sang jazz activist Billy Taylor's song "I Wish I Knew How It Would Feel To Be Free," on her 1967 album *Silk and Soul:*

> I wish I could give all I'm longing to give
> I wish I could live like I'm longing to live
> I wish I could do all the things I could do
> Though I'm way overdue, I'd be starting anew

She performed the song that summer as she toured to the point of exhaustion, fueled by frustration at the events surrounding her, including the passing of her friend Langston Hughes. She had recently set his hard-hitting poem "Backlash Blues" to music, had recorded it, and was performing it regularly as a tribute. The trauma and pace were unrelenting, and her artistry and politics had become irrevocably interconnected.

"The next day one of my friends in SNCC, Rap Brown, was shot and wounded in Maryland. News came through every day of friends getting arrested, beaten, and intimidated," she remembered. The roadwork and the escalating violence wore her down; her mental and emotional health suffered. "But there was no time to try and help because I had to prepare for another trip to Europe, followed by a week in Las Vegas." She did her best to let her anger and grief resolve through her work as she shouted slogans and led sing-alongs from the stage.

One particular incident involving one of Simone's friends is worth detailing for the way it would come to bear on left and right, black and white relations. Thirteen years after the passage of *Brown v. Board of Education* had declared separate schools unequal, H. Rap Brown rallied black citizens and delivered a fiery speech in Cambridge, Maryland, a town where segregation was still a way life. "If Cambridge won't come around, we're going to burn Cambridge down," he said. That evening, the black school burned. There was no evidence that Brown nor anyone in the assembled crowd had set the school alight, but the SNCC leader was picked up on charges of inciting a riot. When Maryland governor Spiro Agnew got involved, his own fiery remarks rendered the incident a symbol of the fight between assertion of black civil rights and white fear. Political historians have noted that following the race-related events in 1967 and 1968 in Maryland, Agnew, previously a moderate, got tough on law and order, which coincided with his rise in politics. Chosen to serve as vice president under Richard Nixon, Agnew later resigned in disgrace following charges of bribery during his governorship in Maryland.

"I wasn't that fond of SNCC, but I was adamant about Mr. Brown's right to say what he wanted, and to act with all the authority granted to him in the Constitution," James Brown writes in his autobiography.[11] He told H. Rap Brown, "I'm not going to tell anyone to pick up a gun," but he supported the H. Rap Brown Defense Fund. James Brown had also supported the efforts of CORE and James Meredith. James Brown was once referred to as the "most dangerous" man in the movement by Stokely Carmichael, due to his appeal and the influence he wielded. Long before he was moved to join the movement, however, Brown was moving and pushing people forward with his music.

Brown's 1964 record "Outta Sight" introduced a new rhythm and a new horn player, Maceo Parker, to the mix, reconfiguring his already singular sound. In the summer of 1965, Brown ushered in the new era of soul, unalterably impacting the sound of music with the irregular rhythm pattern that foreshadowed the birth of funk and characterized "Papa's Got a Brand New Bag," the R&B #1 hit that saw him cross over for the first time in his career. Recognizing a need for leadership from the music community, in 1966 he dropped "Don't Be a Drop Out," urging kids, "Don't be fools, stay in school." "I like to believe the message hit home," he said of his stay-in-school rap. "I had to think it did, or there was no other way I could continue to be an entertainer in such a troubled time."[12]

His stature as a leader—as a musical innovator as well as someone who gave back to the community—grew steadily. Just as the hits kept coming, the showmanship kept showing and the grooves he cut got more grooving—"Cold Sweat," "Licking Stick," "Funky Drummer"—just getting deeper and deeper. JB's trombonist Fred Wesley once said he thought "Cold Sweat" was the funkiest song ever written. Working in the golden age of soul music, Brown was about to open the door to a blacker and stronger sound. He also had an impulse to get further involved during the newly politicized era.

Unpopular as the war was, he wished to entertain in Vietnam—for the black troops who asserted their right to relevant entertainment beyond Bob Hope—and asked his friend Vice President Hubert Humphrey if it could be arranged. The answer was no. "He knew that there was always a worry that a black man might have an agenda for the black soldiers that wasn't exactly what the powers that be wanted," said Brown.[13] Though word was out that in the early years of Vietnam a disproportionate number of black soldiers were sent to the front lines and had died in combat, Brown was more interested in serving the troops than he was in contributing to dissent within their ranks. But for the time being, he would have to be content to serve them from afar as a recording artist instead of as a USO entertainer.

## Black Enterprise, Soul Power

By the mid-1960s Brown and his fellow singers on the soul scene were competing with a new breed of entertainer for the youth audience: singer-songwriters in the Bob Dylan style, Beatle-y boy bands, psychedelicized rockers like Jimi Hendrix, and natural women like Aretha Franklin. While soul music may have been exploding, the changing times and racial issues at hand had the soul men in transition, looking at ways to increase business and secure their financial futures. Payback was still forthcoming for soul's originators.

Though traveling conditions in the South for Solomon Burke and his friends like Don Covay, Wilson Pickett, Otis Redding, and Ben. E. King might have improved from earlier in the decade, they were by no means equal. In fact, it remained dangerous for anyone unfortunate enough to get caught driving while black. Efforts by the NAACP, SCLC, and SNCC on the local and regional levels had brought about the necessary widespread attention to violent racism in the South, and the Civil Rights Act of 1964 had put an end to Jim Crow laws on paper, but ways were slow to change. Nationwide, top-flight performers still remained locked out of certain hotels and restaurants, and were barred from buying in exclusive housing markets. The musicians joked that perhaps a Soul Clan—an alliance like the Ku Klux Klan but without the white sheets and hatred—would afford themselves and the community at large a little leverage.

Crowned the King of Rock 'n' Soul by an enthusiastic DJ in 1964, Solomon Burke is sometimes blackballed (or is it whitewashed?) from the history of soul's high era, but his status as a building block in the tower of its strength is strictly legit. Atlantic Records chief Jerry Wexler called him "the greatest soul singer of all time," and the Rolling Stones were superfans. But Burke recalls, "We were out there performing when the cities and the towns were changing from black and white towns to towns. When it was no longer necessary to go across the track to get a hamburger. When there came the first McDonald's in a town that didn't have a backdoor entrance or sign that said 'for coloreds.' When Kentucky Fried Chicken opened up its door and said there's a front door for the people and a back door for employees. We saw Holiday Inn be the first hotel to integrate and allow blacks into the hotel: one floor, one area . . . We couldn't go into all the pools but we saw that change too."

Responding to new ideas like equality extending beyond the antidiscrimination laws that protected jobs, schools, and accommodations, workers—including artists—were beginning to understand that equal rights under the law must translate into equal economic opportunity. As early as 1966 Burke approached Atlantic's Wexler on the chance that the label might unleash some funds to help him turn his dream of economic self-sufficiency into real-ity. "I said, here we are, and this is the plan," says Burke of the outline he pre-sented to Wexler. "It's Ben E. King and it's Don Covay; it's Joe Tex, it's Wilson Pickett, it's Otis Redding and me. We want to make records, and we need your advice and we need you to give us an accountant and we need someone to help us put it together and we need a lawyer." Conveniently the artists were friends and all under contract to Atlantic Records or one of its sub-sidiaries. Their combined natural camaraderie and collective talent had the potential for their black-owned business empire—potentially comprised of a label, publishing, and real estate holdings—to reach even beyond Motown. And it would give back. Burke's vision included the profits from their soul supergroup flowing back into neighborhoods at risk, bringing franchise busi-nesses, jobs, and scholarships to communities in peril of abandonment and extinction. Working directly with the people who had contributed toward establishing them as singers and great soul voices of their generation in the first place, the Soul Clan would prevail where urban renewal had failed to materialize. It was as lofty an idea as it was bold. "It was time to get on board, buy real estate, invest in those communities before they went down." There was talk of purchasing a substantial piece of land in Alabama. "Into every town we went into we could leave something, give something back to those towns that were giving us the concert support, the record support. This was our fan base." It was community-building in the spirit of nation-building but without the rhetoric that accompanied the power movement's politics. As the Clan saw it, economic stability was the missing piece of the puzzle of inner city instability. Their plan worked toward practical solutions for over-coming joblessness and lack of services that contributed to that instability. Wexler wasn't buying.

"The motor that drove Solomon Burke was a complex mechanism," Wex-ler writes in his autobiography. "Part artist, part hustler, he was a wit and a wonder, always hitting on me for more money, bigger advances, and antici-pated royalties. He knew I knew what was up. And I knew he knew me bet-ter than most. We locked horns, but could laugh about it. Our rapport was strong, even when the money game was most intense."[14]

Burke had indeed lived by his wits and his entrepreneurial skills before, selling sandwiches and popcorn and even carrying a traveling drugstore on the road with him. Originally from Philly, he'd spent the 1950s ministering on the radio and as part of a traveling tent show. The born leader of the House of God of All People, the Bible-based faith conceived in a dream by his grandmother, by the time he was seven Burke was known as the Wonder Boy Preacher. But at the dawn of the 1960s, like his friends Sam Cooke and Otis Redding, Burke became known as a soul singer, one who combined the fervor of traditional gospel with the rhythm and body energy of the newly created rock 'n' roll, itself a mixed marriage of Southern blues and hillbilly music. Burke's charismatic style was derived from the influence of his godfather, Daddy Grace, an emigrant of the Cape Verde Islands who funded his United House of Prayer for All People (of the Church on the Rock of the Apostolic Faith) with sometimes entrepreneurial ventures. Daddy Grace created a line of personal and household products for resale, the profits from which he turned into real estate. Taking his cues from his mentor, Burke sold sandwiches on the old soul revue tour buses; he eventually moved into carrying a road-worthy quasi-drugstore that held elixirs and sundries. To help make ends meet Burke also ran concert hall concessions, operated a fleet of snowplows, and even tended to corpses as a doctor of mortuary science.

Antiquated contract terms and a personal history between Burke and Wexler complicated the compensation situation. "Where I made the mistake was going to him: What do you think, 'dad?' I was remembering him saying to me, 'You can come to me for anything and I'll be here for you.' What I didn't realize then was the family had a limit, there was a gate that closed at a certain entrance." There were other setbacks for the Soul Clan. Burke's voice drops low as he pauses to remember an old friend. "Then we lost Otis. Strange. Really kind of shattered us," he says.

Redding, an undisputed giant of soul, was killed in a small plane crash of indeterminate cause at the end of 1967. Following a period of two high water years for his music, the hot wax he left behind and his soul stature are the indicators that he was just getting warmed up. The energy Redding brought to his performances and the studio combined with the defining elements of soul—the gospel fervor, the funkiness of the R&B—were in synch with the emerging consciousness of the times. The emotional intensity in the delivery of his stone soul classics—"Respect," "Try a Little Tenderness," and "I've Been Loving You Too Long"—course through his live performances. His triumphant appearance at the Monterey Pop Festival in June of 1967, at the beginning of the Summer of Love on the West Coast, was the pivotal point at which Redding expanded his audience to include the youth masses, some of whom were turning on to his brand of Macon-bred soul for the very first time. That he should die at the end of that year at the age of twenty-six is still regarded as a tremendous loss to music. For his immediate circle of friends within the Soul Clan, the loss was incalculable. "It sent Joe Tex into another state of mind to where he went and started doing things that were foolish," says Burke. "It was a struggle. It became Ben E., Don, and Wilson trying to hold the Clan together without a support, without an anchor." Pickett grew disinterested in the venture and made an exit. The Soul Clan would have to reorganize before it would take another shot, but its principle players had created a blueprint for business founded on brotherhood and soul power, though Burke is quick to clarify that soul is not a quality that is exclusive to African American experience. "Well, it's very nice to think that it's a category of race but it's not—it's a category of face: face value. Who you are, what you value, and what you're about. It makes no difference what color your skin is or what country you're from. It has nothing to do with color, it has nothing to do with time, it has nothing to do with a certain world. It's who you are. Tom Jones is soulful. Dusty Springfield is soulful. We can go back . . . Beethoven was soulful. Marian Anderson was soulful. Paul Robeson was soulful . . . Ray Charles . . . c'mon! Kennedy was soulful. Him and Robert together were two soulful brothers, doing their thing, you know, releasing their energies . . . They could say a few words and boom, you felt it. It made a difference. Liberace was soulful. In fact, you couldn't get any more soulful than Liberace."

Just as there were all kinds of soul singers, there were all manner of uses for soul songs, and some of them were getting put to use in some considerably more political situations than its singers would ever have anticipated. NAACP student organizer Fred Hampton joined his local Chicago chapter of the Panthers in 1968 and immediately showed his effectiveness as a community leader. In his efforts to seek social and economic justice for all, at any gathering where young Fred Hampton spoke, you might hear the crowd sing in unison to the Supremes hit "Someday We'll Be Together," as a kind of "united we stand" rallying song. Hampton successfully pursued a truce between area gangs and strove for cooperation between community groups organized for change. He was extremely effective at his health care and feeding program efforts, though these successes increased the FBI's suspicion of him and fueled J. Edgar Hoover's general distaste for the Panthers and other dissenting voices.

A musical group of Panthers called the Lumpen performed the hits of the day, plugging in their own motivational lyrics in place of the original words.[15] Curtis Mayfield's freedom train classic "People Get Ready" became

> People get ready, revolution's coming
> Don't need no ticket, you just load your gun

The rock standard "Louie Louie" was rewritten as

> Oink, oink
> bang, bang

to be sung on the fourth and fifth and seventh and eighth beats of the song's famous melody. Whenever a Black Panther Leader was jailed, it was not unusual to hear an old church melody adapted like the slaves in captivity had done, like this one sung to "Wade in the Water"

> Free Huey Newton
> Free Huey Newton
> Free Huey Newton
> We need our leader free

Like the marching freedom singers in the South, the new generation of Northern strikers and picketers were not coding or signifying to accommodate: they had a message and they were stating it plain. As far as these singers were concerned, "Let My People Go" and "Whitey's Got to Go" were one and the same.

# 4

## Movin' On Up:
## Black Power Rising

A party atmosphere is provided by a hometown Chicago audience. The band strikes up the sound of regality, as if the king and queen were entering, and Curtis Mayfield sets the tone:

> We're a winner
> And never let anybody say
> Boy, you can't make it

"We're a Winner," by the Impressions, was the #1 record on the R&B charts in March 1968, its triumphant sound of pride in motion offering hope for a brand new day. Pushing a little higher, Mayfield issues the affirmation:

> At last that blessed day has come
> And I don't care where you come from
> We're movin' on up (movin' on up)

And it seems there isn't a soul in the room who doesn't want to believe it. A new mood had taken hold, though there were waters still to cross and a river of tears to be shed. There were moments of pride, progress, and inspiration to cheer as the movement kept moving on. It was a time of increased visibility for African Americans in heavily segregated zones, with wins for Shirley Chisholm, the first African American woman elected to the US Congress, and tennis champion Arthur Ashe, with his first victory at the US Open. But 1968 will always be remembered more as a year of upset—for its series of nightmare assassinations and the worldwide protests occurring from Prague and Paris to Mexico City and Chicago—than as a season to celebrate.

The calendar opened with the Tet Offensive, launched by the North Vietnamese in coordination with the Vietcong in an effort to create an uprising among the people of South Vietnam. It was the largest offensive the war had seen, startling in its show of allied strength from the North, and it was returned with massive firepower. After seeing nearly a decade of fighting, the number of Americans in opposition to the war had increased substantially, and by February so had the war's casualties. Troops were spread thin, and though the call went out for more men, objectors and young Americans were delivered hope with the announcement that President Johnson would not seek reelection and that Sen. Robert F. Kennedy would be seeking the Democrat's nomination. And then it was April in Memphis.

"Somewhere I read of the freedom of assembly. Somewhere I read of the freedom of speech. Somewhere I read of the freedom of the press. Somewhere I read that the greatness of America is the right to protest for right," said Dr. King in his final speech, delivered on April 3 to striking sanitation workers of Memphis. "We mean business now, and we are determined to gain our rightful place in God's world."[1]

Delivering the news of Dr. King's murder on April 4 to a crowd at a campaign speech in Indianapolis, Sen. Robert F. Kennedy said, "It is not the end of the violence; it is not the end of lawlessness; it's not the end of disorder. But the vast majority of white people and the vast majority of black people want to live together, want to improve the quality of our life, and want justice for all human beings that abide in our land."[2]

With embers of the previous summer's riots smoldering in the minds of civic authorities, Chicago, Kansas City, DC, Baltimore, Newark, and at least one hundred other combustible cities prepared for explosions of grief and violence—a strange yet inevitable reaction to the murder of the king of nonviolence. In Detroit special measures were taken to install curfews and other means of managing crowds; nevertheless, the Motor City burned for two weeks. In Boston, the job fell to James Brown to keep the peace.

By the time Brown arrived in town, riots had already broken out in Roxbury, and officials were moving toward canceling his concert. Because African American community leaders knew full well that to forestall a James Brown show would be an invitation to further rioting, the mayor's office agreed to televise the concert, advising folks to stay off the streets as part of a peace-keeping effort. Brown, though initially skeptical of the whole idea, went ahead and turned it loose anyway: his impossible combination of tense but fluid music direction and slip-and-slide dance steps formed the bedrock for the hyperemotional vocal expression that was his trademark. Never breaking, always bending, Brown gave the performance of a lifetime to an estimated two thousand in the arena and fifteen thousand home viewers.

Dr. King's murder coincided with Brown's return from Africa, a trip Brown claimed bolstered his confidence in himself as a mighty black leader. "Here I was in a land where black meant something more than 'Hey you,' and 'You're not welcome here,'" he said. He remembered being stunned at the sight of children in the streets carrying James Brown albums under their arms, "Four, five, six different ones . . . they didn't have phonographs to play them on, they just wanted to have the records with them." His performance at the Boston Garden on the night following Dr. King's death is one that cemented his reputation as a showstopping performer. But it was the fervor with which he not only brought home the funk but kept the streets peaceful that was perceived as an all-powerful demonstration of his ability to lead a community in crisis. "If there ever was a night he had to read the crowd right, and use the magnetism of James Brown, that was the night," says the Reverend Al Sharpton. "It was like all of his life was preparing for that night, when the world needed him to connect in Boston."[3] No further rioting was seen in Boston that night; however, in DC the streets were alight. The following night, Brown was asked to make a televised address there, encouraging people to think about Dr. King's message before they acted in further rage. The call for his involvement in inner city riot control became a defining moment for Brown. "There was a lot of suspicion, especially among the national police, the FBI and the CIA about this so-called display of 'Black Power' on my part," he remembered. "If he could stop a riot that easily (although how they came to think of what happened that night was 'easy" I'll never know), he could just as easily start one," he said. "From that moment I knew I was put under national security surveillance. I felt like there were government eyes everywhere, because there were."[4]

"James Brown was the leader of the protest music movement," says John Sinclair. To the black community James Brown was without a doubt a leader, though he never officially endorsed or opposed any particular groups; if anything Brown went more toward the conservative side instead of joining the people in show business who largely leaned left. But as an exemplar of people and power, Brown certainly had the watts, thanks to the acquisition of three radio stations—WGYW in Knoxville, Tennessee (which he renamed WJBE), WEBB in Baltimore, and WRDW in Augusta—which he turned all black. The airwaves boosted Brown's economic base and became an all-access pass to the broadcast of his own music, and black music across the board. His short visit to Africa had done its job of changing his consciousness; there, he'd refused an offer of three million dollars to play a two-night stand in Sun City in apartheid South Africa. "I didn't even want to go there because I don't even want to *see* why I'm not supposed to play it," he writes in *James Brown: The Godfather of Soul*.[5]

Back in the land of the free and the home of the brave, Sen. Robert F. Kennedy was preparing his bid for the presidency, looking as if he would surely be the one chosen to lead his country through the deep water. Like Dr. King, he had grown in favor of withdrawing troops from Vietnam. From his seat on Capitol Hill, he had become a fierce advocate of civil rights and economic justice and the social programs to accompany those ends, supported by a progressive belief within his faith. Following his victory in the California primary election, on June 5, 1968, he too was shot down, two months after the loss of Dr. King.

> Has anybody here seen my old friend Bobby?
> Can you tell me where he's gone?
> He freed a lot of people,
> but it seems the good, they die young

So went the Dick Holler song "Abraham, Martin and John," first recorded by Dion and also done by Smokey Robinson and Marvin Gaye. With America gone insane, these watershed moments did not pass without commentary in song as musical protest, topical expression, outpourings of grief, and social commentary fell like rain. Pianist Otis Spann paid respect with "Blues for Martin Luther King"; Nina Simone performed "Why? The King of Love Is Dead" with stiff upper lip on King's national day of mourning. Artists, as members of the slain leaders' constituencies, were thrown into deep states of shock and horror in the darkness, but soon a new strain of song would come along to light the path to freedom.

The last protest Dr. King organized took place in May 1968. Ornette Coleman appeared at the Resurrection City demonstration in Washington, where the Poor People's Campaign had organized the set-up of a tent city on the Mall. Inspired by Sen. Robert F. Kennedy's idea to organize poor folks and bring them to the capitol, the demonstration was intended to show the impoverished conditions under which people of all races throughout America lived. For more than forty days and nights, Resurrection City's residents would rise and interact with government departments on issues ranging from agriculture to health and education. The action was effectively ended when rain turned the city grounds to mud. When Sen. Robert F. Kennedy was assassinated, organizers lost control of the site. Authorities arrived to bulldoze it.

Up in Detroit, a mood of disturbance also prevailed in the season of discontent. Following an arson attempt on Sinclair's home, the MC5 and the Trans-Love collective decamped to the nearby college town of Ann Arbor, hoping to find some semblance of peace and harmony—which wasn't always easy when the MC5 were involved. The band played its own role in Sinclair's inability to manage the unmanageable; the MC5's Tyner, Kramer, and Davis had run-ins with the law and between past arrest records and constant police hassles, chaos generally reigned wherever they roamed. Bookings were inevitably missed or canceled and police harassment of the band and their scene continued outside of Wayne County. In just one week in the life of the band in the summer of '68, Sinclair and MC5-man Fred Smith were arrested in Michigan's Oakland County (Smith got four days, Sinclair thirty, though he was later acquitted); all five members of the band were arrested following a concert in West Park (and released on $125 bail each); and a concert benefiting the organization American Children with Leukemia was canceled due to warrants against Tyner, Kramer, and Davis. By the end of that week, Ann Arbor had banned all concerts in West Park. Given the circumstances, it would perhaps be unreasonable to expect a trouble-free appearance at the

Festival of Life, in protest of the war, at Chicago's Lincoln Park in August during the Democratic National Convention.

In the spring of 1968, the Youth International Party (Yippie), led by Abbie Hoffman and Jerry Rubin, had announced its intent to hold a protest gathering in Chicago, much to the dismay of law enforcement. An attempt to thwart the permit application for the gathering on park property was put into play. On August 25, three days before the actual riot that would come to define the Chicago convention, the police refused to allow the MC5 onto the flatbed truck on which they were to perform. They proceeded to play without a riser. That evening the five thousand or so who had gathered in the park were rousted and pushed out into the streets of Chicago, as gathering of young people, specifically in protest of the war, was aggressively being discouraged. Men and women of all ages, along with journalists and photographers, were clubbed or tear-gassed by a line of police. An investigation following the event discovered that no warning was issued before force was exerted on the crowd; it was ruled a police riot.

The events in Chicago have been well documented by the journalists, scholars, poets, and the political activists who participated in them. Norman Mailer wrote, "The air of Lincoln Park came into the nose with that tender concern which air seemed always ready to offer when danger announced its presence." He likened the MC5 sound to "an interplanetary, then galactic, flight of song, halfway between the space music of Sun Ra and 'The Flight of the Bumblebee' . . . the roar of the beast in all nihilism, electric bass and drum driving behind out of their own nonstop to the end of mind."[6]

Another riot three days later, on August 28, became the defining moment of the Chicago convention. The initial antiwar protest as conceived by the National Mobilization to End the War in Vietnam (MOBE), SDS, and the Yippies ended in a riot that was broadcast on live television for seventeen minutes. The principals of those organizations, as well as Black Panther Bobby Seale, would later be put on trial for conspiring to start the riots. The display of dissenting young Americans that week in Chicago affected US politics and society from that day forward. Following the defeat of Democratic candidate Hubert Humphrey by Richard Nixon, the United States would never again see young people mobilized for change in such a massive, organized fashion. As the war on dissent escalated, the mood on the street grew hostile; chants of "Peace now" had turned to "Fuck you, LBJ." Mild-mannered and nonthreatening folk-types like Peter, Paul and Mary were beaten up between verses of "This Land Is Your Land."

"Huey said white people who want to help should form their own party," says John Sinclair. The MC5 were perfect additions to the White Panther Party, formed by Sinclair and his close allies. On November 1, 1968, John Sinclair issued the "White Panther State/Meant." Point one of his ten-point program and platform was "Full endorsement and support of the Black Panther Party's ten-point program and platform." All points supported the intention to create a "cultural revolution through a total assault on the culture by any means necessary, including rock & roll, dope, and fucking in the streets." Eight additional points began with the word "free," as in free food, free access, free time, and free the people. "The high priest of the Detroit hippies" had finally found a way to merge his interest in free jazz and black liberation politics with the rock 'n' roll generation's concerns of free love and drugs.

"The actions of the Black Panthers in America have inspired us and given us strength, as has the music of black America, and we are moving to reflect that strength in our daily activity just as our music contains and extends the power and feeling of the black magic music that originally informed our bodies and told us that we could be free.

"I might mention brother James Brown in this connection, as well as John Coltrane and Archie Shepp . . . these are magic names to us," expressed Sinclair in his ten-point platform.

"We did not create the White Panthers, at all. The White Panthers created themselves," says Bobby Seale.[7] "They had some kind of psychedelic program and we ran them out of our office . . . told them we had no time for it. You can blow all the dope you want . . . if we blow it, we blow it, but the thing is, psychedelic programs aren't going to solve the problems of black people. But what happened was, Sinclair really put some politics to it, it came down righteously . . . they turned out to be some beautiful cats and we shook hands . . . They must've been doing something right . . . they put Sinclair in jail and made a political prisoner out of him and they're moving in on the rest of the cats." It wouldn't be long before federal and local law enforcement would catch up with the MC5, who were about to develop a more public profile as recording artists who were perceived to have dangerous intent.

Meanwhile, the Panthers cofounder and media representative Seale was becoming the face of Black Power to the largely white rock 'n' roll audience, many of them constituents of the antiwar movement. By 1968, the Black Panthers would come to replace the student groups, racial equality organizations, the antiwar movement, and all Black Nationalist organizations as the number-one target of J. Edgar Hoover's FBI plan COINTELPRO, the counterintelligence program designed to wipe out all politically dissident groups from inside and out.

"One thing about the Panthers was that it was a paramilitary structure and you took orders," explains Elaine Brown, who joined the party in Los Angeles in 1968. "We didn't believe in having voting, because a bunch of police could unite and come in and vote you out of your own organization," she says. "So we stuck to what we call the democratic centralist idea," a Marxist-Leninist principle. Brown would go on to oversee the newspaper and eventually become the only woman to take a leadership position. She was also the party's official songwriter.

"I worshiped Elaine Brown," says Sinclair. "She was a genius and so revolutionary, she sacrificed her musical career, organizing the party," he says. When *The Black Panther* newspaper hit in 1967, Sinclair added it to his weekly reading list. "It was all part of our propaganda machine, the newspaper, the songs, the art, the poems and anything else we could put out there to raise consciousness," explains Brown. Growing up in Philadelphia, Brown loved the street corner music of the neighborhoods and held dreams of becoming a professional songwriter herself. Moving out west, like so many hopefuls before and after, she wrote poems and songs while working as a cocktail waitress. Friends introduced her to the new black consciousness and encouraged her to get involved. While working on music with children in Watts, she gradually became more interested in learning about the community's cultural affairs and came to join the forming Los Angeles chapter of the Black Panthers. Under order of Chief of Staff David Hilliard and later Chairman Newton, Brown recorded two albums of songs under the direction of avant-garde jazz pianist Horace Tapscott, a contemporary of Don Cherry and Eric Dolphy from L.A.'s celebrated Central Avenue scene. Brown and Tapscott were acquainted from her time in Watts. "Horace always thought music was an answer," says Brown. "He gave me a sense as a singer-songwriter; he validated me. He was a true jazz musician and a great pianist. His musicianship was so big—in an Alice Coltrane tradition of piano playing—and he could sit down and orchestrate a song just as you sang it." Accompanied by Tapscott's Pan African Arkestra, *Seize the Time* was recorded direct to disc, "without any playback and no tracks. Horace's whole orchestra had to be there," explains Brown, whose songs were intended, as was the group's other propaganda, to serve as a clarion call to action. Her poetry turned into songs achieved the right political tones, unified musically by Tapscott's players, who performed in perfect synch with the material. But Brown's *Seize the Time* faced distribution challenges and didn't receive much of a hearing in the commercial market, despite the high level of artistry at work.

"You have to remember, our organization was formed for the liberation of black people, but we also talked about the liberation of the native people, we helped form the American Indian Movement, we supported the Brown Berets, the Young Lords, the Young Patriots . . . we were trying to deal with poor whites," says Elaine Brown. "We worked with women, gays, the handicapped and the environment. We had this larger concern and involvement and that was to free all the oppressed people on this planet. My primary goal was not as a songwriter, it was toward revolutionary change."

## "My Country 'Tis of Thy People You're Dying"

Buffy Sainte-Marie is a singer first, though in the eyes of the government she too was branded as dangerous. "It's not as if I've ever broken the law. I don't have a criminal record, I didn't smoke pot on the White House lawn or take part in violent demonstrations . . . nothing, zero. My record is completely clean." It was sometime in the mid-sixties that her path crossed with the people who founded the American Indian Movement (AIM), an organization created on the Black Panthers model to protect the rights and well-being of all citizens, in this case, indigenous Americans. "I ran into the American Indian Movement people in the sixties. The American Indian Movement was not the first such movement; there were many other groups of Native American people and friends who were trying to bring issues to light and make things better. I first met those guys—Dennis Banks, Russell Means, Eddie Benton-Banai, Clyde Bellecourt—in a parking lot in Minneapolis." She explains that there were people in Boston, New York, and all over "trying to help. But what AIM was doing . . . was making Native American young people aware of their rights," she says. "Normally what would happen was if an Indian was arrested for something, anything, nothing, whatever, he wouldn't know his rights. He wouldn't realize he could get a lawyer. He just went to jail because it was easier than getting beaten up. The American Indian Movement started at that point, and I really admired them for it."

In 1968, the Minneapolis American Indian Patrol was established to confront police brutality in their immediate community, much like the Black Panthers of Oakland and Negro defense leagues in the South had done before them. But unlike the civil rights and Black Power movements that developed through community organizing efforts, the American Indian Movement viewed self-determination and racism through a different lens. At the precise moment the issue of cultural identity had emerged as vital to the health of minorities, from nonwhites and women to the youth movement, the culture of the indigenous people of the Americas was facing virtual extinction and growing more disconnected from the land that was theirs, land that was inextricably linked to their heritage as a people. "Desegregation was not a goal. Individual rights were not placed ahead of Native Nation sovereignty," stated an article from the AIM manifesto.[8]

The first national action that the newly organized Native Nations would take was the 1969 occupation of Alcatraz Island in the San Francisco Bay. The former state penitentiary had housed criminals such as Al Capone and the notorious "Birdman," who famously escaped from the Rock. Under a treaty right that granted use of unused federal land, the island was officially reclaimed by members of All Tribes of the Native Nations—American Indians. Hoping to create awareness for Native American issues like the theft of the land and to call attention to the deception that had been served up to them through the years at the hands of the US government, the Native Nations also had a long-term plan to build a cultural center on the island. Activist John Trudell (of Santee Sioux origin), who is known today as a poet, musician, and actor, was the voice of Alcatraz. Radio Free Alcatraz communicated daily through broadcasts carried by Pacifica Radio stations KPFA in Berkeley and KPFK in Los Angeles. "He is extremely eloquent, therefore extremely dangerous," according to a note in Trudell's FBI file.

Debora Iyall of the Cowlitz tribe was just sixteen and a budding artist and activist living in the middle of the state when she heard the call. With her mother's blessing, she headed for the occupation at Alcatraz. "It was a physically rigorous environment. It was cold and foggy and there was no power except in the generator area . . . The foghorns went off every ninety seconds so you had to figure out how to go to sleep in ninety seconds. I was freezing, I was kinda scared and I was alone." She found community in the sound of powwow music, the sound of which comforted her spirit. Like Buffy Sainte-Marie's early experiences with indigenous music, Iyall says powwow music connected her more deeply to her Native heritage, as did a meaningful contact with an Indian—a woman named Oona. Iyall's parents had divorced when she was two years old. "My dad is Indian and my mom is not. Growing up my older sister and older brother and I were like her little brown kids. People would ask if she adopted us," she says. "Being a kid I always knew all the lyrics to all the popular songs. I loved to make visual art as well, sitting at the kitchen table with watercolors. Definitely the sixties with the loose, psychedelic art meant you didn't have to be super trained or realistic as an artist and that stuff really germinated inside me and made me interested in visual art. Definitely got interested in poetry, checking out the Beats. My mom was quite a reader so when I was pretty young I was reading Aldous Huxley, *Steppenwolf*, thinkers like Alan Watts."

Iyall felt somewhat estranged from her father's Indian side because of the divorce, but her mother nevertheless bought her Native art books, encouraging her to connect with her heritage. Subsequently, "I was always drawn to find out more. I grew up riding horses because my mom's a veterinarian and one of my fantasies about the West and big western skies fed into my identity—feeling part of that Native background and yet not really having much involvement with it at all. When my dad came to visit us, he took us to Disneyland. My mom took us to some powwows up in the Sierras and I remember thinking, 'This is so cool,' seeing people for the first time who physically resembled us kids. I think especially me being really round I thought, 'Here are women that look kind of like me.' I remember a song this woman Oona taught me at the powwow on Alcatraz," she recounts. "She was Indian—and she taught me that little song. I felt like I had these little nuggets of information or culture to hang on to." Like Sainte-Marie, contact with creative Natives helped shape Iyall's own identity as a visual artist, poet, and musician.

The AIM occupation of Alcatraz Island lasted for a stunning nineteen months and was fraught with difficulty every step of the way. Eventually the government brought the stand-off to a close with their firepower and forced a shutdown. The cessation of vital services sent most of the Indian population away while the rest were removed. By the time AIM's "Trail of Broken Treaties 20-Point Position Paper" calling for "restitution, reparations, restoration of lands for a reconstruction of an Indian Future in America" was delivered during a march on Washington and occupation of the Bureau of Indian Affairs during a week in 1972, the operations to disempower the movement as ordered by the FBI were already well under way. AIM was fingered for immediate dismantling under the FBI's COINTELPRO. Following the standoff in 1973 at Wounded Knee between AIM and the Lakota Sioux people against federal marshals, the battle ended in a firefight in June 1975 at Pine Ridge.

"AIM was about community, about the way of the tribe," says Trudell. "AIM's statement was same as Indians of All Tribes/Alcatraz: You have a legal responsibility. Treaties are laws. By the Constitution they're laws," says Trudell.[9]

Trudell served as AIM's chairman from 1973 to 1979. Following a mysterious house fire in which his wife, three children, and mother-in-law were killed, the voice of Alcatraz turned his attention toward poetry and music. Two decades later he released *AKA Graffiti Man*, a combination of spoken word, blues, and rock. He was accompanied by Oklahoma/Kiowa guitarist Jesse Ed Davis, known for jamming with artists from Conway Twitty to John Lennon and many in between. *AKA Graffiti Man* was famously endorsed by Bob Dylan; with Sainte-Marie, Iyall, and his fellow creative Natives, Trudell carried a message for American Indian justice through artistic disciplines. Indigenous music thrives on recordings and at powwows across North America; it is a scene which Sainte-Marie reports is thriving and is perhaps more vital and filled with younger Natives than ever before. Regional sounds and song purposes are too vast to generalize, ranging from the sacred to the everyday, though the unifying qualities of strong voice and drum serve to reconnect Natives with their land and to unite the nations through sound.

## *Kick Out the Jams*

Despite the insanity and turmoil surrounding them, the MC5 were getting some attention from the underground press in New York in the summer of 1968, thanks to Sinclair's friends on the scene. By September the band was signed to Elektra Records and commenced recording their now legendary *Kick out the Jams* album, produced by Jac Holzman and Bruce Botnick. The band set up at the Grande Ballroom with Wally Heider's mobile recording unit and laid down the tracks live. *Kick Out the Jams* is a fine example of what the MC5 was capable of—complete sonic mayhem. Wayne Kramer says, "As I remember we did a lot of covers, and we tried to pick good ones. We used to cover "Reach Out" by the Four Tops. We covered James Brown material; we did a version of "I Put a Spell on You" and Ray Charles's "I Believe in My Soul," which we still do in DKT when we tour . . . We did pick a Bob Dylan song once." Was there a link to the MC5 recording "Ballad of a Thin Man" and Huey Newton's favoritism of it? Perhaps indirectly, says Kramer. "It certainly fit into our worldview. Our purview. Just like the music of Archie Shepp when he put out that record *Fire Music*. We said, yea, the Motor City's burning. With fire music! It all seemed to be part of the fabric of our day."

"We all loved Bob Dylan," says Elaine Brown, Newton's intimate and eventual successor as party leader. "Anyone who writes 'Blowin' in the Wind' gets a free pass to heaven," she says, though that did not mean the Black Panthers sought reciprocal endorsement from him. "We didn't require Bob Dylan to be a revolutionary. I was a revolutionary who wrote songs."

Kramer continues, "Everyone from super-advanced free jazz musicians to Bob Dylan to Black Panther Party to White Panther Party to SDS to women burning their bras . . . the whole generation seemed to be in agreement that the direction everything was going in was wrong. *Basta*. Enough! We want to invent something new."

"I got something they can't never take away," said vocalist Tyner from the stage of the Grande Ballroom in 1968; "I got my anger, baby." The band launched into their freeform jam, "I'm Mad Like Eldridge Cleaver:"

And so you see, a white boy like me, can get mad

Today the MC5 album *Kick Out the Jams* is considered a rock 'n' roll classic, though at the time it was released it didn't take the world by storm as the band hoped it would. Wherever the MC5 traveled, trouble followed. "You pick up the phone and you hear click, clack, clackity click . . . You're sitting in a house where we all lived together working out a song with Rob Tyner, and a police car shines its spotlights on us and runs a siren. You're driving to the gig and funny, the police just happen to pull you over and want you to tear out all your band gear and empty everyone's pockets and put everything back . . . They were in our face. And we had ugly confrontations, violent confrontations with them," says Kramer. It was a combination of the band's habits, their looks, their association with Sinclair, a general intolerance of freethinking hippie types and revolutionary thinkers that conspired on the clampdown on the MC5 and their immediate circle. MC5 didn't want to play music so much as they wanted to change the world with it.

Following its release in February 1969, the album was recalled, pulled off the shelves by retailers for its use of profanity; some markets banned it entirely. The band's West Coast promotional tour proved to be a disaster when band members were arrested in San Francisco for alleged drunk driving and resisting arrest. Out-of-state law enforcement was on their trail, and as tour plans were scratched and their contract with Elektra was dissolved, they entered the studio to record a second album. A third album followed, but by then the band had dismissed Sinclair as its manager. "We lost the revolution," says Kramer, "but I can't look at it as a failure. That's not a fair judgment to make. We came from nothing. We made this whole big stink . . . So it's not fair to say it was a failure. It *is* fair to say that it was a commercial failure and business-wise, it was a failure. But that isn't what we were trying to do anyway. We idolized avant-garde jazz musicians and beatnik poets. We never really aspired to be international jet-set multimillionaire celebrities. We really wanted to grow up and be John Coltrane or Chairman Mao. We related to Eldridge Cleaver and Huey Newton. We really had some grandiose visions of things, which isn't to say that we weren't trying to be successful. We were making records and we did realize that was a way to reach a lot of people. But that wasn't the thing that motivated us."

"We really felt that we could influence the youth of the world with these new thoughts about music and this new way of living and this new kind of politics and this new kind of frame of reference," Kramer says. "We really believed it—totally and completely. You know, I'm not terribly cynical about it now. I still believe that you gotta take a stand and pick what side you're on. I still pick the side of creativity and thinking and of being responsible and following through and self-efficacy, championing what you're trying to do. Which is what we were trying to do in the MC5—we were an advocate for what we believed in. We were, to quote Abbie Hoffman, young and arrogant and crazy and naive but we were right."

The justice seekers and freethinkers who rode for freedom earlier in the decade to a folk, blues, and gospel soundtrack had helped to establish the hippie movement, with its psychedelic folk and acid rock sounds and antiwar peace and love agenda. The crowd also moved to soul, blues, and jazz, from Aretha Franklin to Muddy Waters and Miles Davis, and welcomed a broad spectrum of artists to their scene's central stages at the Fillmores, East and West. But there was one type of rebel music that the revolution generation had not yet fully embraced to accompany them on their quest to upend the status quo, borderline experimentations and other behaviors that distressed Mr. Jones. This was music that was partially rooted in defiance of European tradition while also embracing it; it expanded the boundaries of the musical scale and altered the ear to brain connection and what it could comprehend. Avant-garde or free jazz is perhaps the secret influence on the liberation movement itself, as well as its music. With its sideways burst and blurts, honks and squalls, the music remained for the most part impenetrable to the average listener and definitely far out, even for the mass hippie culture. And yet, these true sounds of liberty were born from an emotional expression of the ultimate freedom—transcendence. Delivered by predominantly black music makers who'd struck out with their new sound in the late 1950s, the idea that tones, notes, and scales could communicate on such a deep level as to affect human and environmental change remained on the margins of thought, though by the time John Coltrane died in 1967, progressive listeners, traditional jazz fans, and overseas markets were starting to come around.

Through his involvement with the MC5, free jazz advocate John Sinclair had became more connected with the rock scene centralized around the Grande Ballroom, a sort of Fillmore of the Midwest where the MC5 served as the house band. The Detroit scene was the most happening of any between the coasts, with its own psychedelic art and liquid light shows to accompany its hardcore, sweat-and-spit-inspired rock 'n' roll. Sinclair arranged for the MC5 to share the bill with Sun Ra at Wayne State, thinking the freaked-out crowd could dig Sun Ra's outrageous performance values and over-the-top presentation; instead they turned ugly at the sight and sound of him. Ra's music was not easy to metabolize for the average hippie, and listeners grew disinterested; much more palatable to them was the MC5's loose, rock 'n' roll interpretation of the avant-garde.

"We tried really hard to school the audience in Detroit, to accept nothing but the best. I think we brought them along," says Kramer. "We had a unique situation in Detroit," he explains. "The music scene was so rich. There was a strong blues subculture in Detroit; John Lee Hooker was from Detroit . . . And then there was the jazz world in Detroit, Barry Harris and the Jones Brothers [Elvin, Hank and Thad] . . . There was the Motown scene and all the studio guys that worked at Motown were as far as I'm concerned the best and most creative recording artists in the world." And Motown as a black-owned business was one of Detroit's if not one of America's most successful models of the American Dream come true.

Ever since around the turn of the decade when Berry Gordy Jr. and Janie Bradford penned "Money (That's What I Want)," Barrett Strong performed it, and it became Tamla's first record to top the R&B charts and cross over to Top 40 in June of 1960, there was no turning back for Hitsville.

> The best things in life are free
> But you can give them to the birds and bees
> I want money, that's what I want

Spurred on by competition with his sisters Anna and Gwen who operated the Anna label, Gordy formed his own label, Tamla, in 1959 and followed with a second label, Motown, in 1960. Soon after Strong's declaration made the charts, Gordy's friend and label vice president Smokey Robinson sold a million copies of "Shop Around" for Tamla with his group the Miracles, and this self-contained black-owned business from the Motor City was well on its way to delivering *The Sound of Young America* to the world. Its specially designed blend of pop and R&B was intended to steer the local singers away from the sounds of the stratified charts of the R&B ghetto and into the

crossover spotlight, where American futures were made. A business and artistic model to the present day, the label's inclusive "sound of young America"
slogan and tremendous and immediate success was a momentous event; it was
an integrationist statement and a miracle in a time of historic racial divide.
Gordy's business plan didn't include a provision for sharing the wealth (and
he famously tussled with some of his musicians over artistic and compensation matters), but Motown became a home, family, and launch pad for some
of black music's biggest stars. Motown could be seen as the very model of
black enterprise as imagined by Booker T. Washington earlier in the twentieth
century or as something less equitable, as in a sharecropping arrangement in
which the farmer only receives a very small percentage of the crop for the
work he puts into the fertilization and maintenance of the land. History has
shown that the reality was somewhere in between; singers and writers were
indeed allowed to grow careers, but the less successful front people and the
behind-the-scenes players who helped shape the sound of the songs were
often left unpaid and unsung. In musical terms and as an entertainment con-
glomerate, Motown was financially and artistically successful as it led and
moved with the times; Black Power–wise, the label was brought kicking and
screaming into delivering more politically motivated recordings. It would be
a while till Motown entered the specifically political arena.

## Black Power Inc.

Far away from the student radicals and free jazz cooperatives and yet simultaneously at work was the idea of Black Power achieved through a program of
economic self-sufficiency. Black Capitalism didn't fly with the Marxist, radical
left, who named it as a way for corporate power to co-opt and neutralize the
movement alongside government programs like the flailing War on Poverty,
perceived by the radical side to be yet another neocolonialist trick. Earlier in
the century, activists had called for black-owned everything and were met
with resistance, though through their efforts a strong black middle class had
emerged. By the mid-sixties, evidence of that progress was diminishing as the
Economic Opportunity Act, designed to assist blacks, instead resulted in joblessness, lack of services, and swathes of cities left shuttered and condemned.
In the season of riots that was the sixties, there was most always an incident

or spark, often involving police violence, that led to escalations of the inner-city eruptions that in some cases could last for days. But during a community investigation into what sparked the five-day Buffalo uprising of 1967, one of its participants stated, "We're just tired of being lied to, that's all."[10] Over and over again, if not caused by direct harassment, riots are often traced back to a trail of broken government promises to deliver programs and renewal that never materialized. The disconnect between what was being said and what was being done was in itself enough to make a community blow.

Black Nationalism and Carmichael's Black Power speech specifically addressed the economic disparity and injustice at hand. But what actions and direction should be taken toward making corrections was up for debate and a source of disagreement that came to threaten the Pride and Power movement's political cohesion. Groups and individuals committed to Dr. King's nonviolent approach that worked within the existing system began to distance themselves from the revolutionaries. A new way of thinking was what was required; whether free food or ownership of franchise businesses, the new economic directive sprung directly from Stokely Carmichael's call for power: "Black people are economically insecure. White liberals are economically secure. Can you begin to build an economic coalition? Are the liberals willing to share their salaries with the economically insecure black people they so much love? Then if you're not, are you willing to start building new institutions that will provide economic security for black people?"[11]

Though Black Capitalism was brought to the table in new language in the sixties and seventies, African Americans and the African diaspora had struggled for centuries, fighting economic exploitation. The idea now was to find something that worked.

"It is important to emphasize that while Black economic power, identity, dignity, economic independence, self-sufficiency and self-determination lay at the heart of some definitions of Black Capitalism, these goals have always defined the goals of the Black liberation struggle," explains historian Kenneth S. Jolly.[12]

Still sitting on his vision for the Soul Clan, singer Solomon Burke had a blueprint to rebuild the urban ghettos with black entertainment capital. His religious training, his sales skill, and his experience as a rock 'n' soul circuit singer and witness to change had led him to his ideas toward advocating economic advancement in the mid-sixties era of new black consciousness; he could see the possibilities of the power in black capitalism and building a benevolent corporate model. But disappointment quickly overtook his vision when Jerry Wexler told him, "Go back and learn some more songs and pay attention to your records and get out there on that road and try to promote these records and stop thinking on that other stuff.'" Burke says, "He didn't want us to be entrepreneurs; he wanted us to be record sellers. And I say no, that's not right." Burke believed Wexler "wanted to keep us in the soul and R&B market and not think about crossing over into pop and not think about buying real estate and having trust funds and scholarship funds and having business meetings and dedicating all of our royalties to one nonprofit organization."

Eventually Wilson Pickett grew disinterested in the Soul Clan venture and exited the fold. Redding was replaced by his protégé Arthur Conley. In 1968, the Soul Clan got as far as recording the single, "Soul Meeting"/"That's How I Feel," but the budget for a full album was withdrawn. Eventually a full-length album was released, though it was filled out by tracks recorded by the Clan's individual members. Unlike the high-energy single, which showcased the group's potential as a collective power greater than its individual parts, the solo material doesn't rise to the occasion and has been declared by soul aficionados as mostly forgettable. "We lost Joe," says Burke, and without him, Burke says the Clan's decline was imminent. Initially the profits from the Soul Clan single were to be set aside for scholarships and endowment plans, but the accounting on that never materialized. It's been forty years since the Soul Clan deal went down, but Burke maintains that the events connected to its demise devastated him. "Those dreams got crushed. And then to take our record off . . . it shattered us," he says. The resistance he received from Wexler became his own dream deferred. Though Burke and the Soul Clan may have been old school, their politics more centrist than radical, they would ulti-mately make inroads for future generations of musicians who would come to harvest the fruits of their labors.

Burke suggests that his dream of contributing to the health of a black econ-omy bought him membership into a less favorable club—one for performers who were allowed to achieve only just so much. He refers to a list of artists whose work, politically motivated or otherwise, was in the process of being suppressed, whether by malicious neglect or by more official means. "I was on that list. It said 'Solomon Burke was not to have a #1 record. He's too arrogant, too smart, and he wants to be more than he is.' I just wanted to be all that I could be," he says. In Burke's case it was nothing so overt as threats or government files. "It wasn't strong-arming. It was just, 'We're not there for you. You guys want a million dollars? What do you want a million dollars for?' I thought we were worth a million dollars. We had a few hits out there . . . I'm sure 'Stand By Me' was worth a million dollars. Don Covay was one of the world's greatest writers, [with] 'Chain of Fools' . . . writing for me and everybody else. Joe Tex was so hot with 'Skinny Legs and All,' Otis Redding, 'These Arms of Mine.' You realize how powerful Atlantic was, that they were able to . . ." Burke never finished the thought.

Burke's story and that of the Soul Clan is representative of the sixties' soul artists who withstood hassles from the power structure of the record industry—and sometimes the US government. What went on behind closed doors, in record label offices or FBI meeting rooms, we'll never know. But there have been documented cases of singers who supported workers' rights, anti-imperialism, and black rights in the forties and fifties, and lesser-known artists in the sixties and seventies, who paid a cost for freedom.

The reasons that Burke's collective alliance did not take off are not easily diagrammed, but there remain certain facts: the Soul Clan and its members were tied to a parent company that would not release its individuals in the name of more personally profitable ventures, no matter how well intentioned. They worked in an era when record labels were in the habit of issuing con-tracts that would be revealed to be akin to indentured servitude. Born from the early recording eras of blues and R&B music, these contractual agree-ments were largely left unexamined by the musicians who signed them until well into the eighties when performer Ruth Brown sought unpaid royalties from Atlantic Records and the label's founder, Ahmet Ertegun. In response to Brown's and other claims, Ertegun, Bonnie Raitt, Ray Charles, and others in entertainment established the Rhythm and Blues Foundation to successfully support recording artists who need assistance later in life because their early contracts were marred by overtly discriminatory and exploitative practices. Under the same umbrella organization, Berry Gordy established the Gwendolyn Gordy Fuqua Fund to aid Motown's heritage artists. That some of rhythm and blues and soul's founders had willingly signed the papers is the most often used defense of the contracts.

The argument that corporate ownership of an artist's creation was like the plantation system was an idea posited in the nineties by folksinger Michelle Shocked (who cited the Thirteenth Amendment, which prohibits slavery) and Prince (who painted "slave" on his face), bringing further attention to the constricting contracts. The dilemma of who fronts the money and the terms of how it's paid back remains unresolved as the music industry struggles to adjust to the age of technology. Though it might be easier for an artist to manufacture and distribute his or her music, payment is still an issue; a new model for the industry is still awaiting revelation. Prince has successfully broken away from the faulty major label system and consistently advocates for artists' rights, remaining vocally opposed to artist-unfriendly arrangements while trying to forge solutions. "In the future it will be unconscionable to even think you can take somebody's creation and claim ownership of it," he said in 2009.[13]

Though the Clan's plan died before it reached the communities, Burke's idea for a benevolent, black-owned corporation would become manifest in later decades as the Soul Clan's chance on change proved to be a down payment toward the security of all musicians who followed. Businesses established by Prince and hip-hop mogul Russell Simmons, for example, operate with an eye on giving back to the community as well as to the up-and-coming artist. The financial empires built by Sean (Diddy/Puffy/P. Diddy/Puff Daddy) Combs and Jay-Z are among the most successful in the entertainment business.

"We accomplished a lot," says Burke of the ideas formed on tour buses and at restaurant tables and eventually brought to completion by professionals who worked within the system. "We got Otis's publishing company organized. We got Wilson's publishing company organized. We learned that BMI was something we could join though we were told that we couldn't. We learned that we didn't have to put other people's names on our songs to get them played. We learned that we had control of our songs—that they couldn't take our publishing—that we had rights."

## "Say It Loud"

Similarly interested in the issue of creating a black economic power base was James Brown, who was simultaneously sticking to his commitment to bring a message to his music: "I Don't Want Nobody to Give Me Nothing (Open up the Door I'll Get It Myself)" was another in his series of empowerment songs. And then came the game changer: upon returning from a trip to Southeast Asia where he fulfilled his long held dream to perform a USO show, Brown wrote and recorded "Say It Loud: I'm Black and I'm Proud" as a response to the murder of Dr. King and to Vietnam; he characterized it as "a rallying cry for peaceful self-pride." Released as a single in March 1969, "Say It Loud: I'm Black and I'm Proud" combined the "we shall overcomes" and point-blank protest shouts with soul power from the ancestral source, the energy of the youth movement, and Brown's own coming to Black Consciousness. With the addition of trombonist Fred Wesley to his revue and a children's chorus on the refrain, the James Brown sound was as fresh and musically revelatory as ever, and more, the record was transcendent. It was musical proof that the journey toward self-worth and the necessary psychological transformation to achieve power had taken place and was within the grasp of anyone with a radio.

"The sheer magnitude of 'Say It Loud: I'm Black and I'm Proud' was an implanted, soundtracked theme into understanding that our minds, bodies, and souls were black and beautiful," wrote rap master Chuck D. of Public Enemy in his eulogy to Brown upon his death on Christmas 2006.

The album *Say It Loud: I'm Black and I'm Proud* included another musical breakthrough track, "Licking Stick," which was foundational to the freshly brewing funk sound. His follow-up, the legendary double live album featuring "Sex Machine," marks a time in James Brown's career that fans and scholars widely agree was a musical watershed—extraordinary in its immediacy and for its influence. The endurance of his work from this period speaks for itself; sample versions of the tracks are used over and over again in contemporary popular music. The excitement, urgency, commitment, and artistry

Brown brought to his work in the sixties has rarely been matched. Michael Jackson and Prince, both children during Brown's late-sixties reign, watched him attentively and eventually brought his standard of excellence to their own high-level work.

"As a seventies B-boy I recall panic on the floors of hip-hop while 'Give It Up and Turn It Loose,' roasted off the 1969 *Sex Machine Live* LP, transfixing the forming rap nation ten years later, as if it were a discovered oil well. While the rest of the disco and rock country had not a clue," writes Chuck D.

Brown had no trouble living up to the nickname Soul Brother Number One. After establishing a circuit for himself in Africa, he would return there a number of times in the decade to come; by the seventies you might have bet on his chance of getting elected on his platform for "Funky President." But Brown's pro-black direction was confusing given his friendships with segregationist governors Lester Maddox of Georgia and George Wallace of Alabama and his endorsement of his friend Hubert Humphrey following the assassination of Sen. Robert F. Kennedy. There is no way to explain the outer contradictions that combined with the elusive magic of Brown's music, its real work done onstage and in studio. Brown was hands on, especially at holiday time during which he found no greater joy than playing Santa, giving away turkeys and hundred-dollar bills. "Santa Claus Go Straight to the Ghetto" was yet another strong statement from him during his growing political song period. Yet in the end, Brown walked away with the feeling that "Say It Loud" was received poorly, believing it cost him his career with the mainstream; he lost the pop audience, the white audience, when his message "went militant." According to Brown, the adoption of the tune by SNCC and the Black Panthers contributed to "obliterating its peaceful and positive message." And yet, he says, "It helped Afro-Americans in general and the dark-skinned man in particular and I'm proud of that."[14]

More than a year after the events at the Democratic convention, folksinger Phil Ochs was called to Chicago to participate as a witness for the defense of the Chicago Eight. Allen Ginsberg, Dick Gregory, and folksingers Judy Collins and Arlo Guthrie, among others, were on hand for a show trial the likes of which the United States has rarely seen before or since. At one point in the proceedings, Bobby Seale was bound and gagged on the courtroom floor; he was eventually dismissed and sentenced to serve four years for contempt. Due to his association with the formation of the Yippies, Ochs was called to the stand by defense attorney William Kunstler. Asked to address the idea the Yippies' brand of guerrilla theater, among other things, he performed a song for the court.

> For I killed my share of Indians in a thousand different fights
> For I killed my share at the Little Big Horn
> I saw men lying I saw many more dying,
> But I ain't marching anymore

Ochs was disillusioned with Chicago and deeply troubled about the state of the union as well as his career. "As you know, I died in Chicago, I lost my life and I went to heaven because I was very good and I sang very lyrical songs. I got to talk to God who said, 'Well, it's all over here on Earth, there's only a couple of days left.'" These were not the utterances of a well man. Toying with leaving behind his image as a folky, topical singer, Ochs talked of reinventing himself, perhaps as a cross between Elvis and Che Guevara. He joked that as Elvis had Colonel Tom Parker, he would hire his own colonel of a manager—Sanders, of Kentucky Fried Chicken fame. The effects of alcoholism exacerbated Ochs's unrest, and he began a dramatic decline.

Though the FBI opened a file on Ochs in 1963, in 1968 he was added to the FBI Security Index, a master list of those perceived to be a danger to national security. His contempt of Richard Nixon was what aroused suspicion of the singer, though it must be said that Ochs was hardly alone in his displeasure with events of the year, which culminated in Nixon's election as president.

Coinciding with the increased interest from federal authorities in singers with dissenting views, an upsurge in violent activity against the Black Panthers started in April of 1968, when seventeen-year-old Bobby Hutton was killed by a peace officer in Oakland. In the government's efforts to neutralize all radical groups, J. Edgar Hoover declared the Black Panthers the "greatest threat to internal security of the country." The following January, John Huggins and Bunchy Carter of the Los Angeles chapter were killed in a shootout with the Black Nationalist US Organization on the UCLA campus. Soon after, the LAPD raided the Panther headquarters.

Elaine Brown memorialized her friends Huggins and Carter in her song "The Assassination" on her album *Seize the Time*, the album she recorded in

Central Los Angeles with avant-garde jazz pianist Horace Tapscott. Brown's songs stand as windows to the world of a revolutionary's experience at the end of the sixties, drawing as they do from her own life and from the day-to-day events within the party—the assassinations, the political discussions and matters of the heart—she turned into songs. "By the time we went to record the songs, most of them were written . . . I used to play my songs leaning so far down into the piano because I was feeling so much." She wrote "The Meeting" following an early encounter with Eldridge Cleaver. The song became better known as the Black Panther Party National Anthem.

"People don't think much of Johnny Mathis but he was my favorite artist when I was fifteen and sixteen. And you know who inspired Johnny Mathis? Edith Piaf," she says. Mathis's and Piaf's notes share the same tragic yet strong and convicted qualities and an otherworldly weariness. The strange tension created by Brown's own vibrato and her session with Tapscott taking place under law enforcement surveillance is palpable on the recording; ironically, you could say it serves the art's severity and seriousness of purpose.

The MC5 definitely felt the heat of having their creative efforts tampered with by surveillance. The fact that their career went so poorly echoes the implosion of their political counterparts, as any attempts to harness a group energy was consistently undermined by counterintelligence. "Maybe I'd be paranoid if I went down that road and asked, did somebody from the administration get to Jac Holzman, tell the president of Elektra Records, this band shouldn't be making albums? I don't know. That's just kind of an open-ended question," says Wayne Kramer of the MC5. "I know the parts of the puzzle I participated in. I know my part in the demise of the band, in terms of my own choices . . . You know, it was a conflagration of forces. We had resistance from the music business—the promoters didn't want to hire us, the record companies thought we were too much trouble. So the money wasn't flowing. We had harassment by the FBI and the Detroit Police Department. Whatever city we were in we would have trouble with the police. We had our own internal conflicts, any one of which could've broken a band in two. After a while it's pretty hard to sustain a positive working environment when you can't get gigs, you can't make records, and the police are up your ass and you're fighting with guys in your own corner. We had trouble with our own people in the movement; that said, we weren't revolutionary enough for the revolution. We would get intense criticism from the super-Marxists: 'How can you guys be in a rock band? You should play for free.' . . . That was the trouble with trying to apply turn of the century Marxism to 1969 rock 'n' roll."

# Rainbow Politics, Woodstock, and Revolution Rock

I f the year 1969 in music is remembered for anything it's Woodstock, though it could also be characterized as the time when rock, politics, and black liberation came together under a multicolored canopy. Fred Hampton called the efforts toward racial and political unity among the black and poor and student population a Rainbow Coalition, but the sweetness and unity associated with visions of rainbows was not sustainable in the period of continued cultural and politic upheaval, and Hampton would not live to see the new year.

"The people were directly involved and affected by what was going on," explains Nina Simone's collaborator Al Schackman. "She wanted to make sure that they were really shaken out of what she felt was their sleep. One of the ways that we did that was like really blasting off on the tune, 'Revolution.'" Pointing to their customized version of the Beatles' tune, "where at the end, we try to set off an atomic bomb, that kind of thing. . . People weren't expecting that out of her at that time . . . I would be playing notes using the slide," he says of the familiar Elmore James "Madison Blues" lick borrowed by the Beatles on "For You Blue," "But in the end, I took that slide and just went nuts on it, totally explosive."

John Lennon and his wife, Yoko Ono, were deeply connected to the peace movement and demonstrated their empathy for the radical counterculture and the Black Power movement. By 1968, as students around the world were becoming radicalized, it was nearly impossible for a group of the Beatles' magnitude to avoid making a statement on youth and world affairs. Activist and educator Angela Davis says she noted the transformation of the Beatles with the arrival of "Revolution." "I don't think he contradicted what many activists felt at that period," she says.[1] Lennon's song was a critique of the violence arising within the worldwide peace, racial justice, and anti-imperialist movements. By becoming involved with artist Ono at the same time, Lennon was transforming personally, and it laid him open to public critique himself. "When I hear the song 'Revolution,' even now, it chokes me up," says Ono. "We were ostracized by the world and the fans too . . . John was daring to speak out," Ono once said.[2] The pair used the occasion of their marriage in 1969 as a way to satisfy the hungry media and wage peace. Observing a change in mood and watching as incidents of violent street protest demonstrations escalated, Lennon and Ono used the bed-ins to appeal to the faction of protestors who thought that violent revolution was the answer.

"Nobody's ever given peace a complete chance before. Gandhi tried it and Martin Luther King tried it but they were shot," said Lennon from the couple's bed at the Amsterdam Hilton. Recorded from their hotel room in Toronto with a roomful of friends and fans, the song "Give Peace a Chance" became the movement's new chant:

All we are saying, is give peace a chance.

Through the end of the war, the couple's stock-in-trade was the creation of one-line slogans, set to music, many of them appropriate for singing in large groups of people on marches and at outdoor gatherings: *Give peace a chance; war is over if you want it.* Some of the song-slogans would be appropriated from the people themselves: *power to the people; free the people now.*

The pair's introduction to the Black Panther Party initially occurred when Bobby Seale and Huey Newton came to the Lennons seeking help. "We told them about our People for Medical Research health clinic, and our Free Breakfast for Children program—we were feeding close to two hundred thousand kids at one point in 1969. John wanted to know how he could support our community survival programs. We rapped a very long time," says Bobby Seale.[3] Yippie Stew Albert also recalls, "Afterward, Huey sent John a letter saying he had listened very closely to 'Imagine' and that the ideas it put forward were similar to his own which he called intercommunalism. John was very proud of that letter. He showed it to Jerry [Rubin] and me."[4]

"Dick Gregory gave Yoko and me a little kind of prayer book," said Lennon. "It is in the Christian idiom, but you can apply it anywhere. It is the concept of positive prayer. If you want to get a car, get the car keys. Get it? Imagine is saying that . . . The song was originally inspired by Yoko's *Grapefruit*. In it are a lot of pieces saying, imagine this, imagine that."[5]

Admittedly, it was getting hard to imagine positively in light of current realities but the Lennon-Ono message was unrelenting: keep on pushing. Part of what branded Yoko "wacko," to use her description, was the couples' insistence at applying a spiritual solution to practical problems. "Music covers the world and it heals the world," she explains. "When you say I love you to the one you love, actually you're saying it to the world and the planet. I think that's *it*," says Ono in reference to the pair's consistent public displays of affection and affirmations of peace. "That says it all."

## Black Woodstock

The spirit of the Woodstock festival—notorious for its record-breaking attendance, definitive sixties lineup, and a live birth in the crowd—was rooted in an unshackling from societal conventions. Intended as a celebration of a new utopian lifestyle, Woodstock was supposed to symbolize the generation that not only valued music and art, but which placed a premium on peace, love, and freedom over chasing the almighty dollar.

"They can't hide us anymore" was the thought that ran through Richie Havens's mind when he saw the crowd that amassed at Yasgur's Farm. Considering the view from the helicopter that delivered him to the gig that day, "I thought, when the pictures come out in the newspaper, they'll see we are now above ground. We're no longer relegated to the underground."

Whether it was destiny or a cosmic hiccup, the musical event that was the climax of the 1960s turned out to be a most auspicious day for Havens as well. Though he and his two-man group were meant to be the fourth act on the bill, they were thrown on first when transportation and other problems put the day's scheduled lineup into a state of flux. Havens's act was all present and accounted for, they were easy to set up, and, most important, they had not ingested the infamous brown acid. Like it or not, it was showtime.

"We landed, they chased me, I went on," he explains. "I went and did my forty minutes, I walked off, and they said, 'Richie, can you do about four more songs?' No one was there to go on. I went back and sang the four songs. I walked off. 'Richie . . . four more?' They did that six times until I realized, I don't have another song. I'm done. I've sung every song I know. It's two hours and forty-five minutes later . . . and that's when I start that long intro, that's me trying to figure out what I'm going to play." After about a minute of freelancing a percussive riff in his distinctive open-D tuning, accompanied by an Afro-Cuban conga beat, Havens cried the word "freedom." He repeated it—freedom, freedom, freedom—for a total of eight times. "I just went with that . . . all of a sudden, 'Motherless Child' came out. I hadn't sung that song in fourteen or fifteen years. I used to sing it early on in the Village."

Before making his way to Greenwich Village in the late fifties in search of the beatniks, Havens sang doo-wop, street corner music popularized in neighborhoods like his own Bedford-Stuyvesant, Brooklyn. "We had a wonderful lead singer whose name was David McCrea. He had the voice of Frankie Lymon but with absolute church soul goin' on. So we had to make a deal with his mother, which was, if he was going to sing with us, we had to sing in the choir of the church. This is how I got to sing some gospel and realized how wonderfully communicative that music is as well . . . in that the people in church who listened to it was moved by it. So I learned from that . . . feeling moved by it myself. We would get together and learn these songs with the McCrea Gospel Singers, songs like 'Call Him Up and Tell Him What You Want,' which of course was referring to God . . . come out and ask for what you need, ask for what you want, tell him what you want. If you need love, that was the idea, you can ask." As he was freestyling onstage in '69, Havens adapted a couple of secularized verses from the song he calls "I Got a Telephone in My Bosom" (a variation on "Jesus Is on the Mainline"), learned during his brief gospel education.

The Woodstock performance, delivered by chance and forever preserved in the recorded and filmed documents of the event, set the stage for Havens to sustain a career in music at a high level—it was the period that marked the end of his beginning of becoming, to use his phrase. For his friend Jimi Hendrix, however, Woodstock would mark the beginning of the end. "Having been the guy who sent him to Greenwich Village to become Jimi Hendrix, I think about him quite often," says Havens, "because I did share that with him." Havens had first witnessed "Jimmy James" in action at an uptown club. He was so blown away by the performance that he told him of the Village, a place where he could go play and fit in, that he needn't settle for a career as a studio musician "at the whim of everyone else—that he could be in his own band." A connection was made between Havens and Hendrix, a pair whose subsequent meetings bind their stories seemingly by fate. Though Havens worked on acoustic and Hendrix primarily on electric, both would go on to perform the triumphant sets that bookended Woodstock weekend. Like most songwriters of their era, they revered Bob Dylan, though his work held a special resonance for Havens and Hendrix, who brought their own unique qualities and insights to the work through their multiple interpretations. It was Havens who first turned Hendrix on to the text of "All Along the Watchtower." "I gave him the words to that," he says. "That's how we started out knowing each other." And it was Hendrix who came up with a cataclysmic mix so definitive even Dylan came to perform the song that way.

Hendrix's breakthrough US performance at Monterey Pop in the summer of 1967 was built on the foundation of the blues he'd come to turn inside out—"Killing Floor" and "Rock Me Baby"—the splash of psychedelic color in his originals "Purple Haze" and "Foxy Lady," and choice contemporary covers, from the mysterious ballad of dubious origin titled "Hey Joe" to Chip Taylor's goofy sludge-fest "Wild Thing" and Dylan's stupendous "Like a Rolling Stone." Just two years later, a weathered and worn-out looking Hendrix turned in a performance that stood in stark contrast to his West Coast coming out. Footage of him in the documentary feature *Woodstock*, portrayed as a lone man, wailing in the breeze in Cherokee-inspired garb, the camera panning the trash-strewn ground as the festival winds down, only underscores the fact that the 1969 rock festival marked the end of an era. But for fans of Hendrix who know his story from here, the images are frankly disturbing. "When I first saw the rushes of the movie in 1970 and I looked at that, I was actually very disappointed in the way it was portrayed," says producer Eddie Kramer, the left hand studio man for Hendrix and recording engineer of the festival.

"Maybe disappointed is the wrong word. Maybe I felt that it was a beginning and an end, as far as Jimi was concerned."

And then there is his bombs-bursting performance of the national anthem. It's Woodstock's defining piece of music, delivered one year after Olympic medalists Tommie Smith and John Carlos raised their fists for Black Power as the national anthem played (the athletes paid for their action by being banned from future Games). Declarations of patriotism, racial and cultural solidarity, and dissent by public figures was dangerous in a time of war; the expressions had a way of backfiring in the land of the free and the home of the brave, though Jimi played on.

"When you think about where Jimi's head was at, he'd spoken about his feelings about the war, and he was totally antiwar. The best thing he could really do to make an impression was to play something that was memorable," says Kramer. "The performance was very searing, very heartfelt. One of the reasons it stands up today is that it's brilliant—from a musical aspect, from an emotional aspect and technically. He's making a statement and it was hey, I'm antiwar. He did it in a few songs—he did it with "Machine Gun." He *was* a political animal." Kramer believes Hendrix's creation of a hippie national anthem may have been speaking to other injustices beyond war, though he declines the opportunity to speak directly to Hendrix's position on race matters, specifically in America. But directly or indirectly, Hendrix, just by virtue of his being, had helped to deliver rock and a young generation's consciousness to new place. That Jimi, Richie Havens, Sly Stone, and Carlos Santana, all rockers of color, prevailed at Woodstock is among the less-emphasized facts of the Aquarian Exposition in White Lake, New York. "Um hum, yea, that's right," says Havens, though that's all he'll say when asked to comment on that plain fact. It is perhaps in keeping with the festival's spirit, steeped in the new age Aquarian doctrine of idealism, humanitarianism, and freedom, that those who experienced Woodstock and live its dream are colorblind. Like Hendrix and Stone, Havens sees Technicolor rather than black and white; he is not one to magnify the racial divide, preferring to keep the focus on similarity and harmony. So too it goes with Santana, who was a twenty-two-year-old guitarist at the time. Originally from Mexico, Santana moved from Tijuana to San Francisco's Mission District on the cusp of the Summer of Love; his bluesy sound equally reflected both worlds. Leading his ensemble through a version of the Afro-Cuban percussive intensive "Jingo," their take on Olatunji's "Jin Go Lo Ba," Santana's accomplished performance at Woodstock was in essence the moment that birthed the Latino rock movement. It was a more serious embrace of cultural heritage and pride as the music moved beyond the innocence of "La Bamba" and "Wooly Bully" and *la raza* was channeled into rock. Bands like El Chicano and Malo, and the multi-ethnic band War, among others, through words and music pushed the national dialogue on minority concerns.

Hendrix was also a rainbow man, living and loving by an esoteric code of magical colors and numbers he devised on his own (while stoking an additional interest in voodoo and its potential to seize power). When it came to the Black Power struggle, Hendrix wasn't specifically an advocate, nor would he touch separatism or anything that didn't promote a harmonious vibration. However, during his famous shows in Berkeley in May 1970, he introduced "Machine Gun" with, "I'd like to dedicate this to all the soldiers fighting in Berkeley, you know what soldiers I'm talking about. And to the soldiers fighting in Vietnam, too." He preceded the "The Star Spangled Banner" by saying, "This is for everybody together, the American anthem the way it really is in the air." Citing "Voodoo Child" as "our anthem," he dedicated the song to People's Park and the Panthers. It was "the strongest public statement he ever made in support of the organization," writes Hendrix biographer Charles Cross.[6] "Every one of his relatives also tell stories of having militants attempting to get near him, and them. Jimi was never one to align himself with anything extreme." Through the years, the stories have circulated—of post-show pressure, exertion and shakedowns for money and the kidnapping. Among the suggested perpetrators have been rogue militants and imposters, bandits and drug dealers, corrupt businessmen and handlers, and agents of the federal government. These extreme situations demonstrate what Hendrix was up against as an agent of change and as a high-profile black rock star living in dangerous times. His position as a charismatic musician of influence, and one of color, was enough to brand him in the eyes of authorities as a potential leader of a rebellious youth movement; his drug bust in Toronto in 1969 coincided with the FBI opening a file on him. Only a little more than seven pages, the file contains very little in the way of discovery beyond two petty juvenile incidents in Seattle. Hendrix was no threat to national security; he was ultimately an artist and a pacifist, and impaired by drugs, rather than a potential leader of a youth brigade in revolt. Besides, he hadn't even captured the black audience's full attention with his music. Though his friends Tundera and Taharqa Aleem had made attempts to involve him in community-based activities in Harlem as part of a larger effort to raise his profile in the neighborhood and gain him airplay on black radio, crossover never happened. Exactly why the wild style of Hendrix was so popular with hippies but not with a more mass African American audience is a mystery Greg Tate investigates in his book *Midnight Lightning: Jimi Hendrix and the Black Experience*.

"A profound irony of Hendrix's career is that even after shredding racial shibboleths by the dozens, he discovered a gate at the country's color-obsessed edge he was not able to bust wide. This being the same gate that has kept black people from embracing him as one of their own to this day. The one that reads, 'Jimi Hendrix was different from you and me. Jimi Hendrix was for white people.' All boundary crossers face the inherent problem of coming back," writes Tate.[7] But there was a project in his musical arsenal that proved to be the exception: Jimi's all-black power trio, Band of Gypsys, featuring Buddy Miles and Billy Cox, found a black audience, "Thanks to the booty-bouncing power of 'Who Knows,' and the twelve-minute antiwar requiem, 'Machine Gun,' whose supernatural flow of ideas has found Hendrix compared to John Coltrane on more than one occasion," says Tate. The album remains touted as a tossed-off contractual obligation project rather than the potential new direction. What the mass black audience failed to get in Hendrix's lifetime would soon be gone for good, though not before Hendrix had made an indelible mark on the culture and on rock music. His genius had not been lost on his fellow musicians, who employed him in their back-up bands and on sessions, as the Isley Brothers did, or wanted to claim discovering him, as Little Richard did. Jazz great Miles Davis and blueser Etta James were outright fans. "He might twist and bend the notes like Johnny 'Guitar' Watson, but his mind was busy exploring the outer limits. That was exciting. By asking 'Are You Experienced?' in his song, Jimi got a lot of people to start looking for an answer," writes James. "I dug the hippies. I related." Having forsaken her earlier involvement with the Nation of Islam as a way to contend with the challenges her life delivered, Etta James endorsed Hendrix and the hippie lifestyle, even if she didn't live it herself. "I saw them as rebels the way

I'd been a rebel, except they were mixing rebellion with love. I liked their attitude. It was a whole generation of young white kids who were interested in sweetness and compassion. They treated black men and women like sisters and brothers and seemed determined to put the racism of their parents behind them. It was naive and idealistic, but hey, why not?"[8] In addition to Hendrix, James mentions her close friend Sly Stone, "the other black man who was a hippie leader."

Like Hendrix, Sly Stone would not maintain the profile of a leader within or without the Woodstock nation, nor would he wear any other tag hung on him during his career, other than the role he chose to play as leader of the band. His extra-large talent and commitment to music, from his days as a gospel family singer to a DJ and producer, led him to the top of the charts, but as his story goes, he became just as familiar with the underside of life. Opening strong, Sylvester Stewart's songs, such as "Stand!" with its burst out flavor, and the funk of "Everyday People," carried a message, all right. His mixed-gender and racially integrated band was a demonstration of backing up message with action. Together they stood, playing circles around the competition until they could play no more, their leader slipping further and further into addiction in the face of the disintegration of a hippie's rainbow-hued impossible dreams. Stone's public persona after Woodstock existed largely in rumors, his largeness gradually dissipating until he projected a fraction of the light he was capable of beaming.

––––––––

Soon after the Woodstock experience, people all over the world would request that Richie Havens play "Freedom." "And I'd say, 'Freedom? Which freedom?' And they'd say, 'You know, "Motherless Child."'" The Woodstock performances captured on the soundtrack and in the documentary feature film had reached audiences all over the world. "This is a big-time change for me," remembers Havens, who to that date had never seen himself perform until the film was in theaters. "It scared me to death, it was just so large. It wasn't me, you know. It was a song. I became a mechanism to get that song out." Havens and his motherless child's song of freedom had indeed carried him a long way from home—from his introduction at Woodstock as a dynamic and commanding solo acoustic performer, to a cross-cultural generational ambassador of socially conscious song and thought. It was in late August 1970, at the second Isle of Wight festival off the coast of England, when Havens saw his friend Jimi Hendrix for the final time. After the concert the pair talked about getting together back in London. Hendrix asked Havens to introduce him to his lawyer. "He said, 'You know, my management is pushing me to keep biting the guitar strings, they call it that, but I want to play music. I want to play the music I taught myself and put it with music that's traditional—that's what I want to be doing.'" But Havens never saw Hendrix back in London. He was pronounced dead a couple of weeks later, in the wee hours of September 18, 1970, a victim of choking following the ingestion of a mixture of pills and alcohol (though circumstances leading up to his death were still being investigated nearly thirty years later).

Time has shown Jimi Hendrix possessed a mind-boggling command of his instrument—technical expertise, emotional quality, showmanship—and a lyrical imagination that could unveil the colors of the dreams within his songs. It would've been enough if that were all he'd done in his short lifetime. But Jimi Hendrix without a doubt did more. As apolitical as he may have appeared on the outside, Jimi Hendrix was a freedom rider. Just as Nina Simone proclaimed herself civil rights, Hendrix was freedom, Do Your Own Thing made manifest. Staking his claim with the pioneer spirit of a Wild Westman, he had set out for the territories a loner, unharnessed by group identification with a race or a movement. "I am what I am, thank God," he sang. "Find yourself first, then find your talent. Work hard in your mind so you can come alive." Armed for the revolution with only a guitar and his "Message to Love," Jimi Hendrix proved himself to be among the most revolutionary musicians and thinkers of his generation.

# The Revolution Will Not Be Realized: The Sound of Black Power Goes Mainstream

As matters of pride and prejudice moved from the underground and began to find a space at the top of the charts, at the end of 1969 the peace-and-love-colored children who created Woodstock were lost in a world that was starting to turn a terrible shade of hate.

Most students of the sixties have been told the decade's final musical act was staged at a racetrack in Altamont, California, and starred the Rolling Stones. A concert-goer, described through the years as "drug-crazed" with murderous intent, was killed there. In these stories that day is framed as a convenient metaphor for the despair and confusion felt at not only the end of the sixties, but the beginning of the long, cold, lonely winter of the early seventies. Altamont was a preview of the darkness that descended at one decade's protracted end, while the storms were still raging and scores were waiting to be settled on the streets at the beginning of the next. And just as sure as the light was changing, so were the songs.

The evil set loose by a series of killings by a madman and his followers in California, the murders at Kent State, the Watergate cover-up in progress setting up the fall of a president, the final curtain on Saigon, and other events have been served up by historians as dramatic and illustrative examples of the many ways and days in which the sixties slowly died. These interpretations of events are tales often told and told again, and they are almost always accompanied and underscored by the music that was created in the chaos of the immediate post-sixties, post-revolution era: "Got a Revolution, Got to Revolution." The music made is documentation of a people who are very much alive; people who will survive, people who have set out to keep on pushing, and who have the power.

> People moving out, people moving in
> why, because of the color of their skin
> run, run, run but you sure can't hide

is what the Temptations sang in "Ball of Confusion (That's What the World Is Today)." Written by Norman Whitfield and Barrett Strong, this was the new sound of Motown, its innocence as good as gone. Marvin Gaye traded in "That's the Way Love Is" for the somber folk rock of "Abraham, Martin and John." "Yester Me, Yester You, Yesterday" was the last of Stevie Wonder's hits to be strung out on love for some time to come. If ever there were a time in which the music going out could be described as old school and the music coming in as new, this was that time. These were new songs for new times— harder times, troubled ones.

In contrast to Motown's core sound, built on a foundation of positivity, these newer songs were not subtle; they directly confronted all the current matters of interest going down. And yet, they were popular, brought to you by Hitsville U.S.A, where the young men and women of Detroit had once literally been groomed at an in-house charm school so that they might transcend their ghetto upbringings and succeed by assimilating.

> Segregation, determination, demonstration, integration,
> aggravation, humiliation, obligation to our nation,
> Ball of confusion!

Affirmation was the new byword at Motown as the label eventually caught up with the 1970s, making its move toward more distinctly black and stronger sounds.

By 1970, Project 100,000, the Defense Department's effort to enlist men from the poorest Appalachian hills to the hardest urban ghettos, had been successful at enrolling those whose lack of education left them off the college track and without prospects. These were the young men, classification 1-A, who were assigned almost exclusively to combat duty, producing the highest percentage of fatalities in Vietnam. "Black people really don't have nothing to fight for," said Muhammad Ali, who remained a vocal player in the anti-war fight following his refusal to serve as conscientious objector on religious grounds. At the time, his statements were met with a mixed response within and without the black communities, but by the decade's end he would find more and more people in accord with his position. "I just don't think I should go ten thousand miles from here and shoot some black people who never called me nigger, never lynched me, never put dogs on me, never raped my mama, enslaved me and deprived me of freedom, justice and equality, and they's black too. I just can't shoot 'em," he said.[1]

Barrett Strong, whose voice had first introduced Motown to an international audience with his hit single "Money (That's What I Want)," was also behind Motown taking it to the next phase. With his songwriting partner Norman Whitfield, they dipped their toes in topical water and found success with the Temptations on "Cloud Nine" ("I was born and raised in the slums of the city"); the more specific "Ball of Confusion" made another Top 10 record for the group. And then they did their magic with "War." The song was a track on the Temptations album *Psychedelic Shack* but was deemed too strong to release as a single, so it trickled down to a Motown second-tier artist, Edwin Starr, leaving him to take the heat should any controversy arise. But there was no controversy and no problem finding Starr's audience or locating people to sing along with his tough reading of a protest song.

> War. Good God! What is it good for? Absolutely nothing.
> Say it again, y'all.

Punctuated by battle-cry guitar and massive drum shots, "War" held the #1 spot on the Top 40 charts for three weeks in August and September of 1970.

That year a poll conducted by a *Time* magazine reporter posed the question, "Should black people fight in Vietnam?" Nearly two-thirds of the 392 black enlisted men questioned answered no.[2] "I read about white folks shooting up Negroes and killing them with the same weapons that they use in the war on the streets of America. With this in mind plus my religious beliefs which is the legal reason I'm not going, I just can't go with that," reiterated Muhammad Ali.[3]

"I believe one of my favorite memories of him was when everybody else stepped forward at the Louisville induction center and he stood his ground. I'll always remember that and I think that should be something that everybody remembers, to stand your ground: what you believe in is more important to you than what everybody says," says Gil Scott-Heron.[4] In 1970, Gil Scott-Heron was emerging as a new black poet. He was barely twenty-two when his novel *The Vulture* was published and his first spoken-word recording, *Small Talk at 125th and Lenox*, was released. "I am a Black man dedicated to expression; expression of the joy and pride of Blackness," he wrote in the album's notes.[5] "I consider myself neither poet, composer, or musician. These are merely tools used by sensitive men to carve out a piece of beauty or truth that they hope may lead to peace and salvation." Scott-Heron was raised in Tennessee by his grandmother. He and his single mother, a librarian, eventually ended up in New York City. He excelled at writing as a teenager and earned enrollment at Fieldston, a progressive Ivy League preparatory school. Upon graduation, he chose to attend Lincoln University in Philadelphia because it was the alma mater of Langston Hughes. As a musician, Scott-Heron's style was conjoined with the word styles of Hughes, as well as those of talkers like Malcolm X and Huey Newton. But it was "musicians more than writers" who inspired him, and he used the rhythms of folk, blues, soul, and jazz to put across the intensity of his emotion. "Richie Havens—what he does with the images and themes, Coltrane—the time defiant nature and thrust of his work. Otis Redding—the way he sings lyrics so that they come through as *sounds*. You can really appreciate how close a saxophone is to the human voice when you hear Otis singing. I sometimes write poetry, in a way, like Otis sings. The sounds form shapes. Like clouds banging into each other. That's how I get loud sounds in my poetry." Scott-Heron also learned from bluesman Jimmy Reed— "You didn't need a string of adjectives to know exactly what his feelings were. He did it by slurring, by drawl, by texture, by phrasing"—and from Jose Feliciano, a hard acoustic guitar-strumming Village contemporary of Havens. He looked to Feliciano for "the way he bends notes. And also his Latin background fits into the neighborhood I'm in. There's a lot of black rhythm down here, but much of it is Puerto Rican." He soaked in all of it, appreciating the atmospheres created by Billie Holiday and the forthrightness Nina Simone brought to the stage. "She was black before it was fashionable to be black."

Scott-Heron took it upon himself to have his poems recorded when he'd seen similar collections by Lois Wyse and Pete Hammil produced by Bob Thiele for his Flying Dutchman record label. Scott-Heron's recorded debut for Flying Dutchman, *Small Talk at 125th and Lenox*, included his poems "Whitey on the Moon," a protest of space program spending; "Brothers," critical of the new breed of street-corner revolutionaries; and "The Subject Was Faggots," an attempt to describe with tolerance the gay scene unfolding in his neighborhood. But it is his poem "The Revolution Will Not Be Televised" for which he is best known, recorded for the 1971 album *Pieces of a Man* and released as a B-side to its single, "Home is Where the Hatred Is," documenting the heroin crisis sweeping inner cities. Scott-Heron and his collaborator Brian Jackson, a flute player and schoolmate from Lincoln, also paid homage to "Lady Day and John Coltrane" on the album, but it was "The Revolution Will Not Be Televised" that became his most visionary and enduring work. Excoriating the media and marketing, it was a rare song that burrowed its way into the collective conscious of musicians—both mainstream and underground—and listeners alike. Scott-Heron and his song would get their due, but at the time his work was caught in a chasm between jazz and soul, poetry and rock, and few knew just what to do with this new poet and basso profundo on the scene. Few knew what to do, period.

As 1970 gave way to 1971, Marvin Gaye asked the fundamental question, "What's Going On?" though the journey from Gaye's interest in black politics to the completion and release of *What's Going On?* was not without struggle. The Motown singer had been known for his stirring soul sides like "I Heard It Through the Grapevine" and "Ain't That Peculiar," which were as peerless as they were apolitical. But the combination of his own consciousness-raising efforts and the return of his brother Frankie from Vietnam had him thinking on a new set of songs. Marvin was changing his consciousness. He'd read *The Autobiography of Malcolm X* and carried it with him in the way books and records were used to accessorize in the late sixties and early seventies. He also changed his look, giving up the bespoke suits for more casual and Afrocentric styles. "Marvin loved the Panthers, though never completely agreed with their politics," writes Frankie Gaye in his memoir. "What Marvin didn't support, actually despised, was their militant and often violent actions, along with their anti-government stance."[6] Just as Motown chief Berry Gordy Jr.

was no fan of Marvin's politicization. The battle between Gordy and Gaye is one of the most famous stories in the portfolio of tales of artist versus record company in a fight for creative control. In the end, Gaye triumphed: by the time *What's Going On* was approved for release even Gordy had conceded that the world was ready to receive a more potent reflection of the voice of black America—the spirit of the times demanded it.

Gaye went on to dominate the sound of 1971, with his follow-up singles, "Mercy Mercy Me (the Ecology)" and "Inner City Blues (Makes Me Wanna Holler)" and had set a new bar for artistic excellence with *What's Going On*. One-off hitmakers the Undisputed Truth sung through the lie of so-called equality in Whitfield and Strong's "Smiling Faces Sometimes," a Top 5 hit in 1971: "Beware of the pat on the back, it just might hold you back."

The following year, the phrase "smiling faces sometimes" was picked up in "Back Stabbers," a hit for vocal heavies the O'Jays, who recorded for the Philadelphia International label. As ambassadors on the love train and exemplars of Kenny Gamble and Leon Huff's trademarked Philly soul productions, writers Gene McFadden, John Whitehead, and Leon Huff delivered a Top 10 song about betrayal—"They smile in your face, all the while they want to take your place, the backstabbers." The Staple Singers also had their say. Moving down the freedom highway since the fifties, the Staples weighed in with "Why (Am I Treated So Bad)" in 1967 before the angry huff of 1971's "Respect Yourself" caught them a hit. The merciful but tense "I'll Take You There"—where *ain't no smiling faces, lying to the races*—still had an edge. It was a #1 record for the Stax label in 1972, and when the God-loving Staples family are singing about trouble with whitey, you know it's time to step up the program for change.

In addition to Motown's new powered jams and in keeping with the atmosphere of tension and release, Gordy also approved the set up of the Black Forum label as an outlet for speeches and other socially and politically minded work; it even had its own tag line, "The Sounds of Struggle." It was a valiant effort to preserve the historicity of the era, though few of the recordings survived the CD revolution. Stokely Carmichael's album of political rhetoric was titled *Free Huey!* after his speech delivered in Oakland on Newton's birthday in 1968. Carmichael outlined cultural imperialism and called out the white man for his relationship to the genocide of Native Americans, among other atrocities, directly linking it to the current challenges facing black Americans.

"We have to understand that we're talking about our survival and nothing else. Whether or not this beautiful race of people is going to survive on earth . . . They can cut all that junk about poverty programs, education, housing, welfare . . . we talking about survival and brothers and sisters, WE gonna survive America! . . . We will survive. Our problem is to develop an undying love for our people," said Carmichael.

The historic Martin Luther King speech "Why I Oppose the War in Vietnam" won Black Forum a Grammy Award for best spoken-word recording. "So I was increasingly compelled to see the war as an enemy of the poor and to attack it as such. Perhaps the more tragic recognition of reality took place when it became clear to me that the war was doing far more than devastating the hopes of the poor at home. It was sending their sons, and their brothers, and their husbands to fight and to die in extraordinarily high proportions relative to the rest of the population. We were taking the black young men who had been crippled by society and sending them eight thousand miles away to guarantee liberties in Southeast Asia which they had not found in Southwest Georgia and East Harlem."

Poetry was also in the mix at Black Forum, from Langston Hughes to Amiri Baraka. As LeRoi Jones, Baraka had documented free jazz as a journalist and was the writer of an Obie-award-winning play on race, *Dutchman*. He was as inspired by the work of Hughes and Malcolm X as he was by the Black Mountain College poets, Allen Ginsberg, and the Beat writers. Beginning in the mid-sixties, the Black Arts Movement and the organization of a Black Arts Repertory Theater/School in Harlem founded by Baraka had contributed to the birth of an unapologetically black style of writing, its creation dovetailing with the Black Power movement's cultural agenda. The 1972 Black Forum release *It's Nation Time—African Visionary Music* offered a sample of Baraka's own Black Nationalist poetry set to music. The track titled "Who Will Survive" is funk as thick as any fatback track, supplemented by a female chorus that might be mistaken for a Motown girl group were the girls not singing, "Who will survive America, very few Negroes, no crackers at all." Baraka's work issued a double-dare to anyone who thought they were going to reap the rewards of change without getting into it or getting involved.

Will you survive in the heat and fire of actual change?

I doubt it

Will you survive, woman, or will your nylon wig catch on fire at
    midnight and light up Sterling Street and your ass prints on the
    pavement?

Though this production wasn't likely to secure a spot on the hit parade,
Baraka's refrain crossed over into the streets and could be heard alongside
"power to the people" at student gatherings and occasions for black unity,
from the yards of Harvard to the docks of Annapolis.[7] It was survival, after
all, that was at the core of the Power movement—the Black Panthers had
established and named their social programs in the name of it and Stokely
Carmichael had proclaimed it: "We gonna survive America!"

Black Forum as a commercial entity would not exist for long, releasing only one 45 single: "No Time," by Elaine Brown. "While the Motown
[Black Forum] label failed to attract large audiences, it was nevertheless significant that the company created an outlet for controversial ideas and black
poetry," writes author Suzanne Smith in her Motown history *Dancing in the
Street*.[8] "Motown decided, strategically of course, to produce this 'forum' on
an obscure label, clearly separate from the company's musical offerings."

## Compared to What?

Also concurrent with soul's solid gold hits and Motown's short-lived political
forum were a string of albums and artists whose sounds took years to emerge
from the underground, buried as they were in the campaign to keep certain
voices down.

Rare groove chasers know the name Eugene McDaniels; his 1971 album
for Atlantic, *Headless Heroes of the Apocalypse* is a standard-bearer for psychedelic soul/funk/jazz rhythms and is borrowed frequently for its samples
(most famously by the Beastie Boys in "Get It Together"). The album is a
fierce statement of black pride, anger, and frustration, equally powered by a
super-soul fever, peace, and ultimately love. It's a showcase for McDaniels's
breadth as a composer, from folky singer-songwriter styles ("Susan Jane") to
proto-rap ("Supermarket Blues"); McDaniels's strongest words are demonstrations of righteous indignation, though he offers spiritual ideas.

The Lord is black, his mood is in the rain, the people have called he's
   coming to make corrections
You can hear his voice blowin' in the wind

McDaniels is the composer of "Compared to What," the 1969 jazz-soul
wartime protest made famous by Les McCann and Eddie Harris: "Possession is the motivation that's hangin' up the goddam nation." McDaniels was
born in Kansas City in 1935, studied at the Omaha Conservatory of Music,
and graduated from Omaha University. After forming a band in the 1950s,
he signed with Liberty Records and hit in 1961 with "A Hundred Pounds of
Clay," followed by five more Top 40 hits, including "Tower of Strength." All in
all, McDaniels had six Top 40 records in 1961 and 1962 before he turned his
focus to writing (he worked closely with Roberta Flack and ultimately wrote
her hit "Feel Like Making Love," among others). By the time he attempted
to launch his solo career as a singing and songwriting artist, McDaniels had
had the time to chew on what he wanted to say and had an intensely unique
way of saying it. He was fearless with his melodies and in his verses. The
instrumentation was a wild combination of folk-funk: electric and acoustic
bass rubbed against guitar, drums, and piano, and they all combined with
lyrics that strike chords of deep recognition. With the fascist-fighting folker's
impeccable style of oration, he injects the song with theatrical and emotional
soul power. As he sings, he evokes images of a man increasingly incensed and
so confused by injustice that he's stretched to the point of losing his mind. His
elegy for the red man, "The Parasite (For Buffy)," dedicated to Sainte-Marie, is
a shining example of his dramaturgical song style that places his subjects in a
social, political and psychological context. But McDaniels's revolution of the
mind is a peaceful one; though he paints pictures of hell and all hell breaking loose, his narrator does not advocate use of violence as a solution. Rather,
violence is portrayed as the problem.

"Supermarket Blues" describes a situation in which a man demands his
money back for a can of peas marked as pineapple and ends up with a beating.
Somehow he even finds a way to inject dark humor into the mess: "I wish I'd
stayed home and got high instead of coming into the street and having this
awful fight." Whatever darkness he's describing, McDaniels's point of view
remains poised and unique; his higher consciousness and keep-on-pushing
spirit bleeds between the notes of each slyly rendered gospel-laced track.

Years later, the white-rapping, Tibetan-Freedom-loving Beastie Boys would turn to McDaniels, nicknamed the Left Rev McD, for a sample.

The jazz-folk project *The Outlaw* is of no less interest: for his solo debut, McDaniels was accompanied by a who's-who of players, including Ron Carter on bass and Hugh McCracken and Eric Weissberg on guitars. He's pictured on the front cover clutching a Bible, flanked by an afroed sister and a severe-looking revolutionary Euro-woman wielding a machine gun, both looking a little like they came straight out of central casting. On that album, McDaniels singled out the "Silent Majority" in one of his characteristically styled rhymes.

> Silent majority, gathering around the hanging tree,
>    negative forces in unity . . . ignoring the call to humanity.

Who's to say if this is what earned McDaniels the enmity of the Nixon administration and landed him on his notorious enemies list; Nixon had courted a so-called silent segment of the population disinterested in countercultural politics, going as far as to speak for them. The lore that goes with McDaniels suggests that Vice President Spiro Agnew personally contacted Atlantic Records and asked for the cessation of his recording career upon the release of *Headless Heroes*. A stealthy compliance to the Nixon/Agnew stance on law and order (and its relationship to racism) could serve as an explanation for the label's reduced promotion and in essence burial of McDaniels as a performing artist, though his valuable services as a writer were retained. Like Solomon Burke described, this was not a case of strong-arming; no home invasions were staged and no personal threats were received. Rather, the heat was turned down on a career that held tremendous promise. Here was a master-class artist whose work had the potential to expand consciousness rather than inure it to present realities. Entertainers without huge bases but with business plans like Burke's and the spiritual, philosophical, or ideological grounding of McDaniels, or folk singing Buffy Sainte-Marie and Len Chandler—were among the artists officially marked dangerous. Without high-powered management on their side, they started to drift from consumer consciousness.

"The reason Bob Dylan probably didn't suffer was that he was just so popular. Look what they did to the Beatles, finding a little bit of weed on them," notes Elaine Brown, who was becoming mighty familiar with all forms of government harassment as a member of the Black Panther Party.

"I mean things had happened to me, but I never thought that there was some kind of blacklisting going on. Who ever heard of that? I don't think very many people, even today, understand how much blacklisting has gone on of artists in the record business," says Buffy Sainte-Marie. She recalls, "What happened was—and pardon my naivete, it's just true—I would go to do the *Tonight Show*, you know, and the producer backstage would say, now you're not going to sing the 'Universal Solider' or 'Now That the Buffalo's Gone.' We just want you to do 'Until It's Time for You To Go,' because we like it better." At the time, she didn't read anything into the change. But, she says, "When I did get the wind that these people were not on the same page as I am, I just wouldn't do a show that tried to be so pushy about what they didn't want. It was never like a big deal. Believe me, people in the White House are very, very discreet about drowning artists, about gagging artists, about denying airplay to artists. They're very discreet about it."

So too goes the story of Little Jerry Williams, an iconoclastic soul singer with some minor hits ("I'm the Lover Man," "Baby You're My Everything") in the early sixties, and a career as a producer, engineer, and songwriter for Atlantic under the auspice of Jerry Wexler. Raised on old-time country radio and trained on the road and in studios, Williams hung out and wrote with the likes of Gary U.S. Bonds, Charlie and Inez Foxx, and Patti LaBelle and the Bluebells. But hardly anyone could have predicted the riot of words and sound going on throughout 1970's *Total Destruction to Your Mind*, credited to the Williams persona Swamp Dogg. In his attempt to turn soul around with his irreverent but pointed views, Williams was a pioneer at fusing rock's blues and country's roots and coming up with country funk. Swamp Dogg preached mind expansion, antiwar sentiment, and equality, alongside frank talk of sexuality, in an attempt to communicate without forsaking his truth or his innate humor. The bold combination didn't earn him any friends in the marketplace nor at Elektra Records, the label to which he was signed for a second album. *Rat On!*, released in 1971, is most often cited for its sleeve depicting the Dogg in ride 'em cowboy position on the back of a white rat. "When they signed me they had one black act on the label [the Voices of East Harlem] and when they signed me, they released that act. It was like one to

a customer . . . They didn't want no more black acts. They told me that."⁹
He was dropped from the label posthaste, he believes, because of his position on the Vietnam War. Williams was part of the Jane Fonda and Donald
Sutherland headlined *FTA*, a satirical song and sketch comedy troupe that
Len Chandler would also travel with. "I was with Jane Fonda . . . we were out
protesting the war and all that and they said, . . . 'We don't need this.' It was
alright for the MC5 to come out onstage and pull their pants down and shit.
It was a very strange company," Williams told author Richie Unterberger in
the 1990s. Swamp Dogg has continued to record, but his most timeless song,
the somber and yearning "God Bless America for What" from 1971, might as
well have been recorded yesterday

> Oh what a joke is the Statue of Liberty,
> With the Indians on the reservation and black folks still ain't free
> Hate, war and distrust is all our forefathers took time to sow
> You see kids growin' up to justify . . . we're tired of singing
> God bless America unless they know what for

"I wasn't trying to help overthrow the government . . . I was just trying to
enlighten people and say what I thought," says Williams.

Those who sang personal and political truths with the power to trans-
form thought and save lives were not put on trial as they were in Pete
Seeger's day. Rather, they were denied exposure for fear that the people too
would take a righteous stance and fight the power. "The Powers That Are,"
as Burke says, saw only one way to deal with musical dissidents—put them,
and others like them, out of business. Deeper involvement with political
organizations would almost assuredly result in a decline if not an outright
ban on an artist's exposure.

McDaniels was able to maintain his career as a writer, behind the scenes;
as of 2011, Williams was continuing to record and self-release material as
Swamp Dogg. Burke left Atlantic behind for smaller concerns like Bell and
Chess, where he continued to work without the major infrastructure in place
for hit making, though times were also changing. The soul revue was going
out of fashion, about to be replaced by more expansive definitions for black
music, a shift in part owing to the Black Power movement, along with soul's
own consciousness raising effects. Artists like Marvin Gaye, Stevie Wonder,

*Poet Langston Hughes took inspiration from jazz; his work affected a generation of folksingers as well as hip-hop's forebears.*
[PHOTOFEST]

*Odetta said, "Folk music straightened my back and kinked my hair."* [PHOTO BY ROMAN CHO]

*Boxer Cassius Clay was inspired by minister Malcolm X and the message of the Black Muslims to become Muhammad Ali. The words of both men run though hip-hop rhyme and culture.* [PHOTOFEST]

*Calypso singer Harry Belafonte worked side by side with Dr. King to bring a musical presence to the March on Washington.* [PHOTOFEST]

*Len Chandler's journey as a topical singer took him from Greenwich Village to Selma, Alabama, and on to Southeast Asia where he sang to Free the Army.* [COURTESY OF PHOTOFEST]

*Nina Simone's early sixties visit to Nigeria opened the door to folk music, while the fight for racial equality in Mississippi and Alabama politicized her brand of song.* [PHOTOFEST]

*Native American folksinger Buffy Sainte-Marie found out she was among Nixon's enemies.*
[COURTESY OF BUFFY SAINTE-MARIE]

*Richie Havens opens his shows with "All Along the Watchtower," the Bob Dylan song popularized by Jimi Hendrix.*
[PHOTOFEST]

*Inspired by blazing rock, free jazz, and radical politics, Wayne Kramer of the MC5 met with obstacles in his efforts to wake up the counterculture.* [ © LENI SINCLAIR (1968) COURTESY OF © WAYNE KRAMER (2011) ]

*John Sinclair was released from prison three days after John Lennon and Yoko Ono, Phil Ochs, Stevie Wonder, Archie Shepp, and others gathered in Ann Arbor for a concert in his name.* [PHOTOFEST]

*Gil Scott-Heron delivers a message to the messengers: "I'm talking about peace."* [PHOTOFEST]

*King of Rock 'n' Soul Solomon
Burke envisioned a supergroup
or Soul Clan, its profits poured
back into the community.*

Yoko Ono and John Lennon: *All they are saying is give peace a chance.* [PHOTOFEST]

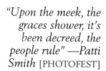

*"Upon the meek, the graces shower, it's been decreed, the people rule"* —Patti Smith [PHOTOFEST]

*Penelope Houston then and now. She took on the pervasive influence of the media in her punk classic, "The American in Me."* [PHOTO BY MARCUS LEATHERDALE, COURTESY OF PENELOPE HOUSTON]

[PHOTO BY PATRICK ROQUES, COURTESY OF PENELOPE HOUSTON]

*Michael Franti went to Iraq with a camera and a guitar and reported back with film and songs. "As an artist, that's my role; to go places, witness, see for myself."* [PHOTO © EBET ROBERTS]

*Debora Iyall joined the Native Americans who occupied Alcatraz Island in 1969; poetry and punk rock gave her a voice.* [COURTESY OF DEBORA IYALL]

*Phranc, pictured here as an art student, found her identity as an "all-American Jewish lesbian folksinger" on the Los Angeles punk rock scene.* [COURTESY OF PHRANC]

and Curtis Mayfield were working on taking their music to a whole new level as they mixed artistry and social conscience, building on their existing commercial successes with the expression of their inner visions. In 1968 Mayfield had established his Curtom label, setting the stage for his seventies soul commentaries. James Brown continued his touring, record releasing and business venturing, all in attempts to get a foothold on his finances, which had previously been in the hands of his recording labels; his persistent trouble with the IRS had his business affairs consistently in upheaval.

A new day had dawned on the future of empowered soul. It was a time of expansion, as black artists from South Los Angeles and the Midwest up to Harlem—the Watts Prophets, Art Ensemble of Chicago, and Gil Scott-Heron—began branching out into folk, jazz, fusion, and funk, their voices steeped in poetry and music inspired by jazz and indigenous music from throughout the world. George Clinton, who like the Isley Brothers had come up through doo-wop and soul channels, took a stand in 1970 with Parliament-Funkadelic, a musical universe of its own that helped birth hard funk. Few of these artists would be considered threats to national security or would be sacrificed the way their sixties counterparts like McDaniels, Williams, and Sainte-Marie had been—but they had their own battles in a musical and political universe that would become increasingly incendiary as the decade turned.

Motown in-house songwriter George Clinton set about updating his own group's image from the old-school Parliaments and fashioning them into a whole new thing. Abandoning the straight-laced soul group look and opting for a buck-wild appearance, the group was greeted with confusion at first, but a new name, a new label, and fresh personnel became Clinton's answer to that: Funkadelic. The band's objective was to get as far out, freaky, and black as possible while turning the undesirable quality of funk into a most desired way of living and way of being—a religion of sorts, an idea he borrowed from Ishmael Reed's experimental novel *Mumbo Jumbo*. Forming a band in possession of extreme musical dexterity that proselytized the funk, Clinton developed a thoroughly underground, largely black following by playing LSD-fueled jams that were of also of interest to the multicultural freaked-out set. Clinton's complete disobedience of the rules screamed liberation. Merging hard rock amplification with deep funk and street poetry with his own language, he turned the standard soul revue into a superjam of color and outrageousness. He didn't stop there. His Parliaments, still vital and keen to work, were engaged in their own kind of transformation, fusing all styles of music from folk to rock to jazz. The Parliaments' album *Osmium* from 1971 was appropriately confusing, but oddly compelling as Clinton's kitchen-sink approach and playful exchange between the Funkadelic and Parliament projects kept him busy and on the rise. Clinton worked to build a Motown or James Brown–like empire of his own. P-Funk's jams are mostly remembered for the party, but its content was root survival, from sex to just plain getting by. "Everybody's Going to Make It This Time" and "Wake Up" from the *America Eats Its Young* album and *Chocolate City* steered the Mothership in a political direction, but the Clinton consortium's charisma and effectiveness was more in its invention and existence than it was in making overly political or discernible message music. "Clinton's absurd brand of black consciousness threw the standard gospel-soul formulas (such as "We Shall Overcome") on their heads, and made Parliament a band to reckon with," writes funkologist Rickey Vincent who explores the funk phenomenon from all sides and in his definitive study of the music, *Funk: The Music, the People and the Rhythm of the One.*[10]

In the maelstrom of the funk and fusion era, jazz auteur Miles Davis made three important albums: *Bitches Brew*, *A Tribute to Jack Johnson*, and *On the Corner*. Inspired by his wife, Betty (Mabry) Davis, *Bitches Brew* informed the funk just as sure as it borrowed from Sly Stone and Jimi Hendrix rock, sounds with which Mabry was well acquainted, opening the door to a world of jazz fusion to follow. *Jack Johnson* explored "black" instrumental themes inasmuch as it borrowed from "I'm Black and I'm Proud," Sly Stone, and inter-cut dialogue from the great boxer and black advocate Johnson. Finally, *On the Corner*, though not particularly well-received at the time, was a forward-sounding collage of drum, bass, and minimalist sound that today is regarded as a forerunner to hip-hop and electronica.

Stevie Wonder channeled the juice from the period and turned himself into a human dynamo. He was just twenty-two when he released *Music from My Mind*, but even the title displayed the increased level of creative control he was allowed at the new seventies Motown. Making full use of the latest synthesizer technology, Wonder was crossing over and well on his way to creating the powerhouse social commentary songs that would become his calling card. Curtis Mayfield must have been thinking along the same lines, but instead of breaking it down he was adding on, with his knack for marrying a prideful and unrepentant black sensibility with reportage from the neighborhood. Powered-up by his solo debut, *Curtis*, for his custom label Curtom, Mayfield continued his post-Impressions journey as a socially conscious solo artist and entrepreneur. In the years ahead, his label would provide sanctuary for the Undisputed Truth as well as longtime trench-marchers the Staple Singers. Mayfield made the transition by introducing more ambitious sounds to his repertoire and loosening up his look, as was the fashion among soul singers. His new output blurred the lines between serious talk, serious rhythm, and over-the-top production in new statement songs like "Move on Up," "We the People Who Are Darker Than Blue," and "(Don't Worry) If There's a Hell Below We're All Going to Go":

> Sisters! Niggers! Whities! Jews! Crackers! Don't worry.
> If there's hell below, we're all gonna go.
> Arghhhhhhhhhhhhhhhhhhh.

Now that's dark—but then that's the funk—and yet wherever Curtis walked, you could count on a hit of joy and a dose of light to lift you up. That's funk, too. In the first blast of the new slappy, bass-happy sound, Mayfield used the medium to deliver his evergreen message to keep on pushing. It was the same message that primed the pump of the Impressions all those years ago, only now Curtis had a new vehicle for his words. Opening the doors of consciousness with *Curtis* in 1970 and following with *Roots*, his 1971 contribution to the further politicization of soulful R&B, Mayfield found a way to reach far more people than ever before with his somber and sophisticated messages: movies. The new songs' themes of urban decay, the ghetto-centered drug trade, and police and vigilante violence lent themselves to a new form of creative expression in the entertainment industry. Though it remains debatable whether the cartoon-like depictions of life in the blaxploitation film genre reinforced stereotypes or successfully lampooned them, the movies definitely had the tunes: Curtis's soundtrack to the Gordon Parks Jr. film *Super Fly* was the blueprint. Perhaps the story of blaxploitation and its lore demands we back up a bit. Auteur Melvin Van Peebles' also wrote the score to his studio film *Watermelon Man* and his independent film *Sweet*

*Sweetback's Baadasssss Song.* The films were the first efforts of a self-trained young filmmaker, but he sure knew the power of combining music with movies. He even had the vision to market a *Sweetback* soundtrack, with music performed by a forming Earth, Wind and Fire, before the movie hit theaters. The film's general plot involves a disadvantaged youth overcoming his circumstances by unsavory means; as a man, he must prevail over further injustice and take on the law. *Sweet Sweetback* was praised by a champion of any brother who resists his own oppression by whatever means necessary, Black Panther leader Huey P. Newton, who also appreciated the film's positive portrait of a Panther character. But *Sweetback* also had its detractors. Since its release in 1971 it has caught blame for launching the controversial blaxploitation craze that thrived throughout the seventies and occasionally rears its influence in revival form. With classics like the score of the blockbuster *Shaft*, composed by Stax man Isaac Hayes; Curtis Mayfield's tunes for *Super Fly*; and Marvin Gaye's songs for *Trouble Man*, blaxploitation remains notable for its high-level soundtracks. Read without the sensational films they accompanied, songs like Bobby Womack's "Across 110th Street" could be received as cautionary tales of gambling with fate and "trying to get over." That's one reason blaxploitation remains problematical: making it out of the ghetto by working the corner is one thing if you're Super Fly, but offscreen the game doesn't usually end in the hustler's favor.

## Weatherman

Taking a stand in art, life, and New Left politics had revealed its consequences for those who were black, as well for empathic working-class liberationists like the MC5. But there was a new strain of white student crusaders who could not be dissuaded from jumping into the fight just as it was peaking. It seemed as if the impossibility of the task at hand only inspired the group called Weatherman, a klatch of student activists, in their fight against racism, classism, and anti-imperialism. In a position paper "You Don't Need a Weatherman to Know Which Way the Wind Blows," a line from Bob Dylan's "Subterranean Homesick Blues," the radical students of Weatherman suggested that a white fighting organization be established in accordance with black liberation principles. Advocating revolutionary communism, their aim was "the destruction of US imperialism" in an effort to "achieve a classless world: world communism." The Weathermen (as the mixed gender collective was alternately known) formed within SDS at their summer convention in 1969, where discussion of the "The Days of Rage" riots in Chicago—an extreme demonstration against the war being planned for October—was met with mixed reaction among members. The actions in Chicago weren't well attended, and by February the SDS was dismantled and the Weathermen were on their own. In early 1970, in the wake of the police murder of Black Panthers Fred Hampton and Mark Clark in the still of the night in Hampton's Chicago home in December of 1969 (ultimately revealed to be part of the COINTELPRO plan) the Weather Underground Organization (WUO), as the group was ultimately known, had declared a "State of War" on the US government, which was the point when former weatherman Mark Rudd says "We crossed over to the politics of transgression."[11] For the next seven years the WUO waged a bombing campaign in retaliation for the violence they perceived the US to have waged on the world. "White youth must choose sides now," declared the Weathermen's Bernadine Dohrn. "They must either fight on the side of the oppressed or be on the side of the oppressor." But the WUO was doomed when its primary tactic of bombing public buildings earned the group public enemy status and the label "domestic terrorists" by the FBI. Choosing targets that illustrated American injustice, former Weatherman Bill Ayers recollects "Maggie's Farm" was the group's code for the Pentagon "again from Dylan, because we said simply, 'I ain't gonna work on Maggie's farm no more.'" Within the organization the Weathermen were known as the Eggplant, as in "The Eggplant That Ate Chicago," a tune by Dr. West's Medicine Show and Junk Band. The original tune's lyric, "You better watch out for the eggplant that ate Chicago for he may eat your city soon," was delivered in a nonthreatening, old-time jug band style. The Weathermen were not especially joking. "We expropriated an entire lexicon of Weather words from the music," writes Ayers.[12] "The Haymarket statue, a Chicago landmark and scene of a number of the group's bombings, was known as 'Bad Moon,' from the Creedence Clearwater Revival song "Bad Moon Rising." "'Rescue' from Fontella Bass's 'Rescue Me' was the name for a two-year effort, finally successful, to break a Black Liberation Army comrade from jail," he writes. "We drew on 'Kick Out the Jams' by the MC5 for names and codes, 'Purple Haze' in tribute to Jimi Hendrix, and 'Volunteers' from the Jefferson Airplane," which features the refrain 'got a revolution, got to revolution.'"

Amidst this rising tide of political mayhem, intensifying sound, and unforgivable blackness there occurred an additional, unexpected development: the return of Bob Dylan to topical songwriting. After Soledad Brother and Black Panther George Jackson was shot down during an alleged escape from prison, Dylan released "George Jackson," a 45-rpm record that reached the Top 40 in 1972 and contains one of his more quotable summations of life in black and white:

> Sometimes I think this whole world
> Is one big prison yard.
> Some of us are prisoners
> The rest of us are guards

Elaine Brown says when she heard the song, "I cried from the first line." George Jackson was a friend of hers. Jackson had made it to California from Chicago, where he'd learned to survive as a young man of the streets. A seventy-dollar robbery landed him in Soledad State Prison—his sentence indeterminate—where he used his time to educate himself. Jackson had studied Fanon as well as Marx and Mao and came to understand the incarceration of poor blacks for the pettiest of crimes in a political context. A leader in moving prisoners to radicalize, Jackson joined the Panthers while on the inside and would become one of their most celebrated members. *Soledad Brother: The Prison Letters of George Jackson*, published in 1971, was greeted with an extremely positive reception by intellectuals and radicals. That Jackson was framed in the Soledad incident, which involved the shooting of three black prisoners and the subsequent killing of a white guard, is a widely held belief. As a vocal celebrity chorus came to Jackson's defense, among those leading the committee was Angela Davis.

As a young politico, Davis was a member of the Communist Party. Born and raised in Birmingham, Alabama, she was formally educated at Brandeis University. While studying French and philosophy in Paris she learned of the bombing of the Baptist church at home in Birmingham that killed the four little girls with whom she'd been acquainted as a child. She continued her studies at home and abroad, eventually returning to Los Angeles in 1969 in the heat of law enforcement's showdown there with the Panthers. "I think the Black Panther Party probably was dangerous but not dangerous in the way that most people assume they might have been," she said later. "Not dangerous because people had guns but dangerous because of its ability to provide an example of standing up to power."[13]

Jackson's politicization during his incarceration had not been greeted with enthusiasm by prison authorities, who had become determined to make his never-ending time served ever tougher. Having moved from Soledad to San Quentin and with the murder of the guard pinned on him, Jackson awaited trial. But when his young Panther brother Jonathan staged an attempt to free three San Quentin inmates from a Marin County courtroom in solidarity, Jonathan wound up dead, as did two of the inmates and the judge in the trial. Davis was accused of conspiracy, homicide, and kidnapping when it was discovered one of the guns used in the courtroom had been registered in her name, though she was eventually acquitted. A year after the courtroom incident and just a few days before his own trial was about to commence, Jackson was shot at San Quentin in an alleged escape attempt; five others were killed in the melee. Tenor saxophonist Archie Shepp paid tribute with his frantic "Blues for Brother George Jackson" on his Black-Powered set *Attica Blues*.

"We loved the fact that Dylan wrote a song about George Jackson," says Elaine Brown. "But it wasn't like the end of the world to have Bob Dylan speak for us. It was more like *he* got to write a song about the life of George Jackson." Brown would write her own song in remembrance of Jackson for her self-titled Motown/Black Forum album also known as *Until We Are Free*, recorded under Party order of Chairman Huey Newton. The album was made with the assistance of Horace Tapscott and produced and recorded by Fonce Mizell and Freddie Perren. It includes the Piaf-like "Jonathan," a tribute to the young Jackson and "All The Young and Fine Men," which was in essence her own tribute to brother George and swings with the Tapscott touch that characterized the depth of *Seize the Time*. But the distribution of the album was hampered by Black Forum's general ineffectiveness as a label. Brown says that though it might have been nice to have a popular black singer, say a Motown giant like Marvin Gaye, play the role of freedom fighter or mouthpiece for her organization, it just wasn't destined to happen. "Though

Marvin Gaye was a wonderful singer who we all loved, Marvin Gaye was no revolutionary and he wasn't going to make black people revolutionary." Nor was Stevie Wonder, who was out on tour with the Rolling Stones, expanding soul's audience while simultaneously moving further into socially conscious efforts with an emphasis on black. "Living for the City," from *Innervisions*, covers rage and racial injustice; while "Higher Ground," told it like the people saw it.

Powers keep on lyin' while your people keep on dyin'

During this time, in the bleakest and darkest period of revolution blues, Sly Stone had stealthily cooked up an album that would come to be considered not only foundational in the creation of deep funk but his most enduring work, his answer to "What's Going On?" Having pioneered psychedelic soul and the borders of funky but brittle commentary with "Thank You (Falenttinme Be Mice Elf Agin)," Stone, like Mayfield, was reaching new peaks in his artistry. Stretching his boundaries beyond peace, love, and party and staring more squarely at their flip sides, Sly could have used his means and the confidence following his triumph at Woodstock to further expand on the creativity and freedom supplied by his star power and deliver the goods while the demand was high. But the story on *There's a Riot Goin' On* was the opposite of that. It was with a case of a post-hippie hangover and under duress that Stone set about painting the odd pictures that turned out to be his most masterpiece. Stories circulated that he felt pressure to capitulate to rogue activist requests to politicize; drugs were also involved. But Stone came through with what turned out to be his commentary on a whole mess of things, from "Thank You for Talking to Me Africa" to the blood ties that bind in "Family Affair." Feeling the horror of a nation reeling from change and projecting his own nightmares— with the aid of substances and hangers-on—Stone created the aural equivalent of a night without end. At once a warbling, slow motion mourning of another dream deferred, part of *Riot's* strength is that no matter in what time, place, or decade you encounter it, its personal vision of dis-integration cuts through and reaches the listener. The revolution hour was haunted, dark, and late; this knowledge hangs on every note. Generally perceived as deeply mysterious to whites and deeply real to blacks, forty years later that may go some way toward explaining *Riot's* status as funk's greatest hit.

It was also in this window in time that quiet and serious Beatle George Harrison made a statement that would have an effect far longer-reaching than anyone could have predicted at the time. Harrison and his musical mentor Ravi Shankar organized the mother of all benefits with an all-star line-up: The Concert for Bangladesh in August of 1971 at Madison Square Garden. Reeling from one of the world's worst cyclones on record, refugees from East Pakistan (Bangladesh)—engaged in an armed liberation struggle from West Pakistan—flooded Shankar's native Bengal region in India, a land still compromised from the great migration during Partition in 1947. Harrison heard his friend's plea, and though he had no previous organizational experience he called on friends Bob Dylan, Eric Clapton, Leon Russell and Ringo Starr. Dylan, making his first public appearance in two years, chipped in "A Hard Rain's A-Gonna Fall" and "Blowin' in the Wind." Harrison offered up "Here Comes the Sun" along with "Bangla Desh," composed for the cause. Bangladesh set a precedent for immediate, organized concert charity in the name of tragedy and political strife, gathering the biggest names in music in the effort to preserve humanity. Though for all of its goodwill and lip service to people of the world, Yoko Ono was specifically invited not to attend the show. She and another number of women with strong humanist and political voices had effectively been silenced.

## Where Have All the Folkies Gone?

"I made the first ever totally electronic, quadraphonic vocal album," Buffy Sainte-Marie says, speaking of the 1969 release *Illuminations*, a watershed space-folk recording. It featured groundbreaking use of processed voice and guitar and a trippy reading of Leonard Cohen's "God Is Alive Magic Is Afoot." "There was nowhere to go except to scoring movies with that kind of approach. It's as if I had a secret life behind my professional persona." Sainte-Marie recorded the theme song to *Soldier Blue*, a controversial film about cavalry–Indian relations. "It became a hit in Europe, Japan, and Canada during the summer of 1971," says Sainte-Marie of the song. "But the movie disappeared from US theaters real fast, so few Americans are familiar with it." In its fictional depiction of a historic massacre that wiped out a village of innocent Cheyenne and Arapaho people, the material was strong in its anti-violence messaging. [14]

Lyndon Johnson's effort to silence Sainte-Marie's music remained effective into the Nixon years when she made the president's famous Enemies List. Though she was still actively recording, her records became harder to find, and as US bookings fell off, so did album sales. Sainte-Marie was satisfied with the way her career had gone throughout the world and put down the US blackout to changing tastes. "That's all I made of it," she says.

In 1971, Lennon and Ono had released "Power to the People" as a single, its general tone and sound echoing the mood of a street protest. Len Chandler knew all about those kinds of songs, had stood in the center of the demonstrations and sung them, but the deep South and New York City were no longer his platforms. In the highly charged climate of protest, racial pressure, and a period of personal change, Chandler gave up his New York base and moved to Los Angeles. Joining Lew Irwin, whom he'd met on the trip to Lowndes County, he became a member of the comedy troupe the Credibility Gap, delivering satirical news on radio station KRLA. Chandler composed topical songs daily and had seemingly found the perfect outlet for his political poetry, though not for long. He transitioned into television and the Newsical Muse, a well-regarded, visionary, satirical news show featuring his songs. The *Hollywood Reporter* called Chandler and the series "a deadly combination for the powers that be."[15] But he was not long for that job either. It seemed Chandler belonged on the frontlines of protest, and he came to perform on military bases in the Pacific Rim in 1971 and 1972 as a featured player in the group of antiwar entertainers led by Jane Fonda and Donald Sutherland, just as Jerry Williams [Swamp Dogg] had done; folksinger Holly Near was also a member of the troupe as was comedian Paul Mooney. *FTA*, or Free the Army, Francine Parker's film about the group and its trip, intercuts reflections and reactions of soldiers in opposition to the war with Fonda and friends' skits. Chandler chimes in with "My Ass Is Mine," the one thing the conformity of army life can't take away. For the most part, the GIs love it, but at one performance on base in Japan, a few disorderly and dissenting soldiers disrupt the show with pro-military heckling. As they attempt to take the stage, the performers stand by until Chandler, with his fearless Freedom Ride experience, leads the room in a raised-fist chant of "Out, Out!" then leads the assembled crowd in a chorus of "Move on over or we'll move on over you, the movement's moving on." Quelling the potential for violence with a nonviolent tactic, Chandler received a universally positive response. He galvanized the mass and united them for a common purpose—leading out the bullies. It was a tremendous demonstration of the power of song.

*FTA* was released in US theaters and withdrawn without explanation within one week in 1972, the same week that Fonda made her controversial appearance in Hanoi. No copies of the film in release were ever recovered and the film was suppressed for 37 years, until early 2009 when documentary filmmaker David Zeiger (*Sir, No Sir!*) brought it back into circulation. Parker passed away in 2007 at the age of 82 and did not live to see *FTA* resurrected, though Zeiger writes that before her death, Parker swore to him that the film's distributor, AIP, had received a call from the Nixon White House. "Is the story true? There's no proof, but I can't think of another reasonable explanation for Sam Arkoff, a man who knew how to wring every penny out of a film, yanking one starring Jane Fonda and Donald Sutherland from theaters at a big loss (and apparently, destroying all of the prints since none were ever found)."[16]

The stories of Len Chandler and *FTA*, the formation and ultimate demise of the Black Forum label and Sly Stone's trips and the creation of a deep, dark funk groove are but reflections of the mood of paranoia, investigations, and infiltrations that permeated the atmosphere. During this wild early-seventies period of transition from decade to decade, there occurred one of the most dynamic cross-fertilized moments between pop culture and the counterculture: the week Lennon and Ono were invited to host *The Mike Douglas Show* in 1972. The Lennon-Onos brought with them Jerry Rubin to explain the Yippies and Bobby Seale to represent the Black Panthers, while the straight-laced and game-faced Douglas displayed tolerance throughout the proceedings, stamping it with his middle-of-the-road approval. The forum gave the maligned Ono a chance to reveal more of her personality, as well as her excellent style, to the curious American public. The Japanese artist was said to have "broken up the Beatles," and there were those who still had misperceptions of her. *The Mike Douglas Show* couldn't have been targeted at a more mainstream audience. And yet, it is where Little Richard performed in a turban, full makeup, and a satin cape his 1970 power anthem "Freedom Blues," and where frequent guest Sly Stone once engaged in a heated discussion on assimilation versus Black Nationalism with Muhammad Ali. The theme of people's liberation was not just an imaginary ideal among those on the far

left, it was unafraid to show its face on daytime television, and apparently
television at the time was unafraid to expose it. So confident were Lennon
and Ono in this period that they'd developed a whole suite of songs—*Some
Time in New York City*—confronting the complicated state of the nation. Produced by Phil Spector and backed by the largely anonymous New York group
Elephant's Memory, the album was certainly companionable for the chaotic
times. "Attica State" referred to the historic September 1971 prison riot, allegedly sparked by the previous month's murder of radicalized prisoner George
Jackson and resulting in the deaths of thirty-nine people, inmates as well as
hostages. There was also "John Sinclair," a song for the White Panther leader
this time around doing "ten for two" on a marijuana conviction.

> If he'd been a soldier man
> shooting gooks in Vietnam
> If he was the CIA
> Selling dope and making hay
> He'd be free, they'd let him be
> Breathing air, like you and me
> Gotta, gotta, gotta . . . set him free

Lennon had written the song to perform at the Free John Sinclair Freedom
Rally in Ann Arbor, Michigan, in December of 1971; the strong show of support resulted in Sinclair's immediate release. Featuring the Lennons as well
as Phil Ochs, Stevie Wonder, Archie Shepp, and speakers and poets like Allen
Ginsberg, Ed Sanders, Bobby Seale, and Jerry Rubin, the concert was of concern to federal authorities, though not simply because of its high profile and
support of decriminalizing marijuana laws. Rather, the authorities surveying
the scene that day had hoped to link Lennon to plans for an upcoming antiwar
concert of some magnitude at the Republican convention scheduled for Miami
in 1972. Yippies and musicians of conscience were counting on Lennon's participation, too. Already projecting a repeat of the 1968 Democratic Convention
in Chicago, authorities were hoping to jam the efforts toward a concert plan,
just as they'd hoped to bring evidence of Lennon endorsing violent actions
there. Not only were the Lennons public advocates of nonviolence, they had
never intended to go to Miami for personal reasons; a report filed by an FBI
informant had even confirmed Lennon as saying he would participate in the

demonstrations only "if they are peaceful."[17] In the end the authorities, reportedly aided by hippie infiltrators and informants, were successful at thwarting the production of a large-scale antiwar concert in Miami, and for all intents and purposes, Lennon's investigative file could now be closed. It wasn't.

Upon the release of *Some Time in New York City* in June of 1972, critics and consumers decreed that a heavy dose of politics with their music was not what the people wanted. The album became the couple's worst-received album in their catalog. "We thought it was really good," says Ono. And in one fell swoop, what had appeared to be optimistic times for anyone involved in the movement turned out to be its very last gasp. Though Dylan had a hit with "George Jackson" and the Rolling Stones wrote "Sweet Black Angel" for Angela Davis, it was Lennon and Ono who took the most heat for supporting radicalism in song. Ono was taking an unfair share of the abuse. "I wasn't heard then. OK, I was heard, and then they trashed me for it," she says. The prescience of the concerns that Lennon and Ono raised in the high era of public protest and their position at the vanguard of musical revolution—raising such ideas as making art and music for peace, standing together, engaging in small acts of human kindness as the actions that change the world—were a threat to national security, but were ultimately rejected by fans. At the time John and Yoko's *Some Time in New York City* was released, critics and fans alike were in agreement that the couple had gone too far in their merging of music with politics. With Lennon's commercial potency at a low ebb and his position on nonviolence now officially committed to a government document, one would think the case against the Englishman and his Japanese wife would be closed. Rather, it marked the beginning of a long hassle with the immigration service under order of the Nixon White House and a dark period in the couple's life that lasted for three years and included Lennon's infamous "lost weekend" interlude in Los Angeles, where all was not lost as he continued to record. He had a romantic liaison with his assistant May Pang and the pair regularly hit the town with their rock star friends.

---

"The LAPD was not very popular among young people in Los Angeles," says Ed Pearl, who in the late sixties and early seventies was still operating the Ash

Grove. "They were beating up hippies—nobody liked the police—they were killing Panthers." With his club's emphasis on traditional music merged with political and social movement, Pearl also worked for the Peace and Freedom Party; between his political alliances, his venue for events, and his access to talent, he was in an ideal position to make the most of the climate for cultural change. He even assigned an employee to take charge of political affairs at the club and began to book events and sponsor workshops. One such effort was devoted to the San Francisco State Third World Student Strike of 1968 to 1969, an unprecedented college closure in a high season of student strikes that called for an end to the Vietnam War as well as for the formation of an ethnic studies program (the latter was achieved and established the precedent for the minority studies programs that exist today). But in these days of raised stakes on matters of revolution, the Ash Grove was increasingly becoming the focus of attention from local and federal law enforcement, and the club's musicians and regulars met some of its more controversial political events with mixed feelings.

"You'd walk in and there would be would be beautiful photographs by Julius Lester. Then you'd go back in and there'd be posters of Chairman Mao and the Chinese proletariat, their arms raised going off into the future," says musician Dave Alvin, who at the time was a teenaged regular at the club. "I'm an FDR union guy—I'm not a Marxist. On the other hand . . . Ed's presentation, while off-putting to some, was intriguing to me. It made you think and it made you put the music into a context—it was more than 'let's get drunk and boogie music.' It was music that came from somewhere and had reasons for existing and you had to ask yourself what those reasons were and all the complicated questions about that."

The Ash Grove had fulfilled its original early sixties mission to become a successful community cultural center. "You had people from East L.A. and South Central there, from Beverly Hills," remembers Dave Alvin. "You really did have the rich rubbing elbows with the middle class and the underclass. That made it really unique as far as clubs. At the Ash Grove there was everybody . . . hippies and radicals and black radicals and Black Nationalists and right wing truck drivers too." Alvin had gone for the music, to hear the legends of the blues, "T-Bone Walker, Big Joe Turner and Eddie Vinson with the Johnny Otis Orchestra . . . still in their prime." But many performances later, the club had provided him a window onto worlds that he otherwise would not have known growing up in suburban Downey, California. He points to the musicians who had arrived at the Ash Grove the previous decade—Ry Cooder, Bonnie Raitt, Taj Mahal—as well as to himself and his brother who went on to combine their love of American music with their labor family background and class consciousness in their group the Blasters and later as solo artists. "Everybody had some kind of sense—not that it was political music—that there was politics involved. It doesn't necessarily have to be Maoist, Stalinist, whatever leftist tag, but it was music whether bluegrass or blues, and it came out of communities. It was all folk music in that sense. And these musics came out of some sort of reaction to circumstances, so you had to think about that. . . . You were just a little more well-rounded. It made the music deeper and richer."

Following a screening of films that took a positive view of Fidel Castro and the Cuban revolution, Pearl received a threat; not long after, the club suffered a debilitating fire. Though the arson was never solved, Pearl maintains it was politically motivated. A year later, in 1970, the club was besieged again, this time by an armed band of men who threatened the employees. "There were only three people there on a late Sunday afternoon and about eight people came in with automatic weapons, shotguns, and a bullwhip, which I assume was for me," says Pearl, who was away from the premises at the time. The cashier escaped, but the bandits tied up two workers and left a trail of kerosene on the floor, setting it alight before getting away. Though the perpetrators were apprehended, according to Pearl they were also released soon after on order of a government agency. Though he rebuilt and stayed committed to musical and political activism, the shattered political and cultural climate of the early seventies could not support Pearl's vision, and in 1973, the club burned a final time before closing its doors for good.[18]

That year, the Staple Singers cut Dylan's "A Hard Rain's A-Gonna Fall" for their album *Use What You Got.*

> Oh what did you see my blue-eyed son
> Oh what did you see my darling young one
> I saw ten thousand talkers whose tongues were all broken
> I saw guns and sharp-swords in the hands of young children.

Ten years had passed since Bob Dylan had first sung his song.

## Get Up Stand Up

Outside America, songs of protest were rising, according to the particular needs of the people. In the United Kingdom John Lennon's former bandmate Paul McCartney and his wife Linda had their own troubles with their first single of 1972. "Give Ireland Back to the Irish" was their immediate response to the Bloody Sunday event in Northern Ireland during which civil rights protestors were shot and killed by the British Army. In return for their song, the McCartneys were banned from their country's airwaves. The following year, they decided on a whim to record their *Band on the Run* album in Lagos, Nigeria, a place which at the time many considered to be among the world's most dangerous following the country's recent civil war.

Nigerian musician Fela Kuti was born into a musically and politically engaged family. His mother was a women's rights activist in the orbit of Pan-African movement leader Kwame Nkrumah of Ghana, founder of the Organization of African Unity (OAU); his father was a minister and educator. With his country at civil war, Fela, as he is best known, did not think to politicize his own music until he'd visited Los Angeles on tour with his band in 1969. There are a couple of versions of what happened on the trip. One says that while playing at an NAACP event he met an American woman who introduced him to the Black Power movement and Black Panther ideology; another version says he read and reread the *Autobiography of Malcolm X* on the trip. He returned to Africa newly politicized and with a mission: "It is my desire to create a new trend worthy of emulation on the music scene, in this country in particular and Africa in general, which will be a pride to the black race," he said.[19] Against the backdrop of his country's Biafran war, he began in earnest his cultural explorations and back-to-roots, anti-colonialist demonstrations against the ruling class. He changed his name from Fela Ransome-Kuti—his slave name—to the more royal Fela Anikulapo Kuti. From there on, Fela injected his sound with a political element and fervor that made him a hero and champion to his country's poor as he created his singular Afro-beat sound. Fela, classically trained and proficient in jazz, dismantled the highlife style he knew and joined it with soul and West African rhythm. Leading his band on baritone sax, keyboards, and vocals, he birthed Afrobeat, a layered, groove-based sound punctuated with horn jabs, female vocals, and guitar;

the jams are continuous, some lasting nearly an hour, accompanied by Fela's resistance messages and traditional rituals

> Them go they cause confusion, cause corruption,
>     cause oppression, cause inflation

"Music is a spiritual thing . . . when the higher forces give you the gift of music—musicianship—it must be well used for the good of humanity," Fela said. Accompanied by a large band and singing and dancing revue, the bandleader appeared onstage in face paint, dressed in colorful suits, shirtless, or sometimes stripped down to his shorts. As he and his band, Africa '70, gained popularity, he created his own party, MOP, Movement of the People, and in 1983 attempted to run for president. "Music is the king of all professions . . . I will be president of this country," he once said. But the stance he took against Nigeria's militaristic regime earned him his government's enmity. "Everybody knows Africa is to be united now to have any headway. If I can take this country then Africa is settled . . . A good government in one African country, the whole of Africa will be liberated. Straightforward and progressive, clean government that knows what it's doing. No diplomacy, no compromises, no agreements . . . no capitalism. Africanism," he said.[20]

The creation of his own republic or kingdom, the commune Kalkuta, and the Shrine, his nearby place of worship and nightclub, attracted undesired attention and he and his people were literally under siege; Fela was imprisoned and beaten. Perhaps the most controversial and confusing aspect of the cultural warrior's agenda was his accumulation of wives—simultaneous marriages into the double digits. Yet despite the incongruities in his justice for all motif, his impact on the global soundscape would go on to be undeniable. "Music is the weapon of the future. Something tells me I'm right," he said.

By 1968 internationally beloved singer Miriam Makeba and Black Power advocate Stokely Carmichael had married and moved to Guinea. Trinidadian by birth, Carmichael had gone through his share of changes since his days as a SNCC organizer turned Black Panther, leaving the Panthers after a year in favor of the Black Nationalism and Pan Africanism movements. He renamed himself Kwame Ture in honor of his Pan Africanist mentors, and remained a suspect of US intelligence throughout his years abroad. Makeba had already paid the cost of singing for liberation when she lost her South African passport in the early sixties; the career she had built in the States subsequently went into decline because of her continued efforts in the name of civil rights and her association with Carmichael. She watched as opportunities for performance and recording dates dwindled until they were essentially blacked out in the United States. "All her bookings all at once? It had to be organized across the industry. A full-blown conspiracy. I could never have imagined my enemies would be so ruthless or so thorough," writes Carmichael.[21]

The pair lived in exile in Guinea where Makeba served as a delegate to the United Nations. The couple divorced in 1973.

Nina Simone, having become more and more disconnected and disenfranchised from America, its politics, and its audiences, took her leave, moving to Barbados in 1970. When Makeba later suggested she move to Liberia, Simone took her advice. Simone claimed she lived some of her happiest days there and wrote "Liberian Calypso" in tribute.

When eighty thousand barrels of oil spilled into the waters of the Santa Barbara Channel in January of 1969, the crude-splattered water, beaches, and birds along the California coast in its aftermath became the symbols of modern eco-disaster. For composer and Beach Boys collaborator Van Dyke Parks, the spill and "the revelation of ecology," as he calls it, was his own invitation to go calypso. From 1970 to 1975, Parks waged awareness of environmental and race matters through the music and culture of the West Indies, making records with the Esso Trinidad Steel band and calypso king, the Mighty Sparrow. "When I saw the Esso Trinidad Steel Band, I saw myself in a Trojan Horse," he says. "We were going to expose the oil industry. That's what my agenda was. I felt it was absolutely essential." Over a five-year period, Parks produced albums by the Esso Trinidad Steel band (1971) and Bob Dylan favorite the Mighty Sparrow (*Hot and Sweet*, 1974); he also recorded his own calypso-inspired works, *Discover America* (1972) and *Clang of the Yankee Reaper* (1976). Born from his passion for popular song and launched at a time when grassroots protest was at an all-time high, Parks had every reason to believe calypso consciousness would prevail. But he hadn't factored in the complications of taking on big oil, nor of touring the United States with a twenty-eight-man steel drum corps from the Caribbean. He was unable to predict that the sessions with Mighty Sparrow would be fraught with rage or that his efforts would arouse the ire of Bob Marley, whose production requests he ignored in favor of calypso's happy/sad steel drum sounds. Parks says it was reggae singer Jimmy Cliff who was of more interest to him than Marley; he helped Cliff secure a publishing arrangement for his songs. "He was a lot more melodic. Jimmy Cliff was a big deal to me," he says. Dylan also recognized there was something about Cliff: He was said to have called the reggae singer's "Viet Nam" among the best-ever protest songs.

In 1971 Phil Ochs made a trip to Santiago, Chile. Just as he had taken an interest in the revolution in Cuba, Chile's political scene and the US involvement there was of deep interest to him, as was the country's elected Marxist leader, Salvador Allende. Ochs immediately fell in love with Chile and its people. As he rambled around, he met the people's singer, Victor Jara, whom he would spontaneously accompany to a student demonstration in progress, deep in a copper mine.[22]

In Jamaica, Pan-African unity advocate Bob Marley was caught in the crossfire of his country's political strife in the seventies. Marley was of mixed-race heritage and identified as black; as a Rastafarian, he believed Ethiopian emperor Haile Selassie was the incarnation of Jah or God. Selassie taught suspicion of Babylon or Western culture, and it is a recurring theme in Marley's songs, as is return to Zion or an African homeland. Taking his cues from Rastafari prophet Marcus Garvey, a pioneer in the movement to decolonize Africa, Marley's songs deliver messages of unity, self-sufficiency, and empowerment. With his band the Wailers he performed to loose perfection, defining the reggae sound. His music and image have become internationally understood symbols of peace and liberation. Bob Marley and the Wailers' 1973 album *Burnin'* featuring "Get Up, Stand Up" is perhaps the best example of how a devotional tune written to honor one's prophet can also stand as an anthem to unite and liberate. Yet with Marley's global recognition and musical crossover appeal came a great burden, as expectations of his political involvement grew more complex as his star rose and he wielded greater influence over the people. "Government sometimes maybe don't like what we have to say because what we have to say too plain," he said.[23]

Though the role of women in Rastafari is generally perceived as subordinate to men, when asked by a reporter if there were any women he admired, Marley said, "Dat woman in America—Angela Davis. A woman like that who defends something; me can appreciate that."[24]

By the time Marley was emerging from Jamaica with his music steeped in the vocal messaging of Curtis Mayfield and the Impressions, the idea of change coming to America had pretty much been laid to rest. The Nixon presidency and the federal authorities worked hand in glove to dismantle the counterculture and were largely successful. By this time the leaders of a movement for a more just and peaceful society had already been assassinated; more radical voices were either in prison, underground, or living outside of the United States in exile. The Black Panthers had ended the sixties at the top of J. Edgar Hoover's hit list as public enemies number one; by the early seventies, they had largely been neutralized, no longer the primary targets of the US government concern. That honor now went to artists John Lennon and Yoko Ono, as the Nixon administration turned up the heat on the counterculture's highest-profile peace and anti-oppression advocates and for three years would do its best to silence them. To deal with a British citizen living in America, the best "strategic countermeasure" was deportation. In early 1972 proceedings to deport Lennon began; in March of 1973 he was given sixty days to leave the United States. Lennon's battle with the US Department of Immigration and Naturalization ended in 1975. Five years after winning his permanent residency, another man of peace was murdered in New York City.

## The End of a Cultural Decade

It has been said on more than one occasion by historians and those who lived through it that the end of the sixties didn't actually occur till 1973. Certainly the high season of protest, liberation, desegregation, organization, social programs, rock 'n' roll and psychedelic soul that defined the ten years since the President Kennedy assassination had wound down. The Aquarian dream of a Nutopia dissolved into the synthetic essence of a society that was more individual, more personal, and less collective, but no less active. Though those who study it or experienced it tend to see the post-revolution blues as a period of disillusionment at social movement and recovery from its fallout, there is no doubt that the chaos of the sixties and its extended wind-down contributed to the creation of an atmosphere in which social justice speakers and equality seekers could take their causes to the next phase. Inspired by civil rights, free speech, the antiwar movement, and especially the veracity of the Black Power advocates who combined cultural exploration with politics, the next wave of minorities had learned to organize and they were preparing to march through freedom's door. With their battle cries and liberation songs borrowed from previous crusades, activists and musicians kept on pushing, till they could reach some higher ground. The sixties and its diverse voices were tough acts to follow—from Nina Simone, Curtis Mayfield, and the Staple Singers, to the former Beatles and Bob Dylan. Freedom's voices had rung from Lagos to Los Angeles, from New York to Santiago, Chile. These representatives of the rainbow coalition, the students, the freaks, the geeks, the poor, the tired, the hungry, and prisoners of society were no longer going to use the back door or the side entrance. Their tactics would be similar: community activism and cultural exploration were now the established roads to empowerment and forward motion. The rights gained by the nation's African American citizens, the people of color who followed, and the students who fought with them, despite the tragedies involved, were a demonstration to anyone seeking power that it could be claimed. It might take time, there might be protest, more eulogies to deliver and memorials to attend, speeches to testify with, literature and culture to be created, and songs to be sung, but these rights for all Americans and disempowered people would be won. No longer content to remain silent, minorities of all kinds, those voiceless masses who had been waiting patiently for their opportunity, had come to liberation's front door and were ready to move forward. Now was their time. Though in case their footsteps pounding on the pavement weren't loud enough to be heard, there would be songs—old songs and new ones—to be sung, moving with them as they marched toward their place in the sun.

# Bridge

As the sixties ended and the seventies began, the lines between decades blurred and so did the boundaries between music and subcultures. Women were organizing a movement of their own, gay liberation was stirring, and as racial minorities exerted pride in their unique heritages, disco soundtracked the new diversity. But as hard disco glittered and rock 'n' roll and funk went glam, there was another a form of music developing that attracted a younger generation with its own concerns. The prevailing stadium-rock culture and a growing complacency found artists flirting with philosophy and gender and mixing it with poetry, rock, reggae, and the politics of identity and rage. This was punk, rebel music, a term borrowed from Jamaica, as both punk and reggae came on hard in the seventies, taking their places on the world stage. Delivered by booming speakers, sound-system style, with microphones, DJs, and MCs, reggae street parties were also front-runners of hip-hop, the final adventure in twentieth-century sound to keep on pushing at freedom's front doors.

The section and artists on deck are representative of the hybridizations of rebel musics disco, punk, reggae, and hip-hop and their ties to economic and social unrest and the discrimination the music and its makers met in the marketplace; occasionally, timelines overlap. As hip-hop enters the picture, there are connections to be made to poetry, social justice, and other rebellious music like disco, funk, reggae, and punk that preceded it, all of it converging with the identity issues that defined the seventies. The musician voices in these chapters speak to their experiences with post-sixties liberation music and for the most part still perform it today. Their stories reflect light on the ideas the new freedoms of the sixties brought, how the struggle for human rights continues, and the way music furthers the movements for economic equality and social justice for all.

# Move On Over: Women's and Gay Liberation at the Punky Reggae Disco Party

When I was little my dad brought me back a little Liberty Bell from a business trip—I was seven or eight. I loved that bell . . . I wanted to go and see it," says the self-proclaimed "basic average all-American Jewish lesbian folksinger" Phranc. A topical songwriter, when Phranc gets interested in something, she writes a song about it.

> They rang it when women won the vote,
>     they rang it when the slaves were freed
> A symbol of democracy,
>     the E-flat peal of liberty.

The Liberty Bell got its name when William Lloyd Garrison's American Anti-Slavery Society adopted it in 1831 as a logo for the cover of their publication *The Liberator*. The inscription on the bell reads: "Proclaim LIBERTY throughout the land to all the inhabitants thereof," attributed to Leviticus. By the time Phranc reached Philadelphia to see the great symbol of American freedom sometime in the middle of the first decade of the twenty-first century, she was a little disheartened, though not exactly surprised, to see that the Liberty Bell was encased in a plastic box. "Not only can it not make a sound, you can't touch it."

For an artist who came of age in the early seventies at the birth of the women's and the gay liberation movements, and who found her voice as a musician in the punk rock era by changing her name to Phranc, freedom is everything. "I was right at the heart of it all: *Sister* magazine and feminist politics . . . gay rights . . . the feminist art movement was just on the brink," says the singer-songwriter and visual artist who was still a teenager named Susan Gottlieb in the seventies. Her personal story of discovering and creating her identity as an all-American Jewish lesbian folksinger uniquely echoes the changes in the musical and political landscape of the new era of liberation— and an extraordinary time in human history.

Germaine Greer and Kate Millett published watershed books that examined the female condition and established that "the personal is political"— espousing that a woman's problems are often an outgrowth of her oppression.[1] In 1970 on the occasion of fifty years of women's suffrage, National Organization for Women (NOW) founder Betty Friedan called for a Women's Strike for Equality. Demanding equal rights be granted to all women, women moved in massive numbers to a proven anthem: "Move on Over or We'll Move on Over You."

The melody of "Move on Over" is recognizable to Americans as "John Brown's Body" and Julia Ward Howe's rewriting of it, "Battle Hymn of the Republic," songs that date back to the Civil War era. Following its heavy usages as an abolitionist song and all-purpose freedom cry in the previous century, Len Chandler updated the theme and put it to work in the name of the civil rights era and antiwar effort. The Lowndes County Black Panthers had also used it as a slogan. And now here it was again—in another striking example of how one song can travel the miles from one movement to the next, without losing its authority or having its message diluted.

> You promise us the vote then sing us we shall overcome
> Hey but John Brown knew what freedom was
> He died to win us some
> And the movement's moving on

Phranc got tuned into the international movement for women's rights on an immediately personal level: she'd discovered *The Lesbian Tide* at a local newsstand and noticed a gathering at her local Westside Women's Center.

"I went to my first lesbian-feminist drop-in rap," she says. Rap sessions had grown from community organizing, and dropping in meant you could check it out. It was the first time she met women actively engaged in working for progress and change. "I went up to the mountains to the Jewish Community Center camp—they had a lesbian retreat. Alix Dobkin, a Jewish lesbian folk-singer, was there. When I went to that lesbian history class and heard Alix Dobkin I thought, that's what I want to be when I grow up."

Dobkin, a mother and a musician, was married to Sam Hood, who'd presided over the Gaslight Club in Greenwich Village—where Richie Havens, Len Chandler, and Buffy Sainte-Marie had worked in early days. "She'd come out as a dyke at thirty, took all of her folk experience, and wrote her songs from a lesbian perspective," explains Phranc. Dobkin's 1973 album *Lavender Jane Loves Women* is widely considered to be the first album in the soon-to-be-defined genre called women's music. There had been others on the folk scene before Dobkin: Maxine Feldman had declared herself a "big loud Jewish butch lesbian" who wrote songs speaking to the lesbian experience. Feldman was comfortable with either gender label and favored men's clothing; she often wore a tuxedo onstage. Performing as early as 1963 in Boston, her song "Angry Atthis" protesting ill treatment of homosexuals was in circulation before the Stonewall Riots in June of 1969, the event that officially marks the beginning of the movement for gay liberation. Immediately following Stonewall activist groups in the New Left tradition began to form a militant alliance for equal rights; one year later, the first Gay Pride parade was held on Christopher Street in New York (today Pride Month is recognized throughout the United States, and in parts of the world, each June).

The versions of how the riot at the Stonewall Inn in Greenwich Village spilled out of the bar and into the streets read like *Rashomon*. Following a slow buildup, explosions of civil unrest generally involve myriad circumstances and a couple of flashpoints that lead to riot; Stonewall was no different. Despite the popular myth, it seems almost certain that the death of Judy Garland and the mass gathering of gay men grieving in public at her funeral was not the emotional trigger for a riot in the Village the next day. More relevant is that homosexuals had long been victims of routine police abuse and raids on the discreet Greenwich Village watering holes where same-sex couples gathered. Described by some of its former denizens as a dingy dive bar, the Stonewall was one of the few in town where men were allowed to dance together to the sound of Motown, girl groups, and Top 40 on the jukebox. In his history of the bar, author David Carter outlines the arrangement between management and clientele—albeit at times an exploitative one—that ultimately served toward the creation of "space, security and freedom," and essential continuity from which a community could emerge.[2] Though not specifically a drag bar, the Stonewall was a place to be *real*; it offered asylum to "street queens," homeless "effeminate" youth, transgendered men, and butch lesbians. As for who or what sparked the riot on the night of June 28, 1969, "I think it is clear that special credit must be given to gay homeless youths, to transgendered men, and to the lesbian who fought the police," writes Carter.[3] Whoever threw the first punch, Stonewall was a historic and unprecedented three nights of street activity and resistance to law enforcement; it stands as the moment one chapter of gay history ended and a new, more militant one began. Greenwich Village folksinger Dave Van Ronk was in the neighborhood celebrating a birthday with a friend when he got caught in a sweep as a passerby. "I had been in antiwar demonstrations where the police descended on us like armed locusts. What I saw was yet another example of police arrogance and corruptions. As far as I was concerned, anybody who'd stand against the cops was all right with me, and that's why I stayed."[4]

## The Politics of Hair

Christopher Street was a world away from Susie Gottlieb's Mar Vista, California, home. Adopted at birth and raised by a very traditional Jewish family, Phranc says she fit in and yet still felt other. She knew she was a lesbian before she was old enough to do something about it, and says, "I needed to leave to become who I was." The drop-in rap is where she says she found "other people like me." "Everyone was about ten years older than me but for the first time ever I felt like I wasn't the only one, I wasn't the only lesbian. I became very political at a young age. I was still going to high school and I dropped out of high school to be who I was because I couldn't be who I was anywhere." Finally in 1974 when she was seventeen, "I came out on Thanksgiving Day that year, and moved out." Predictably, the transition had its difficulties. "I have a great relationship with my parents today but at the time they were not thrilled at all," she says. A friend offered her a place to stay, and she says, "I moved everything out of the house and lived with him but pretty soon I was living on the street in Venice, playing my guitar on the Boardwalk, to make a little bit of money."

During her mountaintop retreat, Phranc had a defining moment: She decided that her outward appearance should match what she was feeling inside. "I saw a slide show one night called *What the Well-Dressed Dyke Will Wear*. There were all these women wearing three-piece suits and it showed [the artist] shaving her head. I changed my name that weekend. Because my name was Susan and everyone called me Susie. I always hated that and I never identified with the name. On a whim and a mountaintop, I changed my name to Franc, like the French franc." Returning home after camp, the metamorphosis from Franc to Phranc continued to take shape. "My hair was all the way down my back . . . when I came back I cut it all off. I went right to Dante's Barbershop—it's still there. There was this dyke there named Bootsie and she gave me a buzz cut. I went to show my friend Punkin my new haircut and I knocked on her door and she said, "Who is it?' and I said 'Franc' and she opened the door and said, 'Franc!' Then she said, 'Wait one minute,' and went in the other room and got a blue baseball cap with a P and she said, "Phranc— P-h-r-a-n-c" and so that's how I got the Ph."

Like the also singularly named Odetta as well as freedom-singing sisters Nina Simone and Buffy Sainte-Marie, Phranc's self-education in her culture was a crucial step in the creation of an identity for herself as a singer, and hair was no small part of that equation. She has worn her flat-top proudly ever since. "Women are expected to look a certain way," she explains. "Cutting my hair gave me the freedom to become who I felt like, and who I wanted to be." Historically hair has been a strong way to assert identity in society. Just as the hippies grew their hair long as an accessory to their nonconformist views, Sainte-Marie wore her long black hair straight, as is the custom of Native women and some Asian women. Straight hair for Caucasian women meant freedom from the tyranny of styling chores—curlers and updos, teasing and hairspray. For African American women, the question of natural or straighten- ing is a debate that has no end. Nina Simone had taken a peek at hair mat- ters in her piece "Four Women" and of course her personal style was always evolving to more accurately reflect who she was becoming as an artist with Afrocentric interests. Activist Angela Davis was known not only for her work, but was recognizable largely by her look, a giant Afro. Odetta, who cropped her hair close in the fifties and let it go natural, believes she was among the first to do so. She was inspired by an interpretive dancer she saw in the fifties in Los Angeles who wore her hair natural while performing a program of African lore.

"I was talking to her but I couldn't keep my eyes away from her hair," Odetta explained as she discussed the politics of hair in the 1970s with WBAI's Celestine Ware.

> Then, the next summer I was a counselor at a camp of some kind and I was in the children's show and I had to keep my hair straight, forgive the pun, for the role on the weekends when I went into Los Angeles. When that show was finished, I got back to the camp and I was a counselor, right, so I went into the cabin thing and the kids were still up. So I said, "Okay, well as long as you're up, cut my hair" and they started getting scared, right? It was straight at this point and so I said, "Okay, that's enough," and I went into the bathroom and washed my hair, and the natural thing happened to it and it's been that way ever since, right? . . . There was a lot of times when I would get on a bus and people would snicker and laugh, and it was very difficult at the beginning. . . . I'm into head wraps now.[5]

## Women's Music

As the women's movement was in its process of developing a visible women's culture that extended beyond hair and the home arts—cooking and crafts, sewing circles and quilting bees—the feminist arts movement was established to introduce reflections of women's lives in art and to make changes in practices within the art community. As an adjunct to both movements, "women's music" was the umbrella term for music about women made and manufactured by women. And just as sure as song was used within the counterculture's peace movement and black liberation's civil rights and Black Power movements, women's music was not just an artistic valve for the struggle toward liberation. These songs cut straight to the heart of women's lives, women who had previously been part of an unseen and unheard minority. It was the time of the pioneers of women's music—Meg Christian, Margie Adam, Cris Williamson, and the women's collective Olivia Records. The core musicians from the peace and civil rights eras—like Holly Near and Bernice Johnson Reagon—pitched in to share their field experience, their powerful voices, and their commitment to human rights as part of a new movement. Near brought to the women's movement a strong folk background and her antiwar movement experience. She founded Redwood Records in 1972 as a forum for politically outspoken singers and continues to perform throughout the world, with a commitment to global activism. In 1973, Johnson Reagon formed Sweet Honey in the Rock, an all African American a cappella vocal group devoted to passing down the gospel and other songs of African heritage (the group continues without Johnson Reagon). Both Near and Johnson Reagon have demonstrated the relevance of bridge building between cultural movements and political movements throughout their respective careers as activists; Reagon's daughter, Toshi, carries on the family tradition of freedom singing.

The women's music movement was largely separatist at the time of its formation, with women occupying all positions in all facets of the music, from its creation to its production and distribution and all functions in between. It was inevitable that a record label by and for women would be created.

Olivia Records was the first independent label devoted to releasing women's music. Founded in 1973 by a collective of women including Meg Christian, Olivia released two pivotal albums that year: Christian's *I Know You Know* and Cris Williamson's *The Changer and the Changed.* "No one was looking over our shoulder," says Williamson.[6] "We pulled people in. We had a little expertise. That's how women's culture was made. No one taught me how to write songs. I did it intuitively." She says her song "Sweet Woman"—"about a woman by a woman"—started to get airplay and as it did, she began to receive feedback from women all around her. She heard stories from women who heard "Sweet Woman" on the car radio and had to pull off the road, so astonished were they to be hearing a musical expression of their experience. Yet Williamson says she was pretty much oblivious to any kind of grassroots musical movement afoot at the time. "I didn't notice it was women at my folk shows. I don't know why . . . I was too busy making art, making a living, getting rid of structure and strictures. I had complete freedom to be poor and make art," she says.

Kate Millet's Sacramento Women's Music Festival, first held in the banner year for women's music of 1973, was the beginning of what would turn into a women's music festival circuit; its most popular stop is the Michigan Womyn's Music Festival, still held annually outside of Grand Rapids.

"I remember being really young and going to those concerts and really, really loving them," says Phranc. "That music wasn't lesbian music and it wasn't really folk music. As much as I love Cris Williamson's albums, and I really loved them, that's not where I connected." Phranc was still a couple of years away from finding her connection to the community. But women's music proved to be the doorway through which women of color seeking liberation from the typical limitations they encountered on the job could pass through. Like Phranc, singer, songwriter, and percussionist Vicki Randle was a teenager during the heady, early days of women's lib. Randle had previously found her greatest opportunities as a background vocalist, but women's music gave her a platform for her own work. "I didn't want to be a singer in some band, doing something that didn't mean anything to me," says Randle.[7] She was among the very few young African American acoustic musicians when she began to perform at political gatherings in the seventies. After years of background singing, by 1992 she became the first female in the *Tonight Show* band. Performing five nights a week on network television as an openly gay black woman with curves was Randle's nightly statement on issues of race, gender, and sexual preference.

## Dorothy Baker's Coffeehouse

As the seventies progressed, the infrastructure for women in the arts was still in the creation phase. In 1973, the Woman's Building was established in downtown Los Angeles as an art and education center with an eye on drawing a through line from the women's movement to its arts community. The Woman's Building leased space to the Chouinard School of Art, which established the Feminist Studio Workshop, founded by artist Judy Chicago, among others. Phranc, along with women artists from all across the country, gravitated to the Woman's Building, which offered work and studio space for artists and actors, along with a bookstore, a travel agency, an office of the National Organization for Women, and Dorothy Baker's Coffeehouse. "I took my guitar there and would play my original songs and the people were so kind to me," says Phranc. "In the hallway on the way to the bathroom the acoustics were right so I played a lot of guitar there and wrote a lot of music. I ended up going to the Feminist Studio Workshop, a two-year program. I learned how to offset press—did printing and silk-screening—but I mostly played my guitar and wrote original music. I was young and I just kind of went for it. I don't know how good any of it was but I was so passionate and I was so angry that I felt I could do anything," she says.

The righteous anger that women had been discouraged from displaying in their day-to-day lives had begun to find an outlet in the artistic expressions of the women's movement, as the fight for women's equality in the workplace and at home was taking center stage. Of course, women had long been on the front lines when it came to the fight for human rights. Whether for racial justice or family welfare, women were accustomed to raising their voices for a cause.

Julia Ward Howe, credited for establishing Mother's Day, had not only written the words to the abolitionist song "Battle Hymn of the Republic," she would later adapt the lyrics to "America" to address women's suffrage. In the Depression and labor movement years, women sang out in the name of workers welfare during the Gastonia Textile Mill Strike of 1929, the Harlan County of Kentucky Miner strike of 1931 and 1932, and the Flint, Michigan United Auto Workers Sit-In of 1936 and 1937. "Bread and Roses" by Caroline Kolsatt and James Oppenheim was among the songs that made the rounds in the labor movement period. In the pre-civil-rights era, Billie Holiday's beautifully rendered interpretation of "Strange Fruit" went straight to the root of modern America's greatest shame:

> Black bodies swinging in the Southern breeze, strange fruit hanging from the poplar trees.

And yet, as the frontline concern of anti-oppression switched focus from race and war to gender-equality issues, the mode of musical expression was also in the process of turning away from the society-driven folk songs that dominated the sixties and early seventies protest eras. A new kind of singer-songwriter emerged to deliver songs of personal fulfillment and self-actualization.

## You're So Vain

With the campaign to wipe out certain dissident voices successfully completed for the most part in the early seventies, by 1975 the general tone toward all things revolution-style had changed dramatically.

"You think Johnson was concerned about some hippies singing about the war or black people singing about peace?" asks Elaine Brown. "What really pushed America out of Vietnam was they got their asses kicked." Having received the message that the sixties effort to upend the power structure ended in more tragedy than triumph, a new group of women, freed by their increasing liberation, set out to take their stand on matters personal as well as political. Though songwriting's earliest female voices—artists like Janis Ian and Buffy Sainte-Marie—would not be vanquished, they were naturally evolving and looking at new ways to put across their ideas following the previous decade's chaos and its mixed reactions to protest movement and its songs. With the war over and poverty matters shunted off to the side, a portion of the pioneering folksingers and songwriting population turned their attention inward, in keeping with the spirit of the Me Decade. Women declared their autonomy, the men of folk famously softened up, and confession replaced aggression in the new era of the sensitive singer-songwriter. Noncontroversial artists like James Taylor, Cat Stevens, Jackson Browne, and Elton John ruled the airwaves alongside the female voices who are now synonymous with the times: Carly Simon, Linda Ronstadt, Joni Mitchell, and Carole King, who came out from behind the scenes from her songwriting partnership with Gerry Goffin and turned it into a record-breaking album for a solo female artist. *Tapestry* included a remake of her song "(You Make Me Feel Like a) Natural Woman," one of Aretha Franklin's string of hits from 1967. The then-new movement in singer-songwriting has been called a lot of things, from wimpy to self-indulgent and worse. It also produced some unforgettable hits from the era and worked as a sort of balm that followed the storm. The music has its diehard fans as well as its severe critics. Though there may be arguments in favor of the singer-songwriter movement's personally political nature, we will not explore them here except to say this: among the singer-songwriters mentioned here as well as others left unmentioned, early personal explorations sometimes led to songs and causes that concerned things social and political in nature. However, their issues of choice were as varied as the individual songwriters themselves and shifted accordingly as the times demanded.

## And Now It's Winter: The Return of the Poets

The energy crisis and recession, the costs from overspending on the war, and a government scandal of epic proportions were fuel for desperate times. Gil Scott-Heron was among the poets, songwriters, and activists who developed his voice and made art of the despair the counterculture experienced in the cold "winter" of 1970 to 1974. With just enough hindsight on the situation, Gil Scott-Heron and Brian Jackson laid down what may be their most inspirational work, *Winter in America*, in 1974. The era of jazz-fusion had arrived and as leaders in a new style of jazz-funk (just one of a number of jazz combinations taking shape), Scott-Heron and Jackson's blend of keyboards and flute stood out as coming from the soul. Scott-Heron distilled the essences of disappointment and the difficulties confronting black America in the immediate post-sixties dream period in songs like "The Bottle," which took on addiction and the ghetto, and "Winter in America," a litany of sixties troubles, its discontents, and the stillness that followed the decade's passing.

Introducing the song to a live audience, he explained, "There used to be an agreement between the seasons, that they would all come and stay about three months, then they would go to wherever seasons would go when they're not where we are—we rarely notice. But one season was unhappy because it seemed as though all of its time was being taken by the other seasons . . . Winter wasn't happy. Fall always stayed too long, spring always came too soon . . . in America winter became very, very unhappy and decided to stay. Winter decided there would be a little bit of winter in every spring, a little bit of winter in every summer, a little bit of winter in every fall and a whole lot of winter in every winter. Till it became a season of ice: Frozen dreams and frozen ideas and frozen progress, all of a sudden, things people needed, frozen just beyond their reach. Winter was unhappy—philosophically, politically, and psychologically."[8]

Ain't nobody fighting because nobody knows what to say.

Having survived the obscenity charges and trial brought about by the publication of *Howl* in the late fifties, poet Allen Ginsberg had chanted his way through the major political events of the sixties, and by the early seventies he set about collecting his own songs, setting them to music. His collaborations with Bob Dylan, his renderings of William Blake, and his own "CIA Dope Calypso," among others, were the substance of *First Blues—Rags, Ballads & Harmonium Songs 1971–74*. Richie Havens, the young poet Ginsberg had first invited to the stage in the Greenwich Village of the late fifties, had devoted his post-Woodstock performances to strumming the songs that caught his ear and turning them into his own self-styled tunes. His melancholy downstroke on George Harrison's "Here Comes the Sun" complemented the long, cold, lonely winter Gil Scott-Heron sang about. But where there's Havens, there is always hope, as the song becomes less social comment and more like a hymn: "And I say, it's all right." Which is not to say that Havens didn't have his own inner-city concerns.

Seeking to bring a little bit of the environmental movement to the blighted urban scene Havens co-created an oceanographic children's museum called the Northwind Undersea Institute on City Island in the Bronx. He conceived the Natural Guard, an organization in New Haven, Connecticut, where kids were encouraged to "guard the natural" in their own surroundings. From a community garden that fed the homeless population to a lead-poisoning awareness campaign, the children were made responsible for identifying the problems and creating the solutions that would have a lasting impact on their community as well as their individual lives. "The most put-upon group is children. It really was based on children using their own community as the endangered environment. The students were told, 'It's up to you guys to tell us what you think the world should be like and we're here to get every tool that's necessary to make it that way.' And that's how they took over their community," he says.

With no particular movement in place, other songwriters turned to environmental wellness, an area where they led when it came to activism, culminating with the No Nukes campaign.

## No Nukes

Following the nuclear accident at the Three Mile Island plant near Harrisburg, Pennsylvania, in 1979, musicians Jackson Browne, Bonnie Raitt, Graham Nash, and John Hall united under the banner MUSE (Musicians United for Safe Energy) for a series of concerts in New York titled No Nukes. The shows (filmed for a movie and recorded for an album) overlapped with a mass protest in town that drew an estimated 200,000 people; it was the beginning of rising awareness about the dangers of nuclear power.

"As the indigenous people we have watched this thing happen on our hemisphere," said John Trudell at the No Nukes rally held in Battery Park in September of 1979. "We have seen them come in and confuse and attack. We understand that the issue is the land. The issue is the Earth. We cannot change the political system, we cannot change the economic system. We cannot change the social system until the people control the land. And then we take it out of the hands of that sick minority that chooses to pervert the meaning and the intention of humanity."[9]

At a time when people were just beginning to understand nuclear power and its potential to negatively impact public health, the disadvantaged communities—whom environmental toxins usually reach first—had already paid the costs. Gil Scott-Heron was hip to the power problem and predicted potential nuclear disaster in "We Almost Lost Detroit," his song about a 1960s failure at a US power plant; he performed it at the MUSE benefit.

> You see, we almost lost Detroit that time . . .
> Odds are we gonna lose somewhere, sometime

Though it was surely an opportunity for musicians and people to unite for a cause, the No Nukes concert, a little like the peace and love generation's last stand at Woodstock, was a collective wave good-bye not only to a decade, but to an era of generational unification and a counterculture who were in basic agreement of common goals and good. Ironically their values were similar, but there was a generational clash between the singer-songwriter, folk-style performers and the cynical "we don't care" kids coming up behind them, while "the natural" state was slipping into retrograde. There was yet another trend competing for a segment of the fractured listening audience, lured by the sparkle and shine of the footlights that lead to the promise of love on the dance floor, by the light of the silvery disco ball.

## The Disco Divide

"With the civil rights and Black Power movements providing not only the inspiration and impetus for the gay liberation movement but also its basic structure, sloganeering, and models for collective struggle, it should come as no surprise that the black music of the period would become the soundtrack to gay liberation," writes author Peter Shapiro in *Turn the Beat Around: The Secret History of Disco.*[10] Though a story not often told, it's worth recalling in an effort to uncoil the confusing legacy of disco—a music rooted in funk, Afrobeat, house parties, and gay discos. As deeply soulful as it was vacuous and hated, its tenure tied to racism, sexism, and homophobia as well as the rapidly shifting trends in the melding of seventies styles.

"Disco's very birth was the result of the big bang between contradictory impulses: exclusion and inclusion, glamour and dilapidation, buying in and dropping out, engagement and withdrawal, earnestness and frippery," writes Shapiro. The chaos was symptomatic of the mid-seventies. "Disco was seen by many commentators as the death knell for community and the harbinger of narcissism."[11] And yet, no music before or since demonstrated such a harmonious convergence of the races and genders with diverse sexual preferences and class backgrounds, working and dancing together on one rainbow-colored dance floor. For a while in the seventies, disco's potential as a harmonizing musical force shone bright. But disco had its detractors, like the aggressive Chicago DJ who fueled the Disco Sucks campaign by staging a Disco Demolition Night at Comiskey Park. Baseball fans were offered discount admission if they brought a disco record to be destroyed. After the DJ blew up the records, a wild mood ensued, and fans stormed the field, nearly destroying it. Any hope of disco's harmonious one-love vibe helping bring peace to the dance floor and spread it worldwide died that night, though disco's influence cannot be that easily dismissed.

As women's music was finding its voice, as soul music was crossing into its ambitious conceptual era, and jazz and soul and funk combined to create fusion, you might say people were less concerned with old-fashioned conventions like touch dancing than they were with breaking out of them. And yet the groove was still very much alive in funk, the James Brown signature style that emphasized the downbeat or "the one" (also a characteristic of the music of the Meters and Allen Toussaint of New Orleans). Brown's music had served as inspiration to musicians on the African continent, contributing to the birth of Afrobeat, which also emerged in the run-up to the disco era, while dance floor records by Sly and the Family Stone and Motown artists slid easily into the disco mix. Basically, if you could dance to it, it was disco, and like the name implies, it was all about the records. Spun at house parties and clubs by DJs, the best of whom mixed on the beat to encourage dancing all night long, disco required no live performances and no stars. In music's high era—before the contemporary cult of the DJ—its fans, rather than its makers, were the focal point. The dancers were elegant and outrageous, and the dance floor was the new melting pot. Whether you were gay or straight, black or Latino, you were welcome to dance.

In 1972 the worldwide hit "Soul Makossa" by Cameroonian musician Manu Dibango became what is now largely noted as the first disco record; its rhythm is steeped in Afrobeat and James Brown funk. The culmination of disco's rise from street phenomenon to nationwide mania was of course *Saturday Night Fever*, the film with the Bee Gees soundtrack. As disco developed, the music became associated with the syncopated bass and a thump-thump beat known as "four on the floor," along with its high-sheen, sophisticated production values that ran counter to rock and folk's esthetics. The lush, orchestrated sound had been forged on the Philadelphia International Records made by producers Kenny Gamble and Leon Huff—as heard on the #1 record "TSOP (The Sound of Philadelphia)" (the theme to *Soul Train*) and "The Love I Lost" by Harold Melvin and the Blue Notes, featuring Teddy Pendergrass. Another #1, "Lady Marmalade" by three-woman vocal group LaBelle, was a disco-era watershed for its boldly sexual lyric fused to the aforementioned New Orleans funk. LaBelle had weighed in early on empowerment statements with their 1973 rock album *Pressure Cookin'* (featuring a medley of Gil Scott-Heron's "The Revolution Will Not Be Televised" fused to Thunderclap Newman's "Something's in the Air," with its references to "the revolution"). The rest of LaBelle's songs were largely written by Nona Hendryx, who stepped out of her role as girl-group vocalist and became masterful at mixing rock, drama, and Mardi Gras into a progressive women's mix. LaBelle spent the earlier part of the seventies working with singer-songwriter Laura Nyro, another front-runner in blending styles, from old school R&B to introspective songwriter ballads with complex melodies. The LaBelle and Nyro collaboration is a prime example of how intersections between artists and styles largely defined the first part of the decade.

Rock and soul bands all got in on the act, cutting their "disco" tracks, while disco itself could encompass everything from KC and the Sunshine

Band's brassy sounds to Giorgio Moroder's synthesizer tracks for Donna Summer and Patrick Cowley's productions for the singer Sylvester. A former child gospel singer, Sylvester James debuted in San Francisco in 1970 as a drag queen named Dooni, performing Billie Holiday songs. By the end of the decade, the triumphant high energy burst of joy, "You Make Me Feel (Mighty Real)" was a bona fide disco anthem. Alongside Cheryl Lynn's "To Be Real" and Gloria Gaynor's "I Will Survive," "You Make Me Feel (Mighty Real)" is not just a disco classic, it remains the standard-bearing ode to sexual freedom and authenticity.

The politics of disco—the opportunity for straights to play elegant dress-up in the face of urban decay, the safe haven for same-sex couples to dance, and a place for drag queens to sashay in plain view in a new age of tolerance—ties disco to the history of resistance music of the ages, from the masked revelry of French renaissance minstrels performed in protest of the treatment of peasants by local lords, to the encrypted songs and performances of minstrels in the slave era, to freedom songs sung by bluesmen and workers and students and militants in the sixties, and the signifying funkateers of the seventies.

The story of Chic and its song "Good Times," on its way to becoming a #1 record just as Disco Demolition Night was taking place at Comiskey Park, underscores these connections. The mixed-gender five-person group, led by bassist Bernard Edwards and guitarist Nile Rodgers, infused each and every one of their songs with what Rodgers calls DHM, or deep hidden meaning. Inspired to write "Le Freak" after being refused admission to the swank Studio 54, the lyric originally conceived as "Fuck you!" morphed into "Freak out!" thanks to the principle of DHM. Rodgers was no stranger to speaking out; he had become a Black Panther at the age of sixteen. Rodgers explains, "I mean, this was all seriously thought-out stuff. We didn't just randomly write this. This was protest shrouded in double entendre . . . If the song didn't have any DHM, we weren't putting it out. We would work on a song until it had a sufficient amount of DHM, and then we were cool with it." He explains the inspiration for "Good Times" came from the Great Depression and the Harlem Renaissance. "I'll tell you, here's 'Good Times' straight up: Al Jolson. 'The stars are going to twinkle and shine, this evening about a quarter to nine and oh, la-la-la-la.' That's how we started." What they ended up with was:

Happy days are here again, the time is right for making friends
Let's get together, how 'bout quarter to ten

"We went back, and we took that, we thought of this guy in blackface and we thought of Count Basie," he says. Back in his day, laws prevented Basie from freely moving through society, despite his status as the Count. "We looked at Al Jolson as saying, 'This is the music of these people . . . that you'll accept me as a white person putting on this makeup and singing it, but if this guy comes up on stage, you'd boo . . . There was no way that I was ever just gonna write a song about partying and dancing. I mean, I'm a Black Panther, what are you taking about? And so it was always about compromise."[12] "Good Times" would go on to become the basic track for the beginning of rap music; it is among the most sampled songs with the most recognizable bass line of all time.

Like the struggle for civil rights, gay liberation was not something that could be obtained in an instant or as the result of one march or demonstration; the road to equality continues to have its obstacles, as did the music's development. But thirty years after the Disco Demolition Night riot tried to take down a musical genre, disco still lives.

## Rock Justice

With rock struggling to find its way between glam rock, punk rock, prog rock, and studio-finished corporate rock, there were still songwriters from the first Greenwich Village wave on the job, doing the work they had always done—performing and writing songs. Phil Ochs celebrated the official end of the Vietnam War by organizing a "War Is Over" rally 100,000 people strong in New York's Central Park on May 11, 1975. The old guard—Pete Seeger, Harry Belafonte, Odetta—turned out to celebrate with him, as did Joan Baez. The singer was having a national hit with her album *Diamonds and Rust*, a collection of her own songs, with covers of works by Jackson Browne, Janis Ian, and, of course, Dylan (the title song is about her relationship with him in the early 1960s). Richie Havens took over his own business, forming a record label, Stormy Forest. He continued to cut originals, along with his versions of familiar songs, particularly those of Dylan: "(It's All Over Now) Baby Blue," "Just Like a Woman," and even the epic "Sad Eyed Lady of the Lowlands."

Havens still opens each and every show with "All Along the Watchtower," its story concerning two outsiders who banter the question, how shall one live life in the face of its inevitable end? But Havens declares Dylan's best tune and his personal favorite is the singer-songwriter's 1975 return to protest music:

> Here comes the story of the Hurricane
> The man the authorities came to blame
> For something that he'd never done
> Put him in a prison cell but
> One time he coulda been champion of the world

Just as when he quit protest music in the early sixties, Dylan had reentered the game and abruptly stopped writing direct protest and topical material again, after the "George Jackson" single in 1971. His early seventies performances were scarce and apolitical as well, save for a walk-on at George Harrison's Concert for Bangladesh. His albums *Self-Portrait* and *New Morning* were reflections of an inwardly directed songwriter, and though he stepped out with the Band for *Planet Waves* and a tour in the new era of big-time rock 'n' roll, he retreated again, against the backdrop of a marital disintegration that famously produced *Blood on the Tracks* in 1975. But by summer of that year, he came out swinging. "Hurricane" sounded as if Dylan were ready to take on not just topical protest but the world, as he spit out the story of Rubin "Hurricane" Carter's triple murder conviction and turned it into an epic ballad about a miscarriage of justice and a not-so-subtle reminder of skin color privilege. Impressed with Carter's book, *The Sixteenth Round*, in which the boxer explains his history as a vocal supporter of black rights and his experience of being framed by New Jersey law enforcement, Dylan was moved to visit Carter in prison. As the story goes, following a five- or six-hour visit, Dylan set about writing the tribute with Jacques Levy, his collaborator at the time. "Look, there's an injustice that's been done and Rubin's gonna get out, there's no doubt about it," Dylan told author Larry Sloman. "But the fact is, it can happen to anybody."[13] "Hurricane" transcends simple topical protest song. Broadcasting as clearly as the pistol shots that rang out in the barroom, Dylan sets a scene and creates a detailed picture of a world unfamiliar to his white majority listeners, showing the status of race relations in Patterson,

New Jersey, circa 1966. The song stirs feelings of empathy and compassion; it becomes a companion for believers in the cause to free Rubin Carter and others wrongly imprisoned.

Following the release of the song as a single in 1975 and the formation of a grassroots movement for Carter's release from prison based on the false evidence used to convict him, the boxer was released on bail and granted a new trial the following year. His conviction was finally overturned in 1988. Dylan and friends performed "Hurricane" onstage every night during their '75 and '76 Rolling Thunder Revue. The event was designed to mimic an old-fashioned traveling tent show. The entourage, including Allen Ginsberg, Joan Baez, Joni Mitchell, and Ramblin' Jack Elliott, rolled into Madison Square Garden in December of 1975. They were joined that evening by singer Roberta Flack and Muhammad Ali for a benefit billed as "The Night of the Hurricane." Ali addressed the crowd. "I'm so glad to see you all with the cause because you have the connection with the complexion to get the protection," he said from the stage. He entertained with some crowd-pleasing, "I Am the Greatest"–type banter, but according to the two main published accounts of the event, Ali's fooling around and endorsement of political candidate John Jay Hooker from the stage was deemed inappropriate at an event whose focus was Carter and prison justice. Far more interesting on this night were Carter's own words, delivered through the house PA via telephone. "Muhammad . . . on a serious note, my brother Bob Dylan once wrote, 'Walk upside down inside handcuffs, throw up my legs and kick them off. Say all right, I've had enough. Now what else can you show me?' " Carter said, quoting from "It's Alright Ma (I'm Only Bleeding)." "Speaking from deep down in the bowels of the state prison of New Jersey, the fact that I'm speaking to you and the other brothers and sisters in the audience, that's revolutionary indeed." Praising the love of his wife and daughter, Carter said his hope was alive. "I knew that if I remained alive, that if I kept myself well . . . I knew they were going to come to my rescue, and tonight, here you are."[14]

## Other Voices, Other Countries

"I didn't even listen to Bob Dylan until I was in my early twenties," explains Phranc. "I didn't even know about Bob Dylan. I got Bob Dylan, Patti Smith, and David Bowie at the same time." Instead Phranc was raised on "the generic liberal music of the late fifties and early sixties: "Pete Seeger's *Songs to Grow On*; Woody Guthrie; Marsha Berman; Theo Bikel; Peter, Paul and Mary. And show tunes: Judy Garland, *Showboat*, *The Sound of Music*." She was also stuck on the topical and parodic songs of Allen Sherman, his roots in Borscht Belt humor and Jewish folklore. "*My Son the Folksinger*, I know it inside out."

Picking up the guitar at the age of nine, she hated the lessons, but she kept playing. The first record she owned was "Hurdy Gurdy Man" by Donovan, then "when I was fifteen someone gave me a Janis Ian record because their older sister had it and they'd heard me play guitar and thought I would like that. That was 'Society's Child,' the record she'd made when she was fifteen, which was very different from the other records she made." Ian had recorded for Broadside in the early sixties and scored a hit in 1966 after three tries with her song about interracial love, "Baby I've Been Thinking," better known as "Society's Child." In return for her success, she received her share of threats and hate mail.

The pressure on Ian as a young woman was simply too great for her to persist and she pulled back from music—that is, until the new women's singer-songwriter's movement of the seventies came along and she was inspired enough to jump back in the game. "At Seventeen" revealed the experience of teen alienation from a woman's point of view, earning her a Grammy Award and a #1 album in 1975. But there are days when Ian feels some remorse about her greatest hit. "I hate to think that 'At Seventeen' is any part of that whole bleeding all over yourself school of songwriting, writing from the internal rather than the external," she says. "At the end of the day, all of our lives are so boring, compared to the grand scheme of things." You might say that the lonely outsider in "At Seventeen" strikes a universal chord for anyone who ever felt the pain of rejection or loneliness. "I would hope so, that would be great," she says. "That's certainly how I approached it. But in my occasional 'my God, what have I created' moments, I don't think so," she says. Ian says she fears she spawned a monster movement in songwriting, a style of writing that saw great commercial success in the seventies as a new singer-songwriter style came to dominate the pop charts. Ian's song was a reflection of her generation—it marked the passage of time for the once-youthful, change-the-world idealists who had grown into a more resigned adult way of life.

Conversely, Sainte-Marie was not one of the songwriters who thrived in the seventies wave of women rising. Instead, she turned her attention toward becoming more deeply involved in activism and educational efforts. She established her Nihewan Foundation to fund Native American study programs and efforts to send Indians to college. She also devoted time to being a mother. In 1976, she and her son Dakota Starblanket Wolfchild, also known as Cody, joined the cast of the public television series *Sesame Street*. The mother and son were the only Native Americans ever to appear on a daily television series for seven years. While on *Sesame Street* she participated in a demonstration of breast-feeding and logged another first in televised history.

*Sesame Street* provided a safe neighborhood for others from the civil rights movement. Maya Angelou, Harry Belafonte, and Stevie Wonder all stopped by, as did the Reverend Jesse Jackson, who delivered his poem "I Am—Somebody":

> I may be poor
> But I am somebody
> I may be young
> But I am somebody
> I may be on welfare
> But I am somebody

Falling away from the mainframe of the movement, in the post-civil-rights era Jackson organized Operation PUSH (People United to Save Humanity) and the Rainbow Coalition and raised a fist for black pride at protests, gatherings, and concerts. Afros got larger and funk got funkier and the community continued the fight for its right to survival. Jackson again recited "I Am—Somebody" at the 1972 Stax Records Wattstax festival, conceived as a "Black Woodstock" and held on the seventh anniversary of the Watts Riots. Motown's Kim Weston opened the show with "The Star Spangled Banner," followed by "The Negro National Anthem," formally titled "Lift Ev'ry Voice and Sing," a freedom song dating back to the early part of the twentieth century. Over the years it had become a custom for it to be played at large, mostly African American gatherings. Following the opening, the Wattstax house was rocked by the soul-gospel of the Staple Singers, Stax giants Isaac Hayes and Rufus Thomas, bluesmen Albert King and Johnnie Taylor, and comedy genius Richard Pryor.

In 1974 James Brown headlined a troupe of musicians including Miriam Makeba, who traveled to Kinshasa, Zaire, to perform during the fight between George Foreman and Muhammad Ali. Ali was attempting to reclaim his position as heavyweight champion of the world following his loss to and Foreman's win over Joe Frazier. B. B. King, Bill Withers, the Spinners, the Crusaders, and Celia Cruz and the Fania All-Stars were also on board for the trip, turning in performances that were as inspired by the motherland as they were by the Zairians themselves who embraced the entertainers with open arms. JB's trombonist Fred Wesley said from the stage, "Now I want everybody to repeat after me. If you don't know who you are or where your place is, just say to yourself, I am—somebody." Brown, with the assistance of Wesley, moved into more album-oriented work rather than concentrating on the hit singles that grew his fame. His song titles from the period, if not the songs' moods themselves, were no exception to the darker reflections: *Reality*, *Hell*, and the landmark funk album *The Payback*.

During the early seventies there was no shortage of matters, inside or out of the United States, from which a topical songwriter seeking to record his times or protest against them could choose. On September 11, 1973, a military coup overthrew president Salvador Allende of Chile; thousands of Chilean people were tortured and murdered in Santiago stadium on order of General Pinochet, including activist and singer Victor Jara. Learning of the atrocities that felled the country with which he'd been so welcome, Ochs immediately set about planning "An Evening with Salvador Allende" at Madison Square Garden, though he initially had trouble finding support for the event. Pete Seeger and Arlo Guthrie were secured, though ticket sales nowhere near matched the Garden's capacity. At the eleventh hour, Bob Dylan agreed to perform.

In the absence of Black Panther Party leader Huey Newton, who was living in exile in Cuba, Elaine Brown continued to lead the Black Panthers in further community works in Oakland. Moving deeper into California politics, she and Bobby Seale ran for public office in Oakland, and by 1977 Black Panther advocacy and voter registration efforts contributed to the election of Lionel Wilson, the city's first black mayor. By 1977, Newton returned from exile to resume leadership; Brown fled Oakland amidst the destruction and confusion of the party's demise at the hands of outer and inner conflict. She considered rejuvenating her singing and songwriting but ultimately elected instead to devote her time to education and activism.

It was during this period that Buffy Sainte-Marie learned about the details of her placement on an unofficial US blacklist. "I found out what had gone on through an interview . . . I didn't know what to say. A second broadcaster . . . I think it was in Cleveland . . . mentioned the same thing and I thought jeez, maybe it's really true. So I got my FBI papers," she says. "I didn't know they made a black magic marker that fat. So the Freedom of Information Act is a joke. All I found out was indeed they were tailing me, there was a lot that they didn't want me to know, but there was nothing I could do about it. By then I had no career in the United States. I had been defeated."

In 1975 the order to deport John Lennon from the United States was overturned. He and Yoko Ono had survived the Immigration and Naturalization Service's inquiry and an eighteen-month separation, and that year their baby boy Sean was born. The Beatle and his conceptual artist wife had the money and goodwill to risk career and reputation, but standing up for their beliefs was its own reward. The immigration case had been a three-ring circus, and Lennon's defiance didn't make it any easier, though in the end his attorney Leon Wildes said, "It became clear to me that he was a guy of major principle. He understood that what was being done to him was wrong. It was an abuse of law. And he was willing to stand up and shine the big light on it."[15]

"I'm real proud of our generation and the fact that we helped to stop a war and put Lyndon Johnson out of business. However, in one way we really missed it, we really blew it," says Buffy Sainte-Marie. "In North America today there are five very highly funded, major serious colleges of war. There's Annapolis, there's West Point, there's the Army College of War, the Air Force Academy, and the Royal Military Academy in Canada," she explains. "There're five of them and we don't have one college of peace of that caliber, of that funding, of that seriousness. So how are we supposed to have peace in this world when our best minds don't even have a university in which to study alternative conflict resolution, but they can study war?"

Phil Ochs had continued to wage his one-man war against the world, which proved to be a losing battle. Under constant government surveillance and suffering from untreated bipolar disorder and alcoholism, he took his own life in 1976. Ochs left an indelible imprint on folk's political evolution;

his name remains synonymous with reportage in song. As if on cue with his departure, a new group of musicians in possession of his fiery spirit took up some of the causes he left behind and prepared the way for the future of protest song. Music was changing again.

## A Brief History of Punk Rock

Upon finishing the art program with the Feminist Studio Workshop, Phranc made a pilgrimage to San Francisco. "I'd heard it was this great queer mecca," she says. The city had been home to freethinkers and outlaws of all stripes since the Barbary Coast Days. Following World War II it had developed a reputation as a city with a world-class gay community, and Phranc looked forward to falling in with the scene there. "I thought I was going to find all these women in San Francisco and that it was going to be great; and what I found was not an incredibly warm community," she says. Understanding friends steered her toward a houseful of iconoclasts who'd formed their own community. "We walked across the street, Howard Street, South of Market, and into this house . . . Everyone was really nice to me. Here were people who were my age, really angry, really smart, being creative, and I felt like I connected much more with them as a peer group than I did with anyone gay or lesbian at that time. I went back to L.A., got my cardboard boxes, and moved everything to San Francisco," she says. "It was the beginning of the whole punk scene." It was 1976, still early days for punk rock, but the scene had been in gestation since the early seventies in New York where rock musicians were working out a rougher, anti–Summer of Love, anti-hippie style of performance that is now generally classified as pre-punk. The minimalist, alienated Velvet Underground may well have provided its icy attitude and two or three chords; the grit rock and urban white blues of the MC5 and Iggy and the Stooges are also notable citations in pre-punk's roots. But of specific interest to this edition of the story are the five cross-dressing, straight, male, white truants who built their repertoire on R&B and the girl group sound of the early sixties, crossed it with garage rock, and called themselves the New York Dolls. Theirs was the sound of the street—dirty, sloppy, often impaired by substances—and because they came from the center of the world, you'd think the rest of the universe would have stopped and paid attention. But they did not (except in England, where the people have historically understood American-rooted sound sooner than people in the States do). The Dolls' primitive, back-to-zero ethos was the nucleus of an insurgent and desperate new music in motion all over Manhattan. The Ramones were four longhairs from Queens who dressed like thugs and played hard and fast; they too paid homage to the black girl group sound of the early sixties. The group Blondie was fronted by a real girl-group-style singer and style maker, Debbie Harry. And it was a snarky poet, Richard Hell of Television and later the Voidoids, who was the first to wear an actual safety pin and scribble on his T-shirt with a pen, the two elements borrowed by New York Dolls manager Malcolm McLaren for the formation of his Sex Pistols—an experiment in Situationist art that actually made good on its promise to create a revolution in music. If punk rock attitude can be summed up in a couple of slogans, those might be "no future" and "we don't care," both lifted from the Sex Pistols song "God Save the Queen," famously performed from a barge on the middle of the Thames on the occasion of the Queen's Silver Jubilee.

All over the world, youth were collectively inspired to take back rock and put it into the hands of their generation, and they did it themselves, without corporations or websites or even a whole lot of love behind them. They did it with spit, muscle, and sweat, and even Sid Vicious's blood, and a couple of copies of *Raw Power* between them.

"It seemed like it had to go back to the three-minute song, something immediate and direct," says the Buzzcocks' Steve Diggle. "And from that people became alive again."

Among punk rock's targets was the comfortable numbness of quotidian life, partially provided by expensively produced (Pink Floyd, the Eagles, Steely Dan, and Fleetwood Mac) and lightweight (James Taylor and Carly Simon) rock. The back-to-basics music style combined with the anti-authority philosophy meant punk was largely a scene without leaders, organization, or infrastructure. It can't be said enough that in the United States there was virtually no commercial airplay for the music and there was very little in the way of favorable aboveground rock press for it either. But self-starting had its rewards.

"People gained confidence in who they were, even ourselves, even with all our insecurities," says Diggle. "It wasn't like we were the big show business act come to entertain people, it was more like . . . These guys are the same as us,'" he says. "It was real people singing about real things and when we go up on stage we just put on guitars and there's no big act."

The do-it-yourself directive also led to the resurgence and proliferation of the self-released seven-inch single, a format that had virtually become extinct with the popularization of seventies album rock. Buzzcocks was one of the first bands of the punk surge in England to release their own record, debuting with their *Spiral Scratch* EP in January of 1977. That spring the Ramones, with the Nerves and Pere Ubu, took the first murmurings of punk all across the USA. Though at the surface the punk pop of the Buzzcocks wasn't political, "It was about personal politics," explains Diggle. "It questioned things on many levels." A song like "Autonomy" was about "self-rule." "And 'Fast Cars' was about the business of having a fast car," he says.

Whether it was the words they sang—at once passionate and dispassionate—the way they sang them, or the fact that they sang them at all, songs like "Fast Cars" telegraphed something that went beyond the speed limit: it confronted individuality and choice in the market-driven culture. "I hate fast cars!" was a radical statement, a rejection of values prized by society.

The Ramones and the Sex Pistols have both been called the Johnny Appleseeds of punk, crisscrossing their respective countries and crossing the Atlantic while punk bands were breaking out like a spotty rash in places likely (London) and unlikely (Akron, Ohio). The Ramones brought their show to San Francisco's Savoy Tivoli in 1976 and inspired a few artists and musicians to form bands of their own. The Sex Pistols did the same, bringing their show to the United States in early 1978, though the resulting media circus marked the end of the Pistols and the death of the early phase of punk. Penelope Houston's band the Avengers opened the last-ever Sex Pistols show at Winterland in San Francisco. Less influenced by the entertainment of the Sex Pistols and the fun of the Ramones, Houston was a punk rocker of the battling kind. "I definitely recognized that Dylan was fighting against the things he saw as wrong but I would say my biggest singing influence would be Patti Smith," she says. The blank generation, a term coined by poet Richard Hell, found its muse, its voice, and its generation's answer to Bob Dylan in Patti Smith, who been there before all of them. Having escaped a New Jersey childhood for the Chelsea Hotel, the young poet was also the girlfriend of photographer Robert

Mapplethorpe, and together they made art before she ever had the idea of making a record. Through the course of her bookstore clerk days and Max's Kansas City nights, Smith emerged an androgynous, rock 'n' roll type with more in common with Dylan and Keith Richards than any woman in rock.

Smith went to the San Francisco Bay Area in 1974—high Watergate season—to perform at Rather Ripped Records on the North Side of the Berkeley campus. At the time it was one of the few places you could buy an independent seven-inch record, what you might call the broadside of the late seventies. Smith's new single was "Hey Joe," the song with which Jimi Hendrix had ended his fateful set at Woodstock in 1969. The A-side began with a poem titled *Sixty Days*:

> Patty, you know what your daddy said, Patty, he said, he said,
> "Well sixty days ago she was such a lovely child, and now here she is
> with a gun in her hand."

The Patty to whom she was referring was Patricia Campbell Hearst, who'd taken the name Tania. The local newspaper heiress had recently been kidnapped by the Symbionese Liberation Army, an armed band of radical militants and just one of a host of urban warriors and terrorists raising hell in the Bay Area during the protracted aftermath of the Summer of Love. Tania had seemingly joined her captors in their clan war, while Smith's "Hey Joe" marked the arrival of the next generation:

> I'm nobody's millionaire dollar baby, I'm nobody's Patsy,
> I feel so free.

From the decaying urbanscapes epitomized by the rotting Big Apple and the Rust Belt cities, and especially in hippie haven San Francisco, the post-sixties air of revolution hung heavy; Smith was the something new that blew in, wild, from the streets. San Francisco would remain the scene of more high times and inexplicable crimes throughout the decade. Home to historic free speech and antiwar movement gatherings in the sixties, the Bay Area continued to be a place where minds behind movement and invention—whether high tech or slow food—converged. Its consecration as a gay mecca at that time is well known, while the role disco music played in the gay liberation movement, and the role San Francisco played in the development of the punk rock movement, remain less documented. Perhaps these stories go some way toward providing these connections, as might the following words on punk's connection to reggae and hip-hop.

## Punky Reggae Party

English and American rock occasionally demonstrated the empire's relation-ship to contemporary worldwide oppression lyrically, though in the beginning those connections were more allusive than direct. The resonance of reggae to young artists on both sides of the Atlantic was born from its mutual concerns of necessity. *The Harder They Come*, the 1972 film starring reggae singer Jimmy Cliff, and its accompanying soundtrack, was one explanation for reggae on the rise. A popular midnight movie, it tells the story of a down-on-his-luck singer who turns to a life of crime. Cliff, on the other hand, had been making a name for himself as a singer and songwriter by more legitimate means. At the time the film was released he'd already recorded five albums of songs, including recordings of his protest numbers "Viet Nam" and Swamp Dogg's "Synthetic World;" *The Harder They Come* was a definite breakthrough. As for his breth-ren Bob Marley, the Rasta man had made previous forays from the island to England and New York. In 1973 Bob Marley and the Wailers launched a full tour of England and the United States. Eric Clapton's recording of Marley's song "I Shot the Sheriff" brought increased international interest in reggae to the wider rock audience. For Patti Smith, listening to reggae music in the early seventies was tied to her explorations as a blossoming musical artist; she even dabbled with reggae sounds on "Redondo Beach" from her 1975 debut.

In London, DJ Don Letts spun reggae records for a punk crowd at a time when there were few seven-inch punk records to mix. As a baby dread, a fan of reggae, and someone born into a bloodline of sound system operators, Letts brought his musical taste and Rasta style directly into the London punk rock dens. Early adopters of the sound include feminist punk trio the Slits, along with the Clash, who specialized in mixing three-chord punk with reggae's rhythm. Letts introduced the band to Marley, who penned "Punky Reggae Party" as a tribute to the scene's outlaw spirit. "I did not understand the atti-tude or school of thought that dictated, 'If you are black, then you could only listen to black music and be immersed in black culture,'" says Letts.[16] The

Clash toasted reggae artists Dillinger and Leroy Smart in their antiracist tract "White Man in Hammersmith Palais," released as a single in 1978. Johnny Rotten's post–Sex Pistols project, Public Image Limited, cloaked in dub reggae, also debuted that year.

The middle and late seventies were an explosive time in Jamaica's history as the Jamaica Labour Party (JLP) and the People's National Party (PNP) engaged in an open war for power. One night in 1976 Bob Marley and his wife Rita were shot in what appeared to be an assassination attempt. Forced into hiding, during this period he recorded *Exodus*, a moving expression of commitment to struggle widely considered to be his masterwork. In 1978, in recognition of his ability to unite through music, Marley was called home to help quell the disturbances erupting in Kingston that had reached gangland proportions. At the One Love Peace concert, he famously brought the opposing party leaders Michael Manley (of the PNP) and Edward Seaga (of the JLP) to the stage, raising their hands together in unity. At about the same time, an original member of the Wailers, Peter Tosh, was making his name as a solo performer; he took a much more critical view of systems of oppression. His 1976 song "Legalize It" is recognized the world over as a marijuana decriminalization anthem. In 1978 Tosh collaborated with Mick Jagger on a skanking version of the old Temptations hit "Don't Look Back." It was a massive move in increasing reggae's worldwide profile and shed further light on Tosh's cause: equal rights for Rastafari. Tosh appeared at the concert, too, though he expressed his displeasure at the party leaders' position on marijuana. Manley served as prime minister until 1980. The country's factions did not unite, but for a moment it looked as if reggae music, or at least Bob Marley, was close to an answer. It was a moment too brief, perhaps owing to bridge builder Marley's death in early 1981 from metastasized cancer (his refusal of the suggested initial treatment conflicted with his religious code). Tosh remained at odds with his country's government and law enforcement for most of his life. In 1987 following a period of retreat then resurgence, he was killed by bandits in a home invasion.

Tosh and Marley and their relationship to politics and the worldwide music community are but a few brief examples of cultural exchange and the impact of rebel music and how it crossed racial, class, and international boundaries with its messages for the people. Aligned with punk and its shared concerns of need, frustration, and oppression, the late seventies and early eighties popularity of reggae held immense possibilities for its crossover success, as bands like Third World, Black Uhuru, and England's UB40 took reggae on tour of the world.

Reggae remains a potent form of musical expression, though like punk, it political roots are less apparent in the commercially accessible records that have found a worldwide audience for the music since its seventies breakthrough.

By the decade's end, the spirit to unify cultures, nations, and causes appeared to be alive and well and ready to march forward. In yet another positive reflection of cultures clashing, in East Los Angeles, the high school friends who formed Los Lobos released their debut album *Si Se Puede!* as a charity record, benefiting the César Chávez and Dolores Huerta–organized United Farm Workers. The band's combination of traditional *corridos*, Tex-Mex, and originals spoke to a young generation of Chicanos; it also caught the ear of punk rockers in Hollywood. By the decade's end, Eastside and Westside were united in a fight for survival. People on the margins of music and political and social movement were going to need to invent new ways and means to be seen and heard.

# Everybody Say Hey! Ho!
# Let's Go: Punk Rock
# Meets Hip-Hop

T his woman singing in a way that no woman had done before . . . She
really broke through the whole gender divide, just cut through it with
what she was doing. It kind of blew my mind," says Penelope Houston,
leader of San Francisco's punk band the Avengers.

Patti Smith's 1975 album *Horses* offered a new window through
which to see the world that had lost its direction and passion during the
post-sixties apocalyptic shut-down. The counterculture's effectiveness had
decreased with the catastrophic losses of its movement's leaders and with
the end of a generation's youth and idealism. Punk attracted the next generation, who didn't know the limits of rebellion, or if they did, they didn't
care. When nineteen-year-old Houston arrived in San Francisco from Seattle in 1977, she found the zeitgeist to be slightly burned out, undefined,
and ready for reshaping. "I didn't have the feeling San Francisco was the
center of anything," she says. "I didn't think of it as an iconic place and I
didn't feel it being stuck in the hippie era, exactly. I didn't see the hippies having much to do with it." San Francisco's inner-city breakdown has
often been blamed on the wreckage from the mass migration of youth to
the city in the sixties rather than on the economic downturn that was a
national phenomenon of the seventies, fueled by the gas and oil crisis. But
the drug and music culture of the sixties lingered there, in some part owing

to psychedelic bands like Jefferson Airplane, the Grateful Dead, and Sly and the Family Stone's identification with the area, and to their fans, like the persistent Dead Heads who made camp in town when the Dead weren't on the road. San Francisco's pride is its tolerance for all comers, its densely populated seven square miles at one time home to the revolution's legacy. The voluntary and involuntary rejects of society—stoned youth, acid casualties, sex industry workers, war-torn veterans—mixed on the streets with Chinese immigrants and newly arrived gay migrants seeking better lives. The freethinkers, imagineers, and Beat poets—Allen Ginsberg, Gregory Corso, and Bob Kaufman—lived together as one body, a family, seeking solace together on the margins. However, African Americans were increasingly becoming absent from the mix. As in other cities, the largely black population that occupied the city's low-income housing units was in the process of being relocated by urban developers, but promised redevelopment projects were slow to materialize—glacially slow, in the case of San Francisco. In the city's Fillmore district, where neglect and gentrification coexisted, the only vestiges of the neighborhood's jazz heritage was in a defunct ice rink, Winterland, turned into a concert venue.

"I wasn't one of those people writing songs like 'Kill the Hippies,' because it was what happened after the hippies that I found more offensive," says Houston. "I felt like what we were doing was busting open the head of corporate rock. It was a blank slate." The world needed new music, and it needed it now.

Like Phranc's experience with lesbian singer-songwriter Alix Dobkin at the mountain retreat, which threw Phranc into the womb of developing women's music, artist Debora Iyall heard punk rock's siren Patti Smith up in the wilds of Humboldt County. She'd come down from the redwoods to witness Smith's inaugural West Coast appearance, an event that kick-started her own direction as a punk poet, musician, and activist. "That was my first turn on to poetry/music culture in a really big way," she says. It wasn't long after, while attending a Fourth of July celebration in nearby Eureka, California, she says, "I got a fortune cookie from the Indochina Peace Campaign booth. It said, 'Art is your fate, don't debate.' I applied to the San Francisco Art Institute and got accepted for January 1977 and moved to San Francisco, just in time to see Iggy Pop at the Boarding House." It was Iyall's third try at the city by the Bay (her first had been as a thirteen-year-old-runaway). Using birthday money meant to buy cowboy boots, "I left on a Sunday night when my family was watching *The Smothers Brothers*; I knew they wouldn't notice for at least an hour." The second time was of course for the Indian occupation at Alcatraz. Both times, she left racial taunts behind in the agricultural town of Fresno. "I remember one girl named Kim saying to me during a softball game, 'What are you?' I didn't know what she meant. And she was like 'What race or nationality are you?' I was really proud and said, 'I'm Indian,' and she said, 'Well I wouldn't be proud of that.' I remember thinking wow, I've never been talked to like this before. As a kid it was like getting socked in the stomach." On another occasion school authorities sent her home for wearing an Indian-style headband (a popular fashion among girls in the sixties). "They said it was disruptive to wear my hair like that. I thought my God, I don't belong here." She left the agricultural community for a college in freethinking Arcata in Humboldt County—where there remains a law on the books stating that all businesses must be locally owned—in the northernmost reaches of the state. "When I went to the campus I realized that I didn't really want to be institutionalized. I thought I'd just get a job and not actually go to school," she says. She worked for the Indian Action county preschool and for the health services, and soon she was learning about Indian people, hanging out with Indian people, and teaching at the Indian school. But poetry was her first love. "I was much more into poetry than anything else," she says.

Moving to San Francisco, Iyall found more of an opportunity to merge her lifelong interests in poetry and activism within the punk movement. "I did march in the gay parade with the gay American Indians, I was always doing a little bit of both, and hanging with both communities," she says, though she felt like a traitor to her hippie roots when she sang along to "Beat on the brat, beat on the brat, with a baseball bat" by the Ramones. But she couldn't help herself: the band from Queens had a sense of humor that appealed to her, serving as relief from hippie fascism of the California coastal towns which have been known to breed strains of "militant vegans" and "hostile pacifists." "Things have to go under for new things to come up. So the hippies, the bell-bottoms, and patchouli had to go, in order for the punks to come up and do something new." It was a split, and once again, "Which Side Are You On?" had a reason to be sung, even though politically punks and hippies were more similar than not.

## The Fab Mab

"My thing is performance," said Dirk Dirksen, overseer and steward of San Francisco's Mabuhay Gardens, not only the city's nightly showcase for punk rock but the hub of its alternative community. Dirksen was an early supporter of the bands coming out the San Francisco Art Institute like Iyall's group, Romeo Void, as well the mixed-gender space-age theatrical band the Mutants, associated with the art scene's first wave of punk. "I always liked them because they were over the top and pushing the envelope, even though they weren't really a punk band," he says. Another showman whose abilities Dirksen admired was Dead Kennedys' Jello Biafra, with whom he remained a lifelong friend. Biafra is San Francisco punk's most famous ambassador and mouthpiece; he is a critical figure at the intersection of punk and politics who still practices a tireless brand of prankster-styled recorded propaganda through his record label and distribution network, Alternative Tentacles. "He stuck his neck out and had the sense to make the shows all ages, which allowed me to get the Dead Kennedys off the ground, since I wasn't 21 when we started," Biafra told the *San Francisco Weekly*.[1] Dirksen also reserved high praise for Houston. "The Avengers wrote some very, very important youth anthems. I told Allen Ginsberg on the night he came to the Fab Mab to see Jim Carroll that I thought punk rock was today's poetry."

The Avengers took the power chords of punk and the rhetoric of revolution and turned it into a riot of their own. Houston's message could at times be obscured by her medium's fury, as in her "We are the One," a generational anthem dressed in punk clothes and attitude that also intimates action.

> We are not Jesus Christ
> We are not Fascist pigs
> We are not capitalist industrialists
> We are not communists
> We are the one

"When I wrote these lyrics, they were a little bit tongue in cheek—the chorus, the laundry list of things we aren't," says Houston. "But one of the things about it—that we are the one rather than we are the ones—is if you look past the general anthemic part of the song, it implies, we are individuals, but we are also the one thing that can somehow instigate change."

Under pressure before each gig to come up with new material, Houston says she often made up words at the last minute, which is how she came up with "The American in Me." "That one was remarkable to me because a lot of times it took me weeks to get something together and that one was like boom, fully formed. It's not as if I studied post-modernism but I think even at this age, there were all these contradictory aspects to our society and our culture and there are certain aspects of that have progressed—technologically, where we're in a much better place than we were 150 years ago. And then there are other aspects of the culture where technology is just totally wasted . . . It's a joke. I was aware of that at the time."

Houston suggests that through art, music, and staying awake, the conscious citizen impacts and redeems the world gone completely wrong. "I think that when you're a teenager, there's an exposure to society that happens when you go away from your family circle and out into the world, high school and college or work . . . a lot of people get confused and search for answers. I remember feeling outraged, that there was so much shit going on, like the Emperor's New Clothes or something." Instead of nodding her head in agreement to those around her and adhering to the status quo, Houston chose to directly confront the discord. "I felt like it was time to point that out and make a noise about it. I had that righteousness that people have when they're first exposed to corruption and hypocrisy that exists in the world and in government. Things aren't black and white, they're gray . . . You try to sort it out and at that point it felt right to rail and to really be loud and opinionated about it. At the same time, I realized there are a lot of different things that motivate people."

Her song the "The American in Me" captured her rage at the power of the media. She recites the song's opening line:

> It's the American in me that makes me watch the blood,
> running out of the bullet hole in his head.

"Boom. I think I was in kindergarten when Kennedy got shot, and the whole nation was focused on this event—focused on it in a way not again until 9/11 happened—on the visual aspect of the event, without really analyzing it. It seemed to me that television was the unifying thing for middle class America and it had this gigantic power—much greater power than I think it should have. And that's one of the things that song is about, how the media influences us to the extent that it describes us as Americans. It was the perfect kind of music to express the outrage I felt. It all kind of came together that way," she says. In "The American in Me," Houston suggests inquiry as an alternative solution:

> Ask not what you can do for your country
> What's your country been doing to you?

However, despite its intention to rally, motivate, or inform, punk rock as a movement was almost over before it begun. "At the time it was recognized as a horrible thing—especially in Britain—and people agreed, *it's just awful*," says Houston. The music's sensational media portrait, in particular the dog and pony show that was the Sex Pistols on tour, left what messages punk had to offer doomed to the margins. It left the Sex Pistols themselves in shards by the time they reached the end of the tour, at Winterland in San Francisco, where Houston and the Avengers opened the show in January of 1978.

Later in the year, dateline San Francisco would rock the headlines again when two tragedies united its citizens under cover of grief. Broadcasting the nightly news on network TV on November 27, 1978, David Brinkley read, "George Moscone, the mayor of San Francisco, was shot dead in his office in city hall this morning. So was Harvey Milk, a city supervisor, both shot, both murdered. Apparently there was no connection here with the Jim Jones cult which is based in San Francisco." Two civic leaders with vision: district supervisor Milk served as the first openly gay man elected under the mayor, who also stood for tolerance by supporting gay rights. Moscone also stood on the side of poor urban dwellers, many of who supported him in his bid for election. But in the sweep of urban development that left poor folks with few options, some of his constituents fell under the sway of cult leader Jones who promised them a better life in the rainbow community they established in jungle of the Guyana republic. Instead they met their deaths there. Given that the tragedies were just nine days apart, the assassinations were grief poured on top of a city already in strife.

At the candlelight march held for the slain officials , Joan Baez sang "Swing Low, Sweet Chariot" the old spiritual, credited to Wallis Willis, a Mississippi Choctaw and former slave, while somewhere else in town, a jukebox played

Sylvester's "You Make Me Feel (Mighty Real)." Six months later came the sentencing of former city supervisor and SFPD officer Dan White: Milk and Moscone's shooter got off with manslaughter behind the Twinkie Defense, so named because he claimed that junk food had warped his mind. This was the spark it took to light the White Night Riot, a battle between the gay community and a police force who acted in protection and service of one of its own.

Biafra and his band memorialized the White Night Riots on the cover of their album *Fresh Fruit for Rotting Vegetables*, which features the biting satire of sing-alongs "Kill the Poor," "Let's Lynch the Landlord," and "California Uber Alles." Far from the anti-sixties sentiment for which punk was known, the music had much in common with the abrasive topical style of Phil Ochs and the 1965 Fugs song "Kill For Peace," to name but two of many dark-humored specialists. However, the satire of punk was often lost on the growing audience for the music's more hardcore side.

## Take Off Your Swastika

Upon leaving San Francisco to return to Los Angeles in 1978, Phranc headed straight to the clubs where the punk rockers met. No longer feeling at home in her lesbian circle of friends, "I wanted punk rock. I started going out to shows. I would put on a little suit and tie and I would go there and try to look so cool though I didn't know a soul." Standing on the street by herself at an Avengers show, she was spotted by a kindred spirit, Edward Stapleton. "He asked me, do you play anything?' And I'm like 'Yea.' He said, 'Good. The band's Nervous Gender, you'd be perfect.'" From playing keyboards in that band she moved on to guitar in Catholic Discipline and eventually landed in Castration Squad. But Phranc's honeymoon period with the early wave of hardcore punks didn't last long; the elements that had initially attracted her to it were diminishing. Though punk wasn't necessarily unfriendly to the gay community, it wasn't necessarily friendly, especially in US hardcore punk strongholds like Southern California, Texas, and DC.

Inspired by the gay pride movement in England, Tom Robinson and his band enjoyed success within the punk milieu with the anthem "(Sing if You're) Glad to Be Gay" while Sex Pistols contemporaries the Buzzcocks were known for non-gender-specific songs that confronted the isolation of its main writer, Pete Shelley. But punk in general operated on somewhat of a "don't ask, don't tell" principle; outpunk was still a decade away.

"Not only did the fashions change but the politics changed," explains Phranc. Where there had been a truth and lightness to the scene—"really fun and really angry; but kind of mock angry"—the mood was now dark. "A lot of makeup, a lot of drugs, a lot of vodka poured into Pepsi cans drunk with a straw so it wouldn't ruin your lipstick." The aggression and negativity of the L.A. punk scene was growing a reputation, not just for the militaristic frat boy types who'd discovered it, but for the scene's macabre and gothic take on the music. Penelope Spheeris documented the times with a keen eye in her film *The Decline of Western Civilization*

"People were wearing the swastikas, which they hadn't been up to that time—because I'm Jewish, I woulda noticed—and it pissed me off," says Phranc. "So I wrote a song called 'Take Off Your Swastika.'" It was Phranc's first topical song and personal reaction to the internationally recognized symbol of hatred that had been adopted as a logo among a certain contingent within the punk scene. The song was addressed directly to them:

> Take off your swastika, it's making me angry
> Take off your swastika, it really nauseates me
> You say, Phranc it's just a symbol, it's just an emblem, it's just a righteous declaration
> But it means a little more to me
> Because I'm a Jewish lesbian, you see
> Because Fascism isn't anarchy . . .

"Up till then I'd been playing electric guitar with Catholic Discipline and Castration Squad and synthesizer with Nervous Gender. So for me to go back and pick up the acoustic guitar again . . . nobody [in punk] was playing acoustic at that time. The reason I did it was because I really wanted the words to be heard. And instead of Dorothy Baker's Coffeehouse, I played it at punk rock clubs."

At about the same time as Phranc's "Take Off Your Swastika," Dead Kennedys came out with "Nazi Punks Fuck Off," a fast and furious diatribe partly inspired by punk's abuse of the circle-A symbol for anarchy. "If you've come to fight, get out of here . . . When you ape the cops it ain't anarchy," wrote Dead Kennedys leader Jello Biafra. "The really amazing thing is people really responded and really listened," says Phranc of her own anti-swastika song. "I remember playing at the Whiskey and seeing a couple of guys taking the swastika off. Not everybody loved it. People would still yell and I'd get heckled and stuff but on the whole it was pretty great," she says.

With the help of a local punk promoter, Phranc put together Folk Hoot Night at the Whiskey, inviting the punk crowd to join her for a night of sing-along favorites on acoustic guitars. The Circle Jerks supplied "He's Got the Whole World in His Hands"; John Doe and Exene Cervenka of X performed "Jackson." "I really wanted my punk rock friends to go acoustic for the night so you could hear everybody. That was the start of my solo folk career. It was also me coming out on stage saying I was Jewish," she says. "I'd been out as a lesbian so I thought why not announce that I'm Jewish too and why not say it all at once and in a way that people could hear it and get it and also know that I have a sense of humor? So since that time I've introduced myself as 'Phranc with a ph and hard c, your basic average all-American Jewish lesbian folksinger.'"

Not all of Phranc's audiences were gracious in their reception of her new persona. "Some of them would give me the finger and yell. Imagine you've got this mosh pit and then you have this dyke up there with an acoustic guitar. There was always someone who wanted to raise some hell and somebody next to them who told them to shut up. I have to say of all my experiences I've had performing, I'd still say 99 percent of them are positive," though she's had her moments. She's fended off coins and burning objects thrown at the sound hole of her guitar. On another night, "instead of singing along to the crowd's part . . . about two thousand people sang, 'f— you.'" But she's never left the stage until she's finished her set. "You cannot make me leave. I am going to do what I'm going to do."

## Rapper's Delight

Michael Franti loved two things: music and basketball. When he wasn't playing one, he was listening to the other, late at night, scanning the frequencies on the dial until he hit a sound he liked. In the late seventies and early eighties the most popular radio station in Sacramento, California, flowed with the smooth sounds of Earth, Wind and Fire and the Commodores, some funkier sides by the Gap Band and Parliament, and the classic grooves of Marvin

Gaye, who was making a comeback at the time. "And then they started to play Sugarhill Gang and Grandmaster Flash and the Furious Five. It was the beginning of rap music," says Franti.

As the initial glow and freshness of punk was starting to dim, another new sound was coming on strong. From out of the parks and into the streets of New York City, rap had announced its existence on the national radar with the success of the Sugarhill Gang's "Rapper's Delight."

> I said a hip hop the hippie the hippie to the hip hip hop
> and you don't stop

Released as a single in 1979, the record was the brainchild of Sugarhill Records' Sylvia Robinson, a musician with a personal history of pioneering. As part of the duo Mickey and Sylvia, she'd sung the 1957 hit "Love Is Strange," penned by the rock 'n' roll originator Bo Diddley. In 1973 Robinson recorded "Pillow Talk," releasing it under the name Sylvia; the song's breathy, orgasmic vocal and orchestrated beat track beat Donna Summer and Giorgio Moroder to the disco show. Now at the birth of rap, the visionary Robinson gathered a group of crack studio players and put three rappers, Master Gee, Wonder Mike, and Big Bank Hank, up front. It was a formula that capitalized on the block-party and public-park phenomenon that was called rap—a combination of DJs playing records, cleverly rhyming on mics, and sometimes break dancing to one ubiquitous turntable break, the bass line of Chic's "Good Times." Chic's Nile Rodgers says he attended "a hip-hop, that's what it was called then," at a high school in Queens with Deborah Harry and Chris Stein of the new wave group Blondie. "All they played was one song, the breakdown to 'Good Times' . . . I didn't know it was going to become a big-time phenomenon," he says. He recalled watching the break dancing in school yards, gymnasiums, and anyplace kids could gather, all of them working out to primarily this one song: "Good Times." When it came time for Englewood, New Jersey's Sugarhill Gang to record, it was only natural they would borrow the sound of the best break beat in town, its isolated thumping bass part virtually incomparable, its screeching string section filling in just fine for turntable scratching. As Rodgers tells it, it wasn't till he heard the "Good Times" track in a disco with the rappers' vocal take on top of it that he made the necessary moves to have his name added to the copyright. But just as Rodgers had wrested his deep hidden meaning from an old Al Jolson song for "Good Times," the inspiration for "Rapper's Delight" wasn't quite that well disguised. Sugarhill's "I'm imp the gimp, the ladies' pimp, the women fight for my delight" sounds an awful lot like "Yes, I'm hemp the demp the women's pimp, women fight for my delight" from "Rap's Poem" by H. Rap Brown. The one-time Student Nonviolent Coordinating Committee (SNCC) leader and Black Panther was nicknamed Rap in the sixties for his verbal skills and his way with the rhyming put-downs beginning with "your mama." The practice, known as the dozens (and its lighter version, signifying) are forms of street battle, wars that are fought and won with words. Blues poet Langston Hughes; jazz poets Gil Scott-Heron, the Watts Prophets and the Last Poets; and even Dolemite, the character made popular by comedian Rudy Ray Moore, had also paved the road that led to the creation of hip-hop's voice, while funk's fat rhythm tracks provided the base for rap's greatest hits. The records were spun on Jamaican-style sound systems by DJs Kool Herc, Afrika Bambaataa, and Grandmaster Flash—the DJ who turned mixing, cutting and scratching records into art.

Like other kids his age, Michael Franti thought he'd try his hand at it. "I'd record those radio shows and memorize the lyrics." Franti's interest in the rhythm and rhyme of rap, still very much in its early-eighties infancy, had him tuning into college radio, in its free-form, high water days; it was one of the few places a wider spectrum of rap was aired. Late one night he found KDVS, broadcasting from the University of California at Davis, which played rap and more. "Right after that there was a reggae show and in the morning there was a punk rock show," says Franti. "Afternoon was a world music show. When I went to the University of San Francisco, my dorm room was above KUSF and I was always going down there, got to know the DJs—sit in, listen in—and heard about all these great shows coming to town and got to check them out. I was equally inspired by the Clash as I was by the Sugarhill Gang and Earth, Wind and Fire," he says, though it would be a few more years before he would make his own kind of music.

## NVR SAY NVR

At first, Debora Iyall and Romeo Void played edgy and uptight musical shapes as a kind of accompaniment to Iyall's poetry. A haunting saxophone sound underscored the singer's complex and abstract themes, it was a study in contrasts and a reflection of the oppression she felt as a queen-sized woman and a Native. Iyall's friend and sometime sound engineer Louie Beeson believed it was Iyall's lack of inhibition and ability to be exactly who she was that drew people toward her band. "They weren't really compromising. Having this big woman there, it was like yea, these guys are for real. It's not a sham. I think that had a lot of appeal." Gay audiences were among the first to embrace Romeo Void, who caught their first break when a twelve-inch dance mix of the song "Never Say Never" became a club hit. "So few bands that had female singers had . . . singers that were trying to be more open in a sensuous way," says DJ Alan Robinson, one of the first to play the record at the I-Beam, a trendsetting rock club that alternated nights from gay to new wave. "Debora was doing that, and it was a time when the music was changing a bit. As one of the first post-punk bands, the lyrics were a little more complex and developed, a little more abstract."

"Never Say Never," a song that rolled through waves of Iyall's free verse, punctuated by the refrain, "I might like you better if we slept together," was conceived around the same time that the HIV/AIDS virus was making news for the first time. The epidemic hit San Francisco particularly hard, though the government was slow to act, its nonresponse serving as a call for activists to organize. Though gains had been made in the area of gay rights and women's rights, both groups remained on the move in the eighties and Iyall's music soundtracked the concerns. Her 1984 hit "A Girl in Trouble" is a female-positive song that addresses women's vulnerability on the street. The issue had been slowly making its way out of the shadows since the Take Back the Night marches that took place in the late seventies. Holly Near sang at the first Take Back the Night march in San Francisco, which focused on speaking out against pornography with the intent to make the streets safe for all women.

"Take back the night, and make it safe for everyone to use," sang Near in her best folky vibrato. In 1984, Iyall hipped up the message and the delivery when she put on her tough girl voice and sang,

> There's a way to walk that says 'Stay Away!'
> And a time to go 'round the long way

Through their liaison with San Francisco label 415 Records, Romeo Void would come to record and be distributed by Columbia Records; the deal gave them exposure, but there was always a battle between the artist and corporate entity over the intensity of the content—and Iyall's larger silhouette. The issues caused strife within the band, and they eventually broke up under the pressure of creative direction and differences. But Iyall had made a contribution to the fiery contemporary discussion on gender and positing the potential of a Native woman as rock star. Phranc was about to attempt the same for the butch lesbian.

Phranc on voice, guitar, and harmonica, recorded her debut album, *Folksinger*, in a small studio in Venice, California. The album included her topical songs, which covered everything from the controversial to now-forgotten slices of popular culture: "Female Mud Wrestling," took on a popular eighties draw at bars and nightclubs, and Phranc declared

> it's stupid, it's embarrassing
> I don't like female mud wrestling

It was simple, direct, visionary social commentary. Though it took another twenty years, eventually this lowlight in modern woman's evolution was called out by third-wave feminist Ariel Levy for what it was: raunch culture that counteracted gains made by women during feminism's second wave. Phranc's "Noguchi" was similarly prescient. It concerns L.A.'s infamous coroner Thomas Noguchi, whose celebrity autopsies and medical examination of Sen. Robert F. Kennedy turned him into something of a minor celebrity himself in the sixties and seventies—well before our age of 24/7 celebrity channel death intrigue.

Phranc's debut album also included the 1964 Bob Dylan song "The Lonesome Death of Hattie Carroll." The song is a true story based on the case of black domestic worker Hattie Carroll, who died as a consequence of a beating by a man of privilege—William Zantzinger—his crime left unpunished. "I was so moved that a song could give me all the information that you could read in a newspaper or watch in a TV show—that a song could deliver all that and impact me so powerfully, and that I could be moved by that experience," she says. "I thought, wow! I can still sing that song today because racism never totally goes away. That song taught me the power of telling a story with a song."

Over the years Phranc became more and more interested in folk's storytelling aspects. "A song can preserve time and memory and history in a way that words or a picture alone can't do; a song can capture it all. It's like nothing else. I'm still very dedicated, to trying to tell the story, do a better job, listen to how other people have told stories, and to really go back and listen to all the old music, like the Harry Smith Anthology," she says, referring to the *Anthology of American Folk Music*. Alternately known as the "Harry Smith Box" after its compiler, the six-volume set doesn't discriminate in its inclusion of music considered "black" or "white." The collection has served as inspiration to listeners and players since its release in 1952; its influence on the original folk revival of the early sixties is irrefutable, just as it is on twenty-first century new folk. A CD reissue of the set in 1997 remains a definitive resource of near-magical resonance to generations of musicians and fans of traditional American music. "It's so interesting that there's a resurgence and new fascination with that collection of music. Why do people keep going back to it? Because it's history in a song." Like any good folker, Phranc reaches back for source material and was happy to discover the old English ballad "The Handsome Cabin Boy," about a female shipmate in male clothing.

Phranc was under recording contract to Island in the eighties. A record label generally known to be forward-thinking back when it signed Bob Marley, the company was flummoxed when it came to marketing Phranc, with her unique appearance crossed with her songbird's voice, even though gender-twisting artists like Boy George and the Eurythmics had found a home on the record charts. For her album titled *I Enjoy Being a Girl*, Island tried a girly, pink-powder-puff promotional campaign. That didn't jibe so well with its leading song, "Bloodbath," Phranc's song on apartheid in South Africa.

> Reagan, Thatcher, Bota, I'm white like them
> and it makes me ashamed of the color of my skin.

The video of the song featured Phranc and a paintbrush, whitewashing everything that stood in her path; it was relegated to airing in the wee hours and specialty programs, as was the custom with videos by new and challenging artists. The music television network MTV had its own personal relationship to apartheid: from its founding as a music channel in 1981 until 1983, black faces were an anomaly in the rotation of videos. It wasn't until Rick James, who was having a mega-crossover hit with "Super Freak," spoke out and Michael Jackson exerted pressure that the channel integrated.

## I Ain't Gonna Play Sun City

There was a time in the eighties when one had cause to wonder whether the civil rights movement had ever happened. A congressional bill to declare a national holiday in remembrance of Dr. King got rolling after Stevie Wonder came out with the song "Happy Birthday" and organized a rally and citizen's campaign to support it. The bill was opposed by Sen. Jesse Helms of North Carolina and Sen. John McCain of Arizona but passed through Congress by overwhelming majority in 1983 (it took until 2000 for all fifty states to observe it). By mid-decade, song was also playing an important role in the worldwide antiapartheid movement, as it had since the earliest days of struggle in Soweto. In 1980, Peter Gabriel dedicated "Biko" to the story of anti-apartheid hero Stephen Biko, the 1960s student organizer who founded the Black Consciousness Movement and is credited with coining the slogan, "Black is beautiful." Following the Soweto uprising of 1976, law enforcement had begun to target Biko more aggressively; eventually he died of massive injuries to the head while in police custody. In 1984, "Free Nelson Mandela" by the Special AKA, formed from the ska band the Specials, was an West African/highlife music–influenced dance club hit. And the heavy MTV rotation of the 1985 recording "(I Ain't Gonna Play) Sun City," an all-star single and album organized by Steven Van Zandt, was successful at raising awareness and funds for antiapartheid causes. Rappers and reggae artists along with Gil Scott-Heron, Jimmy Cliff, Eddie Kendricks and David Ruffin of the Temptations, Ron Wood and Keith Richards of the Rolling Stones, and Bruce Springsteen all raised voices and joined hands for "Sun City" in a "We are the World"–style salute, another celebrity charity recording that year with an emphasis on Africa. Focusing attention on Ethiopia— where famine following a series of insurgencies and a drought had ravaged the land—in the summer of 1985, Irish musician Sir Bob Geldof presented the Live Aid concert. The international telethon broadcast from the United States and the United Kingdom continued a tradition of massive music events in response to international emergency, as first delivered by George Harrison's Concert for Bangladesh in the seventies. Following Live Aid, there would be Farm Aid for US farmers, Live 8 to support the reduction of third world poverty, and Live Earth to increase awareness of climate change. The post 9/11 Concert for New York City and the post-Katrina effort Concert for Hurricane Relief gathered donations with the help of players from all types of music. Using the NBC, MSNBC, and CNBC simulcast of the event benefiting the Red Cross as a platform, Kanye West spoke to what some people were thinking but were afraid to say following the delayed federal response to the disaster in New Orleans in 2005: "George Bush doesn't care about black people." West suggested there was a system in place, designed "to help the poor, the black people, the less well off, as slow as possible."[2] Years after the damage sustained from the hurricane and subsequent broken levees and flooding, New Orleans, a city with a unique musical and cultural heritage, still struggles to rebuild. Detroit and Memphis, cities foundational to America's musical heritage, exist in similar states of neglect.

## Song Reportage in the New Era of Media

In addition to the failure of urban renewal programs and continuing dissolution of social welfare programs, by the early eighties, the Federal Communication Commission regulations established in the forties to preserve diversity and prevent monopolies were in the process of being dismantled with the support of the Reagan Administration. Independently owned and operated radio stations were succumbing as a new era of radio, corporately owned and programmed by consultants, took over. The new trend toward lack of diversity and dissenting opinion laid the groundwork for the contemporary media culture. Market-driven concerns trumped artistic and intellectual impulses on-air, and free-form radio, the type that had contributed to the making of a counterculture, was becoming completely marginalized as alternative media organizations contracted in the immediate post-punk era. "There was no indie radio, there was college radio. That's the only place anyone got played," says Phranc. "Mainstream radio would have nothing to do with anybody who had independent thinking."

College radio stations all over the country, like the ones Michael Franti enjoyed in Northern California, opened their mics to voices like Phranc, Dead Kennedys, Debora Iyall, and Penelope Houston. Regional scenes, away from the urban centers, sprouted bands, and tour routes were mapped out along the college radio network. From KRS-One to the Talking Heads, music makers of the early eighties got their first spins on college radio. All across the country, stations turned over their airwaves to all new forms of noncommercial music, often with strong political messages, that would otherwise have no outlet to be heard. It wasn't unusual to hear contemporary music from African artists like Nigeria's Fela Kuti and King Sunny Ade, British punk from England's first wave like the Slits and the Clash, heavy dub reggae from Jamaica, and home-grown rock 'n' soul from young America, from its small towns to its urban housing projects, come together on college radio.

Today, in the wake of fading broadcast outlets, listeners can still turn to topical songs for news of the era, just as they had once done in the early sixties. Even without a traditional broadcast platform, Phranc's songs had much to say about the times and she continues to document unsung stories in songs. She's advocated for the handicapped ("Handicapped Parking"); she's written about the natural process of aging and death and the expected and unexpected ways in which it can claim our loved ones. She's written about friends taken by the AIDS pandemic and about her grandmothers. She also wrote "Gary," an anti-death-penalty song concerning the imprisonment of the man who killed her brother in 1991. Among her twenty-first century topical songs are "Condoleeza" and "Hillary's Eyebrows," pleas to Secretaries of State Rice and Clinton to adopt policies that work for everyone. In 2008 Phranc received an artist's grant from the City of Los Angeles' Department of Cul-tural Affairs to write songs about her hometown. The titles of those works are for the most part self-explanatory: "Griffith Park Pony," "Growing Old in L.A.," and "Manchester Boulevard" which spans the distance from the beach to South Los Angeles. "L.A. is not all palm trees and picture postcards . . . These songs about Los Angeles, the city I grew up in, are my kind of nostalgic reflections of what's here . . . like people talking on cell phones you can't see. That'll be history someday too."

## Revolution Girl Style Now!

Phranc had survived her Los Angeles youth and went on to inspire the new generation of gay, lesbian, and third-wave feminist musicians involved in grassroots political movements. Queercore and Riot Grrrl both challenged the male-dominated hardcore punk rock scene that bred a particular style of bully—the type Phranc and Jello Biafra had told to take off their swastikas.

In the late eighties and early nineties, the clash of the active fanzine scene and punk music resulted in the launch of two radical movements—Queercore and Riot Grrrl—as responses from members of communities who felt unserved and unheard. Queercore bands like Pansy Division from San Francisco wrote from the perspective of men who could not identity with a dominant gay culture that often encourages conformity. Picking up the thread where Debora Iyall's "Girl in Trouble" left off, Evergreen State College students Kathleen Hanna, Tobi Vail, and Kathi Wilcox of Olympia, Washington, started a fanzine, *Bikini Kill*. Taking inspiration from Queercore's zines and films, Lori Twersky's 1980s rock zine *Bitch*, and their own experiences within an oppressive punk rock culture they started Bikini Kill the band, titling their demo cassette *Revolution Girl Style Now!* Molly Neuman and Allison Wolfe also grew the Northwest culture of zines (theirs was *Girl Germs*), into a band: Bratmobile. Donna Dresch, creator of the fanzine *Chainsaw* and the record label of the same name, was a cocreator of queercore while also maintaining close ties to the DIY punk and indie underground and Riot Grrrl nations. Her band Team Dresch, including Kaia Wilson, Jody Bleyle, and Marci Martinez, recorded "Uncle Phranc" as a tribute.

Uncovering taboo and underreported subjects like rape, sexual abuse, and a woman's right to choose, the Riot Grrrl movement was directly tied to the feminist agenda and espoused radical, revolutionary tactics for change rather than assimilation. "Revolution girl-style now!" was among the movement's slogans, as was the self-defense technique "eyes, knees, groin, throat." The Riot Grrrl bands' arrivals on the punk scene were not necessarily greeted with open arms. "It was pretty crazy back then," explains Kathleen Hanna.[3] "There was a lot of violence and this thing of constantly being told to take off our tops." She remembers having chains thrown at her head and being pulled off stage by her ankles; crew members were assaulted and riots were known to break out at their shows. Riot Grrrl didn't stop at women's rights; fighting against racism and corporations and for environmental protection all fell into riot grrrl's purview as the women involved sowed the seeds of change in the early part of the twenty-first century. Though Kathleen Hanna resisted a leadership role in the movement, she remains actively involved in music for change. Hanna is married to Adam Horovitz of the Beastie Boys—the pioneering three-piece hip-hop group at one time accused of sexism and racial appropriation. Eventually they became better known for their human rights activism, particularly the Tibetan Freedom Concert series launched in San Francisco in 1996 with a bill that featured them with Richie Havens, and Yoko Ono. "The feminist thing is still very, very important," says Ono. "Most people think, 'That's over isn't it?' Of course it's not over!" She is especially happy with the artists who she believes carry on the work that she and Lennon began in 1969. "I really appreciate every one of them," she says, and the feeling is mutual. Alternative musicians including LeTigre (featuring Kathleen Hanna), Antony Heggarty, and Peaches paid tribute on the album *Yes, I'm a Witch*, a remix album of Ono songs. The early Riot Grrrls held up Ono, as well as Phranc, as inspirers to their movement. As a person with a strong identity, Phranc served as a model to the Queercore and Riot Grrrl contingents, though she is not a joiner nor committed to any movement. In 1995, she collaborated with Donna Dresch, Kaia Wilson, and Tobi Vail on an EP titled *Goofyfoot*, released by the Olympia Washington indie-rock label Kill Rock Stars. Five songs in all, it's infused with Phranc's trademark humor: clever covers of "Mrs. Brown You've Got a Lovely Daughter" and "Ode to Billy Joe" meet originals "Bull Dagger Swagger," "Surfer Dyke Pal," and "Goofyfoot," the latter two titles reflecting her passion for surfing Southern California beaches.

Phranc remains very committed to declaring her average all-American Jewish lesbian identity. "I don't say it because it's the biggest part of me or the smallest part of me, it's just one part of who I am. I think that everybody should be able to grow up and be who they are. What has come from that for me—no matter how big a stage, how big a people or how little people I'm playing to—I've always gotten some kind of reaction that has affirmed that is what I'm supposed to be doing. One of my biggest commitments is to keep performing and be of service to the young queer community—it's gone beyond queer now—there are so many challenges." Phranc says that while in many ways she retains a part of the girl from Mar Vista who came out in the seventies, at the same time, "my politics have evolved with my community." Kathleen Hanna suggests that conditions for musicians in the underground punk scene have changed for the better since Queercore and Riot Grrrls, but there is still room to grow. "There's a lot more diversity at shows in general," she says. As a member of the punk-dance band Le Tigre, she no longer encounters the kind of aggression she faced on the hardcore punk scene. As a trans activist, she works to create awareness about a growing segment of the gay, bisexual, lesbian, and transgender community, a large segment of who identify as transsexual. She is also inspired by the new generation of girls making music, who she meets through her work with the Willie Mae Rock Camp for girls, a training ground for the female musicians of the future.

Phranc is often invited to speak on gender identity on college campuses. "People say, 'There's so many role models . . . everyone's out now . . . gay liberation . . . now you can marry . . . Talk to anybody that's coming out right now, they feel exactly the way as I felt when I came out. You still feel very much alone. It's very important for me to be out there. . . . . You never know who's going to hear it."

She believes in the importance of performing in front of a live audience whenever possible. "People are separated by machinery and now it's happening in music. There's no human interaction. Pretty soon you won't be able to pick up a piece of music and look at an image that goes with it," she says. "Right now you pick a song from iTunes, you don't even have to pick all of them you can just pick one. So you don't listen to a whole collection of music by one person—just this much of it—you might not get the whole story. It's disconnecting people from humanity. That's why I love playing folk festivals. That's why I love playing a folk club. It's all that interacting with an audience."

Phranc was asked to perform "Married in London," by Janis Ian, at a friend's wedding. She taught herself the song that grew from Ian's own anger and frustration at the controversies regarding same sex partnership rights in the United States.

"I normally don't get up on a soapbox about things, but I was really furious," says Ian of her initial inspiration for the song. "First I had to watch the Reagan and Bush years co-opt my country and turn it into a place that is not the place my grandparents wanted to come to, and then I was watching as my country turned its back on me and those like me, on every level—politically, socially, economically." It wasn't so much a wedding that Ian wanted as much as she wanted the automatic transfer of her social security and songwriting royalties to her partner in the event of illness or death. "She has no standing. I couldn't even leave it to her children. I was furious." Responding to a suggestion that she channel her anger into song, Ian began to write. "I was writing a song that was really angry and then about halfway through I looked at it and said, 'This is terrible . . . no wonder people don't write angry songs anymore.' It's so rare to hear anything on the level of 'I Ain't Marchin' Anymore,' she says, conjuring the memory of Phil Ochs and his knack for satirically twisting things. "I thought, 'I need to laugh at this,' and so I started to write it, and it was funny." But she found her next challenge was explaining the gravity of the argument to a straight audience, "without scaring them . . . Because that's the trick with something like the gay rights issue. How do you present it without excluding anyone?"

Phranc's inspirer Alix Dobkin was a lesbian separatist. "And when I came out, I was a lesbian separatist too," says Phranc. "I didn't even talk to straight women let alone men." But when she got into punk rock, "I was going against every single thing I was taught and I believed. I loved these boys in San Francisco and thought, 'What's going on . . . I'm a lesbian separatist, and I'm feeling one way and starting to act another.' I moved to a different world so quickly, into the punk rock world. My two worlds collided . . . There were many internal conflicts but what you see is what I am now. I'm a little bit of everything: an out dyke and very committed to saying I'm out as a lesbian every single time I get on stage because I don't know who's going to be in the audience.

"I have a few separatist friends left, who still have a very separatist perspective," she says. "I don't anymore. I've changed my way of thinking to be more inclusive because I always like to be included. That feeling of being on the outside, that despairing feeling of no one is ever gonna get me, no one is ever going to love me, I'm always going to be out here alone, is so painful," she says. Gesturing toward the center of her kitchen in the house she shares with her partner, Lisa, and their two children, "I have love all around me now."

"I am very fortunate that I lived through coming out. If I hadn't found that women's center, if I hadn't read on the back of *The Lesbian Tide* magazine that there was this lesbian feminist drop-in rap on Hill Street and ridden my bike there and found those women, I don't know if I would still be here today."

## The Future Is Now

Punk rock and its men and women, gay and straight, white, red, and brown, grew from a marginalized and maligned society to big business on the world stage. For better or worse, Bono of U2—the rock 'n' roll face for the cause to drop the third world debt—was indoctrinated in punk's do-it-yourself teachings, as was fellow Irishman Bob Geldof, who led the way in matters of musical relief for Africa with Live Aid. Punk rock's reject kids are the organizers of the imperiled world, rallying for hurricane and earthquake relief using Geldof's template for Aid concerts. And yet, as a culture, punk has largely been reduced to a fashion statement—the skinny jeans and leather jackets, spiked jewelry and skull-and-crossbones accessories. These are but superficial, convenient, and very un-punk accoutrements to the music's "make your own carnival" esthetic. Occasionally, punk's root impulses—challenging status quo, wresting power from its abusers and putting it back into the hands of the people—still emerges from the underground. Jello Biafra continues to work as an artist and advocate for counterculture ideas; his record label Alternative Tentacles remains in business after thirty years despite him being charged with obscenity in a trumped-up trial over album artwork. Following a period of persecution by the Parents Resource Music Center, a government committee established primarily to censor music, Biafra has managed to prevail as a free speech advocate, cultural commentator, occasional candidate for public office, and distributor of recorded works from front-burner activists Noam Chomsky, Angela Davis, and Mumia Abu-Jamal, among others.

Green Day, steeped in radical punk philosophy since they were teenage performers at the Berkeley punk collective Gilman Street Project, developed a mass youth audience in the early nineties, when fans of punk-inspired alternative music were grieving the loss of Nirvana's Kurt Cobain. In 1994, Green Day invited queercore band Pansy Division on tour with them. The 2004 Green Day album *American Idiot* was a concept piece, one of few rock albums to critique the dumbing-down of America and foreign and domestic policy of the Bush Jr. administration; Riot Grrrl Kathleen Hanna sat in on the album as guest vocalist on "Letterbomb." A musical based on the album made its way from the Berkeley Repertory Theater to the Broadway stage in 2009.

Both Bono and Green Day have pointed to England's outspoken punk band the Clash as inspirational, though in 2008, it was a young Sri Lankan woman by the name of Maya Arulpragasam who furthered the legacy of punk and Clashman Joe Strummer and his hero Woody Guthrie, creating a controversy while doing so. Under the name M.I.A., Arulpragasam released a song, "Paper Planes," that borrows a sampled loop from the Clash song "Straight to Hell" and features the sound of gunshots and the percussive ka-ching of a cash register. Delivered in Arulpragasam's lazy and lyrical style, the song's message is not apparent on first listen or two, but then misapprehensions are not unheard of in rock—and points have been known to get lost when lyrics and melody are unified in protest. Perhaps most famously, "Born in the U.S.A.," Bruce Springsteen's story of a discarded veteran, was adopted by right-wingers as a patriotic anthem. The tendency to hear style more than lyrics may partly explain why "Paper Planes," a send-up of stereotypes leveled at immigrants, was wrongly perceived: there is just not that much familiarity or empathy for the subject at hand, which can be enough motivation in itself for an artist to write a song in the first place. Confusing matters further is the fact that Arulpragasam hails from London, though she was raised partly in Sri Lanka and in India, by activist parents associated with the fight to liberate the Tamil region of their native country. Today Arulpragasam makes her home in Brooklyn; her story is exemplary of a refugee from a war-torn country, looking for a home. Who better than she to speak to the concerns of immigrants, a marginalized group of citizens inhabiting cities across the globe? Paul Robeson, Woody Guthrie, and Pete Seeger were branded communist sympathizers and put out of work when they sang songs for forgotten people from other lands. Bob Dylan sang of the injustices met by the poor and black, then was criticized when he changed direction. Yes, this business of protest music has been known to be a hassle, so the fact that "Paper Planes" was such a phenomenon contributes to its intrigue. It also found purpose in the mainstream: it was featured in the montage sequence of *Slumdog Millionaire*, a Bollywood-inspired phenomenon that introduced a portion of the mass American audience to the multidimensionality of a developing nation, as well as to the music indigenous to the subcontinent.

Arulpragasam dubs her song a satire, a tongue-in-cheek protest like "Kill for Peace" or "Kill the Poor," though it's also an empowerment anthem as racial stereotypes get reclaimed and are put into service as song lyrics. "It's about people driving cabs all day and living in a shitty apartment and appearing really threatening to society. But not being so," she said.[4] "Because, by the time you've finished working a 20-hour shift, you're so tired you [just] want to get home to the family. I don't think immigrants are that threatening to society at all. They're just happy they've survived some war somewhere." As for the gunshots and cash register ring: "You can either apply it on a street level and go, oh, you're talking about somebody robbing you and saying I'm going to take your money. But, really, it could be a much bigger idea: someone's selling you guns and making money. Selling weapons and the companies that manufacture guns—that's probably the biggest moneymaker in the world."

The British band the Clash, and Joe Strummer in particular, were known the world over for covering the inhumanity of empire building in song. A clash between the police and the youth at the annual Nottinghill Carnival, an annual Caribbean community cultural event, inspired the band's first single. Though "White Riot" would be misunderstood as a white supremacy anthem, that was hardly the story. Clashmen Strummer and Paul Simonon had participated in the riot, tossing a brick for the Jamaican side; their song was an attempt to rouse white and black youth off the dole and into action. The band grappled with its country's complicated history of imperialism and modern-day racism, and though their efforts could be perceived as ham-fisted at times, they were never without passion. The band used the album *Sandinista!* to increase awareness of the battle in Nicaragua, in which the dominant Sandinista National Liberation Front was engaged in what would become a long battle with US-supported counterrevolutionaries. The album's de facto title song, "Washington Bullets," took aim at worldwide bloodshed in the name of peace and freedom, while Strummer called out to his brother in resistance song, "Remember Victor Jara in the Santiago stadium."

It's important to note that the Clash as individuals did not live a life that was beyond reproach; like the MC5, they were a rock band and susceptible to the usual infighting aided by substance abuse that often contributes to perfectly good bands prematurely disbanding.

By opening her song with four bars of "Straight to Hell," Arulpragasam knew what she was doing: it's one of Strummer's most celebrated lyrics, its verses devoted to the plight of the dispossessed. Not exactly sung (perhaps inspired by his friend, poet Allen Ginsberg, who sat in on the recording sessions for the album, *Combat Rock*), "Straight to Hell" is a song to the outsider. It signifies where she stands in society, whether cast-off north of England or in Vietnam. "It could be anywhere . . . any hemisphere . . . no man's land and there ain't no asylum here," sang Strummer. Arulpragasam's additional touch, a child's chorus, borrows from another important anthem: James Brown's

"Say It Loud (I'm Black and I'm Proud)." The depth of that song's impact had once catapulted Brown to a front-seat in community leadership; Arul-pragasam herself has become a symbol of brown people's empowerment. But the dignity of the immigrant as the subject of song is hardly a new theme. In 1948, Joe Strummer's hero Guthrie wrote "Deportee (Plane Wreck at Los Gatos)." The song concerned the treatment of twenty-eight migrant farm workers, their deportation, and their accidental demise in a plane crash as they were being returned to Mexico from Central California. Guthrie was struck by the fact that the immigrants had gone nameless in news reports and that they were buried in a mass, unmarked grave while the American flight crew got full coverage. In tribute, he wrote the unidentified departed what started out as a poem: "Good-bye to my Juan, good-bye Rosalita, adios mis amigos, Jesus y Maria." Ten years later, schoolteacher Martin Hoffman set it to music. Popularized by Pete Seeger, it is still sung and recorded, most famously by the Byrds, Joan Baez, Billy Bragg, and Bruce Springsteen. "Deportee" remains standing not only as a eulogy, but as a statement on the lack of rights and the poor conditions faced by immigrant farm workers to this day. Strummer called up Guthrie ("some of us are illegal, others not wanted") when he jotted down "There ain't no need for ya. Go straight to hell, boys."

"As far as I'm concerned, punk rock was the folk music of its day," says Phranc. "It had all of the emotional and political content that folk music had. It had the passionate lyrics, the anger, the politics, it talked about issues, it talked about classism, it talked about growing up."

After two years on the San Francisco music scene, in 1979 the Avengers said goodnight and good-bye to punk rock; Penelope Houston took a musical hiatus before returning to the stage as an acoustic player. "I think even when I was in the Avengers I told people we were making folk music. It's like people used to play on their porch for their friends and we'd play in garages. But of course people just laughed at that—didn't take me at my word—thought I was being facetious," she says. "What I meant by folk music is we were making music for the people, by the people."

9

# Power to the Peaceful:
# Hip-Hop at the Foot of
# the Mountaintop

"Television: Drug of the Nation" was Michael Franti's first try at hip-hop—and it wasn't traditional. An abrasive and punky combination of poetry and percussion, the song was unmistakably "The Revolution Will Not Be Televised, Part Two." What we see on television—as well as what we don't see—has given Franti something to rap about for more than twenty years. His curiosity about media coverage took him to the Iraq war zone in 2007 with a guitar and a camera, just so he could see for himself and document for the rest of us what we were not allowed to see. Developing his voice as a performing songwriter and activist against the backdrop of the nearly thirty years that extended from the election of Ronald Reagan to that of Barack Obama, Franti has evolved from Beatnig to a Disposable Hero of Hiphoprisy, to leading Spearhead and fronting the Power to the Peaceful movement. "What I've found in terms of activism is, it's never hard to get people to care, but it's hard to get them to show up, year after year after year," says Franti.

The original "New Black Poet" Gil Scott-Heron's percussive statement on the media's ills dated back to 1970, and yet its sentiments were no less relevant in 1988 when Franti sliced it, diced it, and put the ideas back into popular rotation. By that time Scott-Heron had been out of the recording game for at least four years—dropped by his record label—though not

01

before he'd left a few choice words for Ronald Reagan, who he painted as the right-wing's B-version of John Wayne, come to return the USA to the so-called good old days: [lyric]

> You go give them liberals hell Ronnie . . .
>    civil rights women's rights gay rights all wrong.
> Call in the cavalry to disrupt this perception of freedom gone wild.
> God damn it, first one wants freedom then the whole damn world
>    wants freedom.

Protesting Reagan's bid for reelection, Scott-Heron pointed to the former actor's links to the screen in "Re-Ron," as in, "We don't need no Re-Ron." In "B Movie," Scott-Heron wraps his edgy wit around his tale of a country sold down the river.

> In the last 20 years America has changed
> from a producer to a consumer and all consumers know
> when the producer names the tune, the consumer has got to dance.

Franti's "Television" was similarly concerned with a media-generated reality. Popular on the San Francisco club scene, "Television" owned the dance floors and local public airwaves; when it was released on Jello Biafra's record label it was such a rapid seller that the first pressing couldn't meet the demand. Franti's homage to Scott-Heron riffed on "the political economy of the mass media" as described in the then newly published *Manufacturing Consent* by Noam Chomsky and Edward S. Herman. It delivered the sobering facts, accompanied by a crushing, industrial hip-hop beat.

> Television is the reason why
> less than 10 percent of our nation reads books daily,
> why most people think Central America means Kansas,
> socialism means unamerican and apartheid is a new headache remedy

Allusions to Scott-Heron's song throughout rap, rock, and in the popular culture are so prevalent they border on cliche: the revolution will be "digitized," the revolution will be "synthesized," but so far, the revolution has not been "organized." One ill-fated ad campaign suggested the revolution *will* be televised. Franti's interpretation of the theme underscores Scott-Heron's in that as it suggests a necessary parsing of media-generated "reality" from truth. The bluster of his music, poetry, and politics commanded listener attention, as did the vehicle with which he delivered his message: referencing San Francisco's connection to the Beat movement in literature, his band the Beatnigs was confrontational, its intention explained in a scrappy, fanzine-like insert tucked into every album.

> The word "nig" is a positive acronym derived from the word "nigger" and is used by the members of the Beatnigs. "Nigger" (a description of the stereotypical ignorant, lazy black person) has long been used as a tool of degradation against African Americans. Other dehumanizing words are used to describe other ethnic groups but because "nigger" is the most common of all these words, "nig" has taken on a universal meaning in describing all oppressed people who have actively taken a stand against those who perpetuate ethnic notions and discriminate on the basis of them. The importance of shortening the word "nigger" as opposed to creating a new word is that nig serves as a constant reminder that things have not and will not change until we change them. It is vital that we remember that in the eyesight of the majority of people in America we are still spics, chinks, kykes, dykes, queers, sandbugs, punks, hippies, white trash, cripples, bitches, old people, wops, and niggers. And let us not forget it . . . because they will not let us forget it.[1]

Of course things have changed dramatically since 1988: the majority to whom the Beatnigs refer are now only but a small but vocal minority in a multicultural society. Words once classified as hate speech can be heard not only in the rhetoric of both sides, they have been subsumed into the culture at large, masquerading under cover of free speech.

## Hip-Hop in Action

While the Beatnigs worked with words while consciously merging punk with rap in San Francisco, the group N.W.A—short for Niggaz With Attitude—issued a wake-up call to the world with a sound grown from their home base in South Central Los Angeles. Their 1988 album *Straight Outta Compton* was a collection of raps concerning life on the streets, set to beats so tough that the hearing impaired could likely feel the rumble of their urgency. Dr. Dre, Ice Cube, Eazy-E, MC Ren, and DJ Yella were immediate critical and commercial sensations and full-blown enemies to law and order. Their stories of ghetto life, racial profiling, and other forms of police harassment suggested reality. Though these were tales as old as time, they were chillingly prophetic in Los Angeles in the nineties.

The insurgent sound of N.W.A would come to define gangsta rap, as would the group's tussles with the law that echoed the gangsta lifestyle described in their songs. Courting controversy wherever it went, founding member Eazy-E touted his gang membership and told how drug sales contributed to bankrolling his music career. Ice-T, the L.A. rapper of the same vintage, told similar tales involving his outlaw past. Life-of-crime stories were the foundation on which gangsta was built, often aided by a litany of homophobic, misogynistic, anti-Semitic remarks and violent scenarios. The style would grow to dominate hip-hop culture well into the twenty-first century. N.W.A's most controversial track, "Fuck Tha Police," was of course an attempt to expose the practices of racial profiling and police brutality in Los Angeles, yet what started as a protest song was perceived as a taunt, and it was no time before the LAPD and the FBI stepped up efforts to shut them down. When ad hoc groups like the Parents Music Resource Center—the Washington wives who had formed earlier in the decade in hopes of stamping out risqué music—and the press got involved, the group's days were numbered. Unraveling from the pressure put on them, N.W.A's uniquely talented members eventually went their separate ways, experiencing different degrees of commercial success. Much of their time offstage was spent publicly feuding with each other and fending off the law, but they had birthed the sound of gangsta and made way for Dr. Dre's West Coast G-funk style that would dominate California hip-hop for the rest of the decade.

Before N.W.A came along and altered hip-hop, in the late eighties New York's KRS-One of Boogie Down Productions (BDP) and the Chuck D–led Public Enemy had spearheaded the movement toward rap consciousness, with an eye on waking up the masses though education. This was hip-hop with an intention to inform not only with reality reportage—and a slightly lighter hand on homophobia, sexism, and profanity—but with hard information.

"Hank Shocklee and I were hanging a flier of a gig we were promoting and we put a picture of Malcolm X on front of the flier," says Chuck D. "This guy came up to us as we were stapling the flier on the pole and he said 'I'm down with checking you out . . . who's this Malcolm the tenth?' We looked at each other like, this dude doesn't even know who Malcolm X is? We had to reconnect the dots. We knew who Malcolm X was from people like the Last Poets and Gil Scott-Heron." Chuck D wanted to work in the tradition of music with a message. He remembered the time when "music in general would not skip a beat when what needed to be said, had to be said."[2]

KRS-One (Lawrence "Kris" Parker) of BDP lost a friend to violence when Scott La Rock, his collaborator, was killed in a shooting incident. Taking action, he decided to reflect a more positive message in his work by following his group's *Criminal Minded* debut with *By All Means Necessary*, its album art duplicating the famous photo of Malcolm X at the window. Parker laid down his philosophy as a blueprint for conscious hip-hop.

> The way some act in rap is kinda wack
> And it lacks creativity and intelligence
> But they don't care cause the company is selling it

Parker also formed the Stop the Violence Movement, raising awareness of hip-hop youth at risk. He remains an advocate of nonviolence and education, earning himself the nickname the Teacher.

Public Enemy's sonically startling debut, *Yo, Bum Rush the Show*, pointed to a collective revolution of the mind, but when word came down through record industry channels that it was "too black" the question came back, for whom? The criticism fueled Chuck D's case against a racist America, and with like-minded individuals in his corner, like filmmaker Spike Lee and Public Enemy's appointed "media assassin" Harry Allen, he took an even stronger stance when he hit hard with *It Takes a Nation of Millions to Hold Us Back*.

The album opens with "Countdown to Armageddon": "This time, the revolution will not be televised . . . consider yourself forewarned." With raps about underreported phenomena like the US prison-industrial complex and the ineffective response to 911 calls from the projects, Chuck D's words were set to unifying tones of sirens, chains, and the slamming of prison doors. Loading up their imagery with Black Panther–style rhetoric and the accessories of a Black Power heritage, Public Enemy positioned themselves as new radicals. Its name was a direct reference to the time when J. Edgar Hoover identified organized efforts toward Black Power as public enemy number one. Chuck

D's initial public enthusiasm for Black Nationalism was the antidote to what he perceived to be black complacency. Organizing the group in militaristic fashion, assigning titles to its members, posing with toy guns, and resuscitating Malcolm X's credo "by any means necessary," Public Enemy repopularized Afrocentricity, an idea that had cooled off in the American consciousness.

Public Enemy was making its statement in the era when Michael Jackson went to visit Ronald and Nancy Reagan at the White House and the economy was enjoying a boom time. But as Chuck D never fails to point out, the R&B era—as in Reagan and Bush—meant hard times for another set of folks. Raising his voice in resistance, he was out there blowing the whistle on America the beautiful, a place where the idea of a holiday in honor of Dr. King could still be met with rejection. He pushed back with "By the Time I Get to Arizona":

> I'm on one mission
> to get a politician
> to honor or he's a goner
> by the time I get to Arizona

With "Fight the Power," the theme to Spike Lee's *Do the Right Thing*, he said it plainly another way:

> Most of my heroes don't appear on no stamps
> Sample a look back you look and find
> Nothing but rednecks for 400 years if you check

The theme shared its name with "Fight the Power Pts 1&2," the 1975 Isley Brothers hit:

> When I rolled with the punches I got knocked on the ground with all
> this bullshit going down . . . fight it, fight the power

Public Enemy set the bar high for the new age of protest music. Since *It Takes a Nation's* release in 1988, it has stood as a classic recording. Chuck D remains a historian and hip-hop advocate who refuses to be crushed by manipulation, the media, or marketing trends. That Public Enemy also spawned the minstrelsy-styled clowning of reality TV star Flava Flav is one of its contradictions—and a great example of how there are few things in life that can be reduced to simple shades of black and white.

## From Black Rock and Afro-Punk Back to Roots

Sometime in the post-disco/punk/MTV era, it came to the attention of a group of freethinkers that black music was in danger of being shackled and thrown into a trick bag, as it was in the days before desegregation, psychedelia, fusion, and funk.

In the spirit of the Black Arts Movement, Vernon Reid, Greg Tate, and Konda Mason formed the Black Rock Coalition (BRC) in 1985 as a cultural community for people interested in giving back freedom to all forms of black artists.

Though the seventies had supported black experimentation to some degree, it wasn't so long after the death of Jimi Hendrix and the disappearance of Sly Stone and his band that many black rockers crossed over. Prince had made it to the top, and Nile Rodgers got most of the guitar gigs, but why did so few black rock artists cross over into the stratosphere when real rock 'n' roll had been invented by black folks? The BRC, in its attempt to make corrections, called the music business on its racism and the limitations it put on black artists who sought to be more experimental and to take chances. The BRC supports recording, performance, and distribution opportunities for progressive black artists, from every generation, like writer/performer Nona Hendryx, who came up with groundbreaking singing act LaBelle, to artists diverse as Cassandra Wilson, Erykah Badu, Lenny Kravitz, Mos Def, and the genius Prince. The BRC also supports group efforts, like OutKast, the Roots, and TV on the Radio. These artists are the heirs of the original rockers—Ike Turner, Little Richard, Chuck Berry, Fats Domino, and the great Bo Diddley, who had been the first to declare that R&B stood for "rip-off and bullshit." He and his fellow rockers had fought the fight, they'd survived segregation and the Chitlin Circuit, and they had done or were doing their time. They outraged church people and horrified the frozen chosen—they'd done their job and given us rock 'n' roll. As the next generation of "Boogie Chillen" comes to claim their legacy, Black Rock helps create the space for them to make an impact and to have their say.

In early seventies Detroit, three brothers—David, Bobby, and Dannis Hackney—traded in their R&B suits and started to blast out punk rock. They called their band Death—named so because they had lost their father, as well as Dr. King and Sen. Kennedy in 1968. Their song "Politicians in My Eyes"—"They could care less about you, they could care less about me"—features punk's standard staccato rhythms and the sophisticated melodies and machine guitar styles of Hendrix. Sparking some local interest and impressing crowds wherever they went, the legend goes Death was offered a recording deal by music industry giant Clive Davis. But when asked to change their name to something more inviting, Death went the punk rock way: No was the answer and that was their end. Not a word was heard from Death until thirty years later, when Bobby's sons, rockers themselves, heard a cult had grown around their dad's and uncles' singles from the seventies. Released in 2009, *For All the World to See* was the revelation that the collectors raved about—some of the most searing rock 'n' roll music that you will ever hear, black, purple, punk, or otherwise. Death are the original Afro-punks. Acknowledging the debt to the loud and fast Bad Brains and stage-diving Fishbone, what began as a loose organization of black punk fans, skaters, and BMX bikers embraces all forms of alternative expression among black punks. Message boards and an annual festival serve as a way for the community to develop further liberation consciousness. The Afro-punks may just be the groundbreaking black musicians of the future, those unbound by chart and radio format stratifications and discrimination at the label and payment level and all forms of marginalization in the market place.

The Wondaland Arts Society is the latest consortium of black artists working together in a demonstration of education and experimentation combining to create excellence. An exemplar of the Wondaphenomenon, Janelle Monae challenges herself to incorporate the esthetics of James Brown and Jimi Hendrix as well as classical music and the values of show tunes and standards into a mix that's earned her kudos from discerning listeners.

———

Adhering to no particular doctrine, the emphasis of Michael Franti's music was based on an elevation of the mind, landing him among the artists labeled conscious. Fueled not only by rap but now punk and reggae, his music hovered on the edges of acceptance, a condition that wasn't new to him. While growing up one of two black kids adopted into a white family in a largely white community of Sacramento, California, "I always felt like an outsider," he says. "My childhood wasn't a real happy one. My father was an alcoholic. That brought a lot of tension and anger into the household." Picked on at school and unhappy at home, he was a fist-fighter and a wrestler. "I was an easy target because I'd get pissed off," he says. But Franti took solace on the basketball court as well as in music. "Music is the thing I'd do. I'd go to my room with my cassette player, tape songs off the radio. That's what got me through," he says. He also took a personal interest in history. "The book that changed me the most when I was a kid was *Roots* by Alex Haley."

*Roots* is the family saga of Kunta Kinte, abducted from his home in Africa and turned into a slave in the United States. "I had no idea of that whole legacy and experience. It wasn't part of my experience or education. When I read it, I was so moved. I took it on as my experience," he says. In high school he got into Malcolm X and read his autobiography, a collaboration with Alex Haley. "And again, I was so moved, not so much by his political ideas but by his transformation—from street thug to more skilled gangster, getting busted, going to jail, his conversion to Nation of Islam, becoming this powerful educator and orator and then going to Mecca and coming back and saying it's bigger than Islam, it's bigger than black and white. He had this whole new world perspective. I've always been fascinated by viewing how people change in life," he says.

For twenty-two years Franti says he didn't know who or where his parents were. "When I met my mother—my girlfriend and I were expecting a child— I'd searched for two years." He found his birth father was African American and Native American and his mother was Irish, French, and German. "I found out the reason she gave me up for adoption was that her family was racist and never would have accepted a brown baby . . . When I found my father's side of the family I met my grandmother." Franti's grandmother had spent her life working as a domestic, and she told him stories of her own grandmother, a woman who had experienced firsthand the atrocities of slavery. Franti wrote her, and the words she passed onto him, into a song:

> When things get tough, don't sweat it
> Sometimes you just have to let it
> And sing out a song so strong
> That even a bad dream couldn't bring harm

Franti says his grandmother had also been given up as a baby girl. "She was given up by her mother but was rescued by her grandmother. Her grandmother was a freed slave and her grandfather was a Native American man—his tribe was Seminole. He was a veterinarian and he'd travel around the countryside on horse, taking care of animals. He'd be gone for thirty days at a time or so and when he'd come home he'd ride into this little valley they lived in and he'd call out, give a loud scream, so they'd know he was coming from a mile a way. She said to me, 'You know, your voice is exactly like his.'

## The N-word

When Franti and friends named their band Beatnigs, it was at a time when the relatively new practice of studying the postmodern era's ethics and aesthetics, especially in relationship to consumer culture, had begun to gain ground at the university level. Since the student protests of 1968 and 1969 that were largely responsible for the implementation of minority and cultural studies programs, examinations into the social, political, and cultural phenomena among minorities in relationship to the dominant culture remains a relatively wide-open field. Cultural studies are an occasionally still controversial part of contemporary college curriculum; postmodern ideas like the reclamation or expropriation of hate speech fall into this broad category of analysis. By the eighties the repurposing of the n-word was in the air on campuses and the Beatnigs were part of that confrontational new wave, but examinations of it had been going on since the sixties when comedians Dick Gregory and Richard Pryor and activist H. Rap Brown used it to spotlight racism. Nonblack artists Yoko Ono and Patti Smith controversially used it in their seventies' work to promote feminism and express revolutionary solidarity respectively. But the persistent use of the word in the late twentieth and early twenty-first centuries within the hip-hop community and outside of it, particularly when whites use it, is cause for further controversy. Community leaders suggest that hate speech and dehumanization of people are connected—that language is a way to keep people enslaved. These are the elders who worked for the eradication of the word and don't buy the idea that it signifies camaraderie and loyalty or that it can theoretically be reclaimed. As recently as 2007, New York City proposed a ban on its use punishable by city ordinance, though cooler heads prevailed when even the word's high-profile detractor, Dr. Cornel West, agreed that censorship is not a viable solution to matters of the spoken word, even when it comes to the longstanding problem of hate speech. An individualized, self-imposed moratorium on its use was mooted as a long-term solution. Whether in retirement or circulation, the n-word remains a reminder of America's history of violence.

After a long hiatus, Gil Scott-Heron reemerged in the nineties to deliver his "Message to the Messengers" to the new gangsta rappers.

> The first sign is peace
> Tell all them gun totin' young brothas that the man is glad to see us
> out there killin' one another
> We raised too much hell when they was shootin' us down
> So they started poisoning our minds trying to jerk us around

But it would be the original rapper's last message for some time to come: addiction nipped at his heels and he was sentenced to serve time for his illness, on drug charges.

Following the dissolution of the Beatnigs in 1992, Franti retitled and rerecorded "Television" as "Television: Drug of the Nation" with his next venture, the conscious hip-hop group Disposable Heroes of Hiphoprisy. In the recast "Television" he examines the reinvention and softening of the media's language during wartime, inspired by the splashy coverage of the first Gulf War. Franti heard the words "friendly fire" and "collateral damage" used to describe the loss of human lives, and it disturbed him. The proliferation of nonstop cable news in the nineties meant that the war in the Persian Gulf was the first to be brought to you live on the 24/7 news. A major difference from the war in Vietnam was that all images of civilian death or soldiers returning home in caskets were censored. The news also had a practice of christening each news event with a catchy title. Sold to viewers by media personalities coiffed within an inch of their lives, the stories reporters continued to miss were usually those involving the highly combustible conditions of poverty, government abandonment, and police harassment at home, like the stories told by N.W.A in South Los Angeles. The job of reporting had been left to hip-hop music, compelling Chuck D to famously declare rap as black America's CNN. But as much as there were those who wished to blame the explosive expression of N.W.A and gangsta rappers like them for the violence, they were only the warning shots rather than the cause of the big story in urban rebellion of 1992. Historic riots were sparked by the acquittal of four white police officers who had beaten motorist Rodney King excessively following a high-speed chase. The whole world watched the L.A. riots, broadcast live from the ghetto for six days straight.

———————

Disposable Heroes opened a series of large arena shows on rock band U2's Zoo TV Tour, and Franti slammed the band's fans with his update of "Television: the Drug of the Nation."

> Race baiting is the way to get selected
> Willie Horton or will he not get elected?

Back in 1988, the far right had used a misconstrued vision of the left's position on crime and punishment as an on-air advertising tactic against Michael Dukakis in the election of George Herbert Walker Bush. Today "Willie Horton" still stands as an example of how racism and fear continue to affect the campaign trail. At the time Franti was on the road with U2, Bono attempted to reach then-president Bush on the telephone nightly (he never got through). Other songs in the Disposable Heroes' repertoire included "The Language of Violence," concerning the story of a young victim of hate speech and murder (years before Matthew Shepard made headline news). "Death is the silence in this language of violence" turns on the AIDS activist slogan "silence equals death," then spells it out plain.

> Words can reduce a person to an object
> Something more easy to hate
> an inanimate entity, completely disposable,
> no problem to obliterate

Conscious rap from this point forward would remain focused on the underground, its eyes on the lives of people and movements on the verge. Franti's songs and his audience were a little like the hip-hop equivalent of the Pacifica Radio Network in contrast to the sensational scenes reported on in vivid color by CNN and South Central's gangsta rappers.

"In hip-hop there was a lot of antigay sentiment, and I thought it was so hypocritical," says Franti. "In the early nineties, I wrote a song about AIDS." It had become clear that HIV/AIDS did not discriminate along economic, sexual preference, or color lines and was not exclusive to gay men and intravenous drug users; more than any other racial minority, African Americans were feeling its spread the most and by 1996 it had become the leading cause of death of African Americans aged twenty-five to forty-four.[3] In 1991 basketball hero Magic Johnson had announced his retirement from the game when he learned he'd contracted the virus; his increasing candor put him at the forefront of the HIV/AIDS awareness movement. But four years later, the death of N.W.A's Eazy-E of complications from the virus caused shock waves in the hip-hop community, demonstrating the depth of misunderstanding about the disease. Franti's way into the subject for a song came from personal experience.

"The first version I did was kind of dissing the government because they weren't responding to the AIDS crisis. And then something happened which was I went to get tested for HIV. I sat down in my room and waited for the results to come back for a few days. And I thought, how's my life gong to change if my test comes back positive." He called the song "Positive."

> I'm readin' about, how it's transmitted,
> some behavior, I must admit it,
> who I slept with, who they slept with,
> who they, who they, who they slept with . . .

"Being an artist, I've met so many creative people from the gay community. It was a startling revelation to me at eighteen, nineteen, coming from a straight, Christian community, to have all these friends who were gay and I didn't even know it. I saw how AIDS was affecting people who I knew and cared about. Their families were turning their backs on them," he said, "because they were gay and had a disease. Their own flesh and blood, people who were supposed to care about them the most, turned their backs on them. That's really what made me want to write 'Positive' and the 'Language of Violence.'"

Writing "Positive" opened a door to an aspect of songwriting which Franti hadn't much explored. "I realized something," he says. "Songs don't have to be like 'fuck the government,' to borrow a phrase from my buddy Zack from Rage Against the Machine. You don't always need to do that," he says. "The ones that get you to raise your fist in the air, they're good to get you riled up. But . . . sometimes you write a song that's more quiet and gentle or about something that's happening inside of you. And those songs tend to be the ones that I've found are the most powerful."

Franti, of course, is not the first artist to note this. Back in the seventies when the movement among songwriters had turned gentle and inward, one of the songwriters most accused of oversensitivity and too much introspection was Jackson Browne. By the mid-eighties he had taken a great leap into directly confrontational music. Continuing his involvement with antinuclear and environmental causes, he wrote about the consequences of Ronald Reagan's economic policies and the administration's Iran–Contra affair on the album *Lives in the Balance*. But like John Lennon and Yoko Ono's *Some Time in New York City* in the seventies, Browne's album was not immediately received with open arms. The people had largely already spoken and they were saying "don't mix your leftist politics with my rock music." Yet for artists like Ono, Franti and Browne, music and political point of view have been and remain inseparable.

"It's a mass self-hypnosis that we're engaging in," says Browne. "People know more about baseball players' contracts than they do about policies that govern the fate of our children's lives in twenty years," he says.[4]

## The Return to Consciousness

In the period after the L.A. riots and the gangsta explosion, with a few notable exceptions the job of conscious hip-hop artists did not pay so well. Like all categories of music, over time hip-hop developed its own subset of flavors, with regional sounds and a fusion of styles from crunk to hyphy, while the audience for the conscious style remained relatively small. Common, Talib Kweli, Mos Def, and political rap's the Coup along with the old school's Chuck D and KRS-One stay on a message to make a difference. Mos Def was particularly outspoken during the Katrina disaster and Bush II presidency; he's made an effort to return hip-hop to a forum where political and social issues are confronted, and he promotes the idea that black musicians are the rightful heirs to rock 'n' roll invented by their ancestors. Chuck D would like to see women get involved. "When women group up as a collective . . . nothing can stop a collective of women . . . I think across the world women are still looked upon as second class citizens no matter how many Beyonces come up or Latifahs do their thing . . . For women not to be involved in hip-hop is terrible."[5]

Franti came of age seeing the changes brought by tax cuts and Reaganomics, the births of hip-hop and punk rock, and the spread of HIV/AIDS, watching friends die while the president would not speak the disease's name for another three years. He's gone from living in a no-computer zone to adapting to a daily existence in which technology is part of the fabric of life. Today he feels moved to work for peace and nonviolence through music.

By 1994 Franti had formed Spearhead, its name shared with the 3rd Armored Division of the US Army. Incorporating music and reportage, a Spearhead show feels more like a celebration than a mass rally these days, but Franti's commitment to substance is by no means lightweight. Following the public's protest before the war in Iraq in 2003 and the building clampdown on dissenting opinion and the disinformation campaign regarding weapons of mass destruction, Franti went to see for himself what was going on in Baghdad.

"One day we were on a tour bus and I was watching the news, right after the war started. A general was talking about a bomb they were using, a 'bunker buster.' A big bomb, fifty thousand pounds that would drop down and could explode five stories below the earth . . . I thought, Baghdad is a city of five million, four million more than where I live in San Francisco, and if someone were to drop a bomb that day here, there would be thousands of people killed. But they're telling me on the news, *no one is dying, no one is suffering, these are 'smart bombs.' We're smart people and we know we aren't only blowing up buildings where people aren't.* I thought, this is bullshit. I kept hearing about the economic and political cost but no one was talking about the human cost," he says.

Responding to a challenge from a friend who suggested he go to the war zone to see for himself, Franti took a guitar and a video camera, and with a small group of friends he walked the streets of Baghdad, playing music for people. "When I look back on it now, it seems crazy and irrational but at the time it seemed important."

Franti returned with footage from places that most US citizens knew little about; that footage was cut to make the film *I Know I'm Not Alone*. Franti had been inspired by the book *An Act of State* by journalist William F. Pepper, who asserts that in early 1967 he'd opened his personal files on Vietnam for Dr. King and discussed with him its cost to Vietnamese civilian life and culture. Stokely Carmichael had also talked through matters with him for some time, but it was shortly after seeing Pepper's photos that King would deliver his "Beyond Vietnam" speech, officially aligning the civil rights and antiwar movements.

"And a year from when he spoke out, to the day exactly, was when he was assassinated. What that told me was that people seeing images from war is important," Franti says. "If people in America had seen what was happening with the Holocaust, it wouldn't have gone on. If people had seen what was happening in slavery, it wouldn't go on. If people were seeing what was happening in Darfur, Palestine, South America, Haiti. If I can do that through film or song . . . As an artist, that's my role, to go to places, witness, see for myself."

Franti had also been tuning into the idea that instead of expanding the media, deregulation had delivered fewer ideas, fewer solutions, and fewer minority interests to the public airwaves. He's observed the ensuing millennial crises unfolding, such as unattended environmental matters and the incarceration of a disproportionate number of black men in the United States, and has cared to comment on all of it. In 1998 he founded the Power to the Peaceful Festival in San Francisco, a one-day music and social awareness happening, initially called to bring attention to Mumia Abu-Jamal's death row conviction and to educate on matters of social justice.

Abu-Jamal, better known as Mumia to the worldwide community of human rights activists who support his case, is a former radio journalist and Philadelphia cab driver. As a teenager he joined the Black Panthers; at the time of his conviction in 1981, he was president of the Philadelphia Association of Black Journalists. He was sentenced to death row, where he has remained since 1983, for allegedly killing police officer Daniel Faulkner. Despite eyewitness testimony to the contrary and evidence of racial and judicial bias he remains a death row prisoner—his most recent appeal for a retrial was denied in the spring of 2009. He reports from his prison cell at 175 Progress Drive via poems, books, and radio broadcasts. He speaks about matters of police brutality, racism, and incarceration without rehabilitation. The Spearhead album *Stay Human* was a concept album about the death penalty in America; Franti used radio call-in segments to tie together the story of a black activist awaiting execution.

Since 1998 Power to the Peaceful has evolved into a nonprofit organization devoted to fostering cultural coexistence, nonviolence, and environmental sustainability through arts and music. Power to the Peaceful has its own logo— a brown raised arm clenching a daisy in a power-fisted salute. Through the festival, his live performances, and his recordings, Franti attempts to inspire people to stay committed to change. In 2007, Power to the Peaceful staged an event in Rio de Janeiro, Brazil. Rio is famous not only for its beaches, music, and celebration of Carnival, but also for its extreme gap between rich and poor and its high-density slums. Franti brings the music wherever he travels, from Rio to Iraq to maximum-security prison San Quentin in the Bay Area, where he and Spearhead performed for inmates. Not all of his fans agree with the matters he chooses to support, but he says the criticisms have helped him to become a better communicator.

"I don't play music to reward people and I don't play music to punish people. I play music because I believe music is a healing art and that it can be an opportunity for people to pass through whatever it is they're going through in their life," he says. "For some people it's the pain and sadness of death. For other people it may be the healing of remorse or regret about the things they've done. For other people it might just help them get into the next minute or into the next day."[6]

## Calling All Rebel Rockers

Around the time he was completing *All Rebel Rockers* in 2008, Franti was invited to Los Angeles by his friend Zack de la Rocha to perform at a tribute to Bob Dylan. De la Rocha is also a musician and activist as front man of Rage Against the Machine, the rap-metal band known primarily for its abrasive music and political activity. Rage Against the Machine is committed in song and action to antiglobalization, immigrant rights, and the Zapatista cause in Mexico, among other political and human rights causes. The band had taken a hiatus during the majority of the Bush II presidency, but by 2007 they pulled out of retirement. During the break, the band's core of vocalist de la Rocha and guitarist Tom Morello (who also performs solo as the Nightwatchman) had been involved in their own politically potent musical ventures and actions, specifically for immigrant rights in Los Angeles. At a contentious immigrants' rights reform rally, Morello was arrested, along with four hundred fellow marchers who had gathered in the name of low-paid airport hotel workers. In 2006, de la Rocha stood in solidarity with the growers at the South Central Farm in Los Angeles—as did Willie Nelson and Joan Baez—in an effort to save the largest urban farm in the United States from a political real estate development deal. (They were unable to achieve their immediate goal to keep the farm growing and watched as it was bulldozed.) Morello has been an active campaigner for peace; when it was revealed that rock music was being played at continuous high volume as a means to torture prisoners at Guantanamo Bay Detention Center, he and a small group of musicians gathered and filed suit against the US government. Though nothing came of the suit, the legal action provided an opportunity for a continuing dialogue toward the closure of the torture camp. Morello and Wayne Kramer took their music to Madison, Wisconsin, in the winter of 2011, standing with workers in the fight to retain their collective bargaining rights. Rage Against the Machine has frequently been in the position of defending the words of their songs and of their band members; the rhetoric of revolution is not easily metabolized by the corporate media, but the band has remained unrelenting in holding the line against human rights violations of all kinds.

"This system has become so brutal and vicious and cruel that it needs to start wars and profit from the destruction around the world to survive as a world power," says de la Rocha, speaking to the concerns of those involved in the antiglobalization movement.[7]

Morello and de la Rocha's band and Franti each make different music, but their lives have interesting parallels. They were born between 1964 and 1970, to boomer parents (and in the case of de la Rocha and Morello, politically active ones); all are of mixed race heritage and are representative speakers for multicultural America.

The Dylan tribute at which de la Rocha and Franti were set to perform was hosted by the Skirball Cultural Center, an institution devoted to exploring the connections between Jewish heritage and American democratic ideals. Its mission emphasizes inclusiveness while working toward building a society in which people of all ethnic and cultural backgrounds can thrive. Prior to his appearance there, Franti had taken his cues from Alex Haley, Malcolm X, the Clash, and Bob Marley; he had not done Dylan and it meant he had to cram. "He wasn't part of my musical landscape," Franti says. Out of the hundreds of Dylan songs on offer, he chose the double-entendred sixties anthem "Rainy Day Women #12 & 35" and the rhyme-intensive Beat-driven salute to the counterculture underground, "Subterranean Homesick Blues." "I think 'Rainy Day Women' is very political," says Franti. "Although the chorus sounds like a stoner song, he's talking about the society stoning you as an individual. *I would not feel so all alone, everybody must get stoned,* I think that's a powerful political statement—to be among the misfits who are freethinkers." Franti wrote his own song for "all the freaky people," "Stay Human":

> I speak low but I'm like a lion roarin'
> Baritone like a Robeson recordin'
> I'm giving thanks for bein' human every morning . . .
> Every flower got a right to be bloomin'

## Stay Human

Since at least the forties, a battle joining federal and local law enforcement against peace and human rights activists, in particular against black, female, and gay advocates, has raged on. Actor, singer, and activist Paul Robeson, whose inspiration Franti called on in "Stay Human," was a man of extraordinary charisma, substance, and talent in multiple disciplines; he led on the sporting field and on the stage as a Shakespearean dramatist. He was also a freedom singer who threw in his hat with peaceniks and labor organizers, pitching in with songs and oratory, devoted to raising awareness of worldwide fascism, racism, and white supremacy. Labeled a communist for his relationship to the dispossessed, in particular to colonized people of color whom he supported in their struggles for liberation, his passport was revoked for most of the fifties. He was subjected to extreme surveillance for most of his lifetime, and the controversy surrounding him resulted in a dwindling fortune and lack of a platform for his liberation ideas. Robeson's FBI file approaches three thousand pages and is among the fattest files complied on an actor-singer. In an appeal to the courts to regain his passport in 1956, the brief filed on his behalf stated, "The weapon of turning a searchlight on the white man's inhumanity to the black man in America helped to win emancipation a century ago and it is equally necessary in order to help realize the thirteenth amendment today."[8] In 1961 Robeson allegedly attempted suicide in a visit to Moscow; his son Paul Robeson Jr. has reason to believe the event had more sinister implications. It became a climactic event in what looked to be Robeson's ultimate neutralization. Robeson's story of the passion he brought to combining art with politics remains among the most dramatic ever told.

In the intervening years from Robeson to Franti, there have been artists who have conducted their careers and activism just as staunchly, some whose names are known— poets like Nikki Giovanni, artists like actor/poet/musician Saul Williams, intellectuals like Dr. Cornel West—and others whose work remains less celebrated. Those who merge words with music to sing against injustice or tell stories through songs fulfill an important function in the world: they have chosen to celebrate life.

"The spirit of life is almost nonexistent in the perceptual reality of the society that we're in. They got religion, they got civilization, they got military, they got politics, they got education, they got all this stuff, but they don't have the spirit to live," says musician activist John Trudell.[9]

The truth sayers in music's politically active wing use their words and experiences to affirm life in attempts to free the listener's minds, to make them think about their relationship to the world, and how they will survive it. Michael Franti, the musicians profiled here, and countless others, their praises sung and unsung, gather in earnest in the tradition of musical protest, railing against the conditions for those whose lives are lived in the balance. Such ancient traditions of singing and dancing and honoring the earth come together under one banner toward survival of the human race—all creeds, nationalities, races, and genders. Lead Belly and Woody Guthrie, Odetta and Bob Dylan, Len Chandler and Buffy Sainte-Marie, Phranc, Yoko Ono, Richie Havens, and Michael Franti have all followed a command to sing for those who can't sing themselves to freedom. They have known and felt the conditions of the outsider looking in and they have delivered the outsider's feelings in song.

"There's so much of that in the country we live in—so many amazing people are left out," says Franti. "This always led me to want to stick up for people who were unheard."

# Coda

More than half a century has passed since the bus rides, the sit-ins, and the marches for voting rights, desegregation, jobs, and peace. Perhaps the civil rights movement, Black Power, women's liberation, and gay rights sound like causes from another dimension. They are not. People all over the world await deliverance from violations of their civil liberties and human rights, including right here in the land of liberty. War, poverty, and racism are still with us, and it's expected they will be as long as the interests of a few trump the survival needs of the many. Today we must add environmental blight to the list of concerns confounding today's truth speakers, justice seekers, and freedom singers. And yet, there exists no one effective, organized mass movement of people, marching and singing their way to solutions toward freedom and equality.

"There's no clear thought being exercised right now in the American public," says John Trudell, musician, poet, Voice of Alcatraz, and former leader of the American Indian Movement. "They're allowing the insanity of the leaders to make decisions that really are not in the best interest of the public, they're not in the best interest of the children of the public, they're not in the best interest of the grandchildren of the public, they're not in the best interest of the Earth, they're not in the best interest of anyone."[1]

The number of writers delivering unfiltered news in the form of a song are few compared to the explosion of bands and singers in the world today—more than at any other time in history. For the musicians for whom art and progress are inseparable, there is always work to be done. Buffy Sainte-Marie, Yoko Ono, and Richie Havens are still singing for peace. Tom Morello and Wayne Kramer stand together on the frontlines of a progressive movement based on shared musical and political concerns. Chuck D and Archie Shepp forged a similar cross-generational alliance when they collaborated in performance and on a track for Shepp's album. In 2007, Ornette Coleman won the Pulitzer Prize in music for his album *Sound Grammar*, a culmination of his work combining free expression of the mind, body, and spirit through music. "People don't realize it, but there is a real folklore music in jazz. It's neither black nor white, it's the mixture of the races and folklore has come from it," he writes in his Harmolodic Manifesto.[2]

"Now that I am older I realize I can't change the world, but I still believe that if anyone can, it is the artist," said Nina Simone before her death in 2003. "It is always through art that society changes—not politics or even education. Art, and music especially, speaks to people more than government and education. Why do you think great nations have patronage for their artists?"[3]

In the course of writing this story, I had hoped I would find the exact time, place, and forces within the whirlpool of American history that drown out the voices of protest as time marched on. Instead I found songs, and more songs, waiting for another turn to be sung.

# Acknowledgments

This book could not have been completed without the cooperation of the following, along with others who I regret I've forgotten to remember.

Thank you to the musician activists, their representatives, and to all who sat for interviews specific to the project or related articles, especially the late Solomon Burke, Buffy Sainte-Marie, Len Chandler, Richie Havens, Michael Franti, Phranc, Penelope Houston, Debora Iyall, Janis Ian, Laura Love, Ed Pearl, Al Schackman, Wayne Kramer, John Sinclair, Elaine Brown, Dave Alvin, Don Letts, Eddie Kramer, Steve Diggle, Van Dyke Parks, Mikki Itzigsohn, and Lincoln Meyerson.

Three cheers and a hearty thanks to all the other singers, songwriters, authors, historians, journalists, filmmakers, webmasters, statisticians, politicians, orators, poets, preachers, and prophets whose work was quoted herein.

Thanks to Jocelyn Hoppa and Angela L. Zimmerman at *Crawdaddy!* who both agreed to assign and publish stories on musicians whose lives are intertwined with politics. Portions of the interviews can be accessed at crawdaddy.com.

To Yuval Taylor, Michelle Schoob, Mary Kravenas, and especially Susan Bradanini Betz at Chicago Review Press and Lawrence Hill Books, thanks—again and again.

I thank my family and friends for their love, especially those who showed wild enthusiasm and special sensitivity, and guided me at critical junctures: Mary Coleman, Diane Conor, Leora Chamberlain, Charles R. Cross, Jill Ebersole, Neil Feineman, Ron Franklin, Karen Gordon, Nadine Jolson, Alan Korn, Mary Lou Muir, Leslie Parness, Kevin Sullivan, Pat Thomas, and Richie Unterberger.

*Amour, honneur et reconnaissance* to Peter Case, whose words and music inspire me and without whose support this work could never have even been attempted nor brought to completion.

# Notes

## Intro

1. Tim Weiner, "The Last Word," *New York Times*, December 3, 2008.
2. W. E. B. DuBois, *The Souls of Black Folk*, in *Three Negro Classics* (New York: Avon Books, 1965), 209.

## Chapter 1: Freedom Now

All quotes in this chapter from Len Chandler, John Sinclair, Al Schackman, and Richie Havens are taken from author interviews unless otherwise noted.

All quotes from Archie Shepp are taken from Steve Schwartz, "Archie Shepp: the Original Fire Music," WGBH, Boston, June 3, 2008, www.npr.org/templates/story/story.php?storyId=91086057, unless otherwise noted.

All quotes from Odetta are taken from Tim Weiner, "The Last Word," *New York Times*, December 3, 2008, unless otherwise noted.

1. Alex Hayley and Malcolm X, *Autobiography of Malcolm X* (New York: Random House, 1964), 280–81.
2. Julius Lester, *Look Out, Whitey, Black Power's Gon Get Your Mama!* (New York: Grove, 1969).
3. Odetta, her remarks to the audience, McCabe's 50th anniversary concert, Royce Hall, UCLA, October 3, 2008.
4. Ron Rosenbaum, "The Playboy Interview: Bob Dylan," *Playboy*, March 1978.
5. Tiny Robinson and John Reynolds, *Lead Belly: A Life in Pictures* (London: Steidl, 2008), 105.
6. LaShonda Katrice Barnett, *I Got Thunder: Black Women Songwriters on Their Craft* (New York: Thunder's Mouth Press, 2007), 182.
7. Amiri Baraka [formerly LeRoi Jones], *Blues People: The Negro Experience in White America and the Music That Developed From It* (New York: Morrow Quill Paperbacks, 1963).
8. Dizzy Gillespie and Al Fraser, *To Be, or Not . . . to Bop* (Garden City, NY: Doubleday, 1979), 288–300.
9. Frank Kofsky, *Black Nationalism and the Revolution in Music* (New York: Pathfinder, 1970), 64.
10. Ibid., 65.
11. Etta James and David Ritz, *Rage to Survive* (New York: Villard, 1995), 112.

12. Johnny Otis, *Upside Your Head! Rhythm and Blues on Central Avenue*, (Middletown, CT: Wesleyan University Press, 1993), 143–44.

13. Nina Simone and Stephen Cleary, *I Put a Spell on You: The Autobiography of Nina Simone* (New York: Da Capo, 2003), 67.

14. Bob Dylan, *Chronicles Volume One* (New York: Simon & Schuster, 2004), 86.

15. Ibid.

16. *Jimi Hendrix Voodoo Child*, directed by Bob Smeaton, part of *West Coast Seattle Boy* box set (New York: Sony Legacy, 2010), DVD.

17. Dylan, *Chronicles Volume One*, 60.

18. Robin D. G. Kelley, *Thelonious Monk: The Life and Times of an American Original* (New York: Free Press, 2009), 330–343.

## Chapter 2: Everybody Knows About Mississippi . . . Goddam!

All quotes from Ed Pearl, Len Chandler, Buffy Sainte-Marie, Richie Havens, and Al Schackman are taken from author interviews unless otherwise noted.

1. LaShonda Katrice Barnett, *I Got Thunder: Black Women Songwriters on Their Craft* (New York: Thunder's Mouth Press, 2007), 149.

2. Ibid., 152.

3. Nina Simone and Stephen Cleary, *I Put A Spell on You: The Autobiography of Nina Simone* (New York: Da Capo, 2003), 98–100.

4. All quotes from Bernice Johnson Reagon are taken from "The Songs Are Free," *Bill Moyers Journal*, November 23, 2007, www.pbs.org/moyers/journal/11232007/profile3.html.

5. George Breitman, *Malcolm X Speaks* (New York: Grove Weidenfeld, 1965), 68.

6. Richie Havens with Steve Davidowitz, *They Can't Hide Us Anymore* (New York: Spike, 1999), 150.

7. Eric Burdon, *Don't Let Me Be Misunderstood* (New York: Thunder's Mouth Press, 2001), 288–289.

8. Steve Schwartz, "Archie Shepp: The Original Fire Music," WGBH, Boston, June 3, 2008, www.npr.org/templates/story/story.php?storyId=91086057.

9. Ibid.

10. Frank Kofsky, *Black Nationalism and the Revolution in Music* (New York: Pathfinder, 1970), 224.

11. *Ash Grove Burning*, directed by Aiyana Elliott (Los Angeles: Ash Grove Film, 2008).

12. Taj Mahal and Stephen Foehr, *Taj Mahal: Autobiography of a Bluesman* (London: Sanctuary, 2001), 90.

13. Joni Mitchell and Buffy Sainte-Marie, *Buffy Sainte-Marie: A Multi-media Life*, directed by Joan Prowse (Canada: Cinefocus, 2006), DVD.

14. Curtis Mayfield, *Poetic License: In Poem and Song* (Beverly Hills: Dove Books, 1996), viii.

15. Timothy B. Tyson, *Radio Free Dixie: Robert F. Williams and the Roots of Black Power* (Chapel Hill: University of North Carolina, 2001), 288.

16. Robert F. Williams chronicled his shocking fight with and flight from Southern racism in his 1962 book *Negroes with Guns* (New York: Marzani & Munsell, 1962; reprint, Detroit: Wayne State University Press, 1998); his was a lifelong freedom ride that took him from the United States to Cuba and ultimately China.

17. Magnificent Montague and Bob Baker, *Burn, Baby, Burn* (Champaign: University of Illinois, 2003), 90.

18. Ibid.

19. Schwartz, "Archie Shepp: The Original Fire Music."

20. John Lewis with Michael D'Orso, *Walking with the Wind, A Memoir of the Movement* (New York: Simon & Schuster, 1998), 292.

21. Dave Van Ronk, "Green Green Rocky Road," *Dave Van Ronk Memories in concert 1980* (Sparta, NJ: Vestapol, 2004), DVD.

22. Bassist Bill Lee played on records by Harry Belafonte, Odetta, Bob Dylan, and many other artists in the early sixties and continues to compose music and record. He is the father of filmmaker Spike Lee. Guitarist Bruce Langhorne worked frequently with Bob Dylan and is said to be the inspiration behind "Mr. Tambourine Man." He worked with Harry Belafonte, Richie Havens, Peter LaFarge, Olatunji, and Buffy Sainte-Marie among others, and appeared at the March on Washington.

23. Sonia Sanchez has written of and been quoted on multiple occasions as being at odds with law and government forces. Sonia Sanchez and Joyce A. Joyce, *Conversations with Sonia Sanchez* (Oxford: University of Mississippi Press, 2007); Claudia Tate, *Black Women Writers at Work* (Continuum, 1983).
24. Cordell Reagon was murdered in his Berkeley apartment in 1996; the crime remains unsolved.
25. James Baldwin, "The American Dream and the American Negro," *Collected Essays* (New York: Library of America, 1998), 715.
26. Telegram from Langston Hughes to Len Chandler, October 24, 1966, 12:15 a.m.

## Chapter 3: The Rhythm of the Rebel

All quotes from John Sinclair, Wayne Kramer, and Al Schackman are taken from author interviews unless otherwise noted.

1. James Brown, *I Feel Good: A Memoir of Life and Soul* (New York: New American Library, 2005), 137–165.
2. Stokely Carmichael and Michael Ekwueme Thelwell, *Ready for the Revolution* (New York: Scribner, 2003), 661.
3. Bobby Seale, *Seize the Time: The Story of the Black Panther Party and Huey P. Newton* (New York: Random House, 1970), 186.
4. Carmichael and Thelwell, *Ready for the Revolution*.
5. Nina Simone and Stephen Cleary, *I Put a Spell on You: The Autobiography of Nina Simone* (New York: Da Capo, 2003), 117.
6. Mance Lipscomb and Glen Alyn, *I Say Me for a Parable: The Oral Biography of Mance Lipscomb, Texas Bluesman* (New York: Da Capo, 1994), 311.
7. Frank Provenzano, "The Beat Moves On: John Sinclair," *Detroit Free Press*, October 26, 2004.
8. Steve Schwartz, "Archie Shepp: The Original Fire Music," WGBH, Boston, June 3, 2008, www.npr.org/templates/story/story.php?storyId=91086057.
9. Martin Luther King Jr., "Beyond Vietnam: A Time to Break the Silence," April 4, 1967, Riverside Church, New York City, www.stanford.edu/group/King/liberation_curriculum/speeches/beyond vietnam.htm.
10. The total number of fatalities in the Detroit riots is generally recorded as forty-three. Simone and Cleary, *I Put a Spell on You*, 113.
11. Brown, *I Feel Good: A Memoir of Life and Soul*, 137–165.
12. Ivan Solotarrof, "Pleas, Pleas, Pleas: The Tribulations and Trials of James Brown," *Village Voice*, February 21, 1989, in *The James Brown Reader: Fifty Years of Writing About the Godfather of Soul*, ed. Nelson George and Alan Leeds (New York: Plume, 2008).
13. Brown, *I Feel Good: A Memoir of Life and Soul*, 137–165.
14. Jerry Wexler and David Ritz, *Rhythm and the Blues: A Life in American Music* (New York: Knopf, 1993), 153.
15. Michael Torrance, "The Lumpen: Black Panther Party Revolutionary Singing Group," It's About Time, Black Panther Party Legacy & Alumni, www.itsabouttimebpp.com/Our_Stories/The _Lumpen/the_lumpen.html.

## Chapter 4: Movin' On Up

Quotes from Debora Iyall, Buffy Sainte-Marie, Elaine Brown, Wayne Kramer, Solomon Burke, and Len Chandler are taken from author interviews unless otherwise noted.

1. Martin Luther King Jr., "I've Been to the Mountaintop," April 3, 1968.
2. Robert F. Kennedy, "On Martin Luther King's Death, April 4, 1968," *Ripples of Hope: Great American Civil Rights Speeches*, ed. Josh Gottehimer (New York: Basic Civitas, 2003), 319.
3. *The Night James Brown Saved Boston*, directed by David Leaf (Los Angeles: Shout! Factory, 2008), DVD.
4. James Brown, *I Feel Good: A Memoir of Life and Soul* (New York: New American Library, 2005), 137–165.
5. James Brown and Bruce Tucker, *The Godfather of Soul* (New York: Thunder's Mouth, 2002), 264.

6. Norman Mailer, *Miami and the Siege of Chicago* (New York: Plume, 1986), 144, 142.
7. Bobby Seale, speech from CD included with *Guitar Army Rock & Revolution with MC5 and the White Panther Party* (Los Angeles: Process, 2007).
8. Laura Waterman Wittstock and Elaine J. Salinas, "A Brief History of the American Indian Movement," www.aimovement.org/ggc/history.html.
9. *Trudell*, directed by Heather Rae (Metuchen, NJ: Passion River, 2005), DVD.
10. "Preliminary Report on the Disturbances in Buffalo June 26–July 1, 1967, by the staff of the Store Front Education Centers," *The Buffalonian*, www.buffalonian.com/history/articles/1951 -now/1967riots/index.html.
11. Stokely Carmichael, "Black Power," October 1966, *Ripples of Hope: Great American Civil Rights Speeches*, ed. Josh Gottehimer (New York: Basic Civitas, 2003), 296–303.
12. Kenneth S. Jolly, *Black Liberation in the Midwest* (New York: Routledge, 2009), 123.
13. Prince. Interview with Tavis Smiley, PBS, April 27, 2009, www.pbs.org/kcet/tavissmiley /archive/200904/20090427_prince.html
14. Brown and Tucker, *The Godfather of Soul*, 200.

## Chapter 5: Rainbow Politics, Woodstock, and Revolution Rock

Quotes from Al Schackman, Yoko Ono, Richie Havens, Eddie Kramer, and Charles R. Cross are taken from author interviews unless otherwise noted.

1. *The U.S. vs. John Lennon*, directed by David Leaf and John Scheinfeld (Santa Monica, CA: Lions Gate Films Home Entertainment, 2007), DVD.
2. Ibid.
3. Jon Weiner, *Come Together: John Lennon in His Time* (Urbana and Chicago: University of Illinois Press, 1984), 180.
4. Ibid., 181.
5. David Sheff, *All We Are Saying: The Last Major Interview with John Lennon and Yoko Ono* (New York: St. Martin's/Griffin, 2000), 212.
6. Charles R. Cross, *Roomful of Mirrors: A Biography of Jimi Hendrix* (New York: Hyperion, 2005) 273, 296.
7. Greg Tate, *Midnight Lightening: Jimi Hendrix and the Black Experience* (Chicago: Lawrence Hill Books, 2003).
8. Etta James and David Ritz, *Rage to Survive* (New York: Villard, 1995), 193, 177.

## Chapter 6: The Revolution Will Not Be Realized

Quotes from Ed Pearl, Len Chandler, Buffy Sainte-Marie, Elaine Brown, Van Dyke Parks, and Dave Alvin are taken from author interviews unless otherwise noted.

1. "The Black Athlete," *Say Brother*, WGBH broadcast, June 19, 1969, http://openvault.wgbh.org /saybrother/mla000938/index.html.
2. Gerald Gill, "Black Soldiers Perspectives on the War," *The Vietnam Reader*, ed. Walter Capps (New York: Routledge, 1991), 178.
3. "The Black Athlete," WGBH.
4. *Muhammad Ali Through the Eyes of the World*, directed by Phil Grabsky, TWI, 2001, televised movie.
5. *Small Talk at 125 and Lenox*, Gil Scott Heron, recorded in 1970, Flying Dutchman Records, 1995, compact disc.
6. Frankie Gaye and Fred Basten, *Marvin Gaye, My Brother* (San Francisco: Backbeat, 2003), 80.
7. Sule Greg Wilson, *The Drummer's Path: Moving the Spirit with Ritual and Traditional Drumming* (Rochester, VT: Destiny Books, 1992); Ken Gormly, *Archibald Cox: Conscience of a Nation* (New York: Da Capo, 1999), 213.
8. Suzanne E. Smith, *Dancing in the Street: Motown and the Cultural Politics of Detroit* (Cambridge: Harvard University Press, 2001), 230–232.
9. Richie Unterberger, "Interview with Swamp Dogg," September 1998, archived at Perfect Sound Forever, www.furious.com/perfect/swampdogg.html.

10. Rickey Vincent, *Funk: The Music, the People, and the Rhythm of the One* (New York: St. Martin's Griffin, 1996), 239.
11. Mark Rudd and Ishmael Reed, discussion at City Lights Bookstore, San Francisco, April 22, 2009, www.c-spanvideo.org/program/MarkR.
12. Bill Ayers, "Weather Underground Redux," blog post April 20, 2006, http://billayers.wordpress .com/2006/04/20/weather-underground-redux/.
13. *The U.S. vs. John Lennon*, directed by David Leaf and John Scheinfeld (Santa Monica, CA: Lions Gate Films Home Entertainment, 2007), DVD; To begin to fully understand the formation of the Black Panther Party, its duration, and its impact, along with the story of COINTELPRO and the other factors that conspired to dismantle the Party, it's suggested one consider the facts presented in the wealth of Black Panther–penned literary biographies and memoirs as well as the mass of published dissertations on the subject. Many of those titles are noted in the bibliography.
14. Notes on *Soldier Blue* from Buffy Sainte-Marie website, www.creative-native.com.
15. Colette Wood, "The Newsical Muse," *Hollywood Reporter*, July 20, 1970.
16. American International Pictures (AIP), specialized in sixties teen-exploitation (dragstrip, horror, and juvenile delinquent films); in the seventies they produced the blaxsploitation films *Foxy Brown* and *Blacula*. David Zeiger, *Sir, No Sir!*, 2005, www.sirnosir.com/FTA.html, DVD.
17. Most of what is published about John Lennon's FBI file was uncovered by Weiner in this book and its follow-up, *Gimme Some Truth* (Berkeley: University of California Press, 2000); Jon Weiner, *Come Together: John Lennon in His Time* (Urbana and Chicago: University of Illinois Press, 1984), 200–207.
18. Further reading on the Ash Grove fires can be found in the articles by Robert Hilburn, "Sand Runs Out on Ash Grove," *Los Angeles Times*, December 15, 1973, and Rebecca Kuzins, "The Last Coffeehouse," *Los Angeles Magazine*, February 1985.
19. Tejumola Olaniyan, *Arrest the Music! Fela and His Rebel Art and Politics* (Bloomington: Indiana University Press, 2004), 24.
20. *Fela Kuti: Music Is the Weapon*, directed by Stephane Tchalgadjieff and Jean-Jacques Flori, (Universal City, CA: Universal Imports, 1982), DVD.
21. Stokely Carmichael and Michael Ekwueme Thelwell, *Ready for the Revolution* (New York: Scribner, 2003), 654; Miriam Makeba with James Hall, *Makeba: My Story* (New York: Plume, 1989).
22. Marc Eliot, *Phil Ochs: Death of a Rebel* (New York: Omnibus, 1990), 205.
23. Ian McCann, *Bob Marley: In His Own Words* (London: Omnibus Press, 1993), 37, 79.
24. Ibid.

## Chapter 7: Move On Over

Quotes from Phranc, Buffy Sainte-Marie, Elaine Brown, Janis Ian, Yoko Ono, Steve Diggle, and Don Letts are taken from author interviews unless otherwise noted.

1. Germaine Greer's book *The Female Eunuch* (New York: Farrar, Straus and Giroux, 2002) and Kate Millett's *Sexual Politics* (Champaign: University of Illinois Press, 2000) were among the defining texts of the women's movement. Additionally, Carole Hanisch's essay "The Personal Is the Political," originally published in *Notes from the Second Year: Women's Liberation*, 1970, asserted as well as coined that phrase, which remains in popular usage.
2. David Carter, *Stonewall: The Riots That Sparked the Gay Revolution* (New York: Macmillian, 2005), 74–76, 155, 156, 174, 263–266.
3. Ibid.
4. Dave Van Ronk with Elijah Wald, *The Mayor of MacDougal Street* (New York: Da Capo, 2005).
5. Celestine Ware, interview with Odetta, May 27, 1971, WBAI Pacifica Radio Archive, www.pacific aradioarchives.org/pdf/transcripts/transcript.
6. Cris Williamson, panel discussion, 50th Anniversary of the Ash Grove, UCLA, April 2008.
7. Vicki Randle, panel discussion, 50th Anniversary of the Ash Grove, UCLA, April 2008.
8. Gil Scott-Heron and His Amnesia Express, *Tales of Gil*, London, March 14, 1990 (London: Sanctuary Visual Entertainment, 2002), DVD.
9. John Trudell, *No Nukes*, directed by Daniel Goldberg and Anthony Potenza (New York City: Warner Bros. Pictures, 1980), VHS.
10. Peter Shapiro, *Turn the Beat Around: The Secret History of Disco* (New York: Faber and Faber, 2005), 117.

11. Ibid., 30.
12. Nile Rodgers, "Happy Days Are Here Again," recorded 1929, EMI Robbins Catalog, http://empsfm.org.
13. Larry "Ratso" Sloman, *On the Road with Bob Dylan* (New York: Three Rivers Press, 1978), 27–35, 48–51.
14. Remarks by Hurricane Carter from concert recording, December 8, 1975, retrieved from Wolfgang's Vault, www.wolfgangsvault.com/the-rolling-thunder-revue/concerts/madison-square-garden-december-08-1975-set-1.html.
15. Leon Wildes, *The U.S. vs. John Lennon*, directed by David Leaf and John Scheinfeld (Santa Monica, CA: Lions Gate Films Home Entertainment, 2007), DVD.
16. Don Letts, *Culture Clash: Dread Meeets Punk Rockers* (London: SAF, 2007).

## Chapter 8: Everybody Say Hey! Ho! Let's Go

Quotes from Penelope Houston, Debora Iyall, Phranc, Michael Franti,and Yoko Ono are taken from author interviews unless otherwise noted.

1. J. Poet, "Dirk Dirksen Godfather of SF Punk Scene, 1937–2006," *SF Weekly*, December 6, 2006, www.sfweekly.com/2006-12-06/music/dirk-dirksen-151-godfather-of-s-f-punk-scene/ poet,j.
2. Kanye West, "A Concert for Hurricane Relief," NBC, MSNBC, CNBC simulcast, September 2, 2005.
3. Kathleen Hanna quotes from GritTV with Laura Flanders, webcast, February 17, 2010, http://lauraflanders.firedoglake.com/2010/02/17/kathleen-hanna-three-dimensional-role-model/.
4. Clark Collis, "M.I.A. 'Paper Planes,' and coasting to fame on 'Pineapple Express,'" *Entertainment Weekly*, August 26, 2008, www.popwatch.ew.com/2008/08/26/mia-interview.

## Chapter 9: Power to the Peaceful

Quotes from Michael Franti are taken from author interviews unless otherwise noted.

1. The Beatnigs, *The Beatnigs*, Alternative Tentacles Records, 1988, compact disc.
2. Chuck D Talks About Artists of the Civil Rights Movement, *Let Freedom Sing!: Music of the Civil Rights Movement* (Des Moines, IA: Time Life Entertainment, 2009), compact disc boxed set, www.youtube.com/watch?v=I0RvHNugBl0.
3. "Statistics," San Francisco AIDS Foundation, accessed November 9, 2010, www.sfaf.org/hiv-info/statistics.
4. Anthony DeCurtis, "Jackson Browne: Talking with the Great Pretender," *RollingStone.com*, April 17, 2007, audio interview, www.rollingstone.com/music/news/jackson-browne-talking-with-the-great-pretender-20070417.
5. "Chuck D on Music of the Civil Rights & Women in Hip Hop," *Let Freedom Sing!: Music of the Civil Rights Movement* (Des Moines, IA: Time Life Entertainment, 2009), compact disc boxed set, www.youtube.com/watch?v=kcPV5_iuLCo.
6. Michael Franti, "San Quentin: Episode Six," in a discussion on his YouTube channel FrantiV, www.youtube.com/watch?v=0fMUMp8lhwU&feature=user.
7. Zack de la Rocha, Rock the Bells concert, July 28, 2007, New York City; www.youtube.com/watch?v=mMuWTsEZRLo.
8. Office Memorandum to J. Edgar Hoover from Warren J. Berger, April 2, 1956, http://foia.fbi.gov/robeson/robes13.pdf.
9. *Trudell*, directed by Heather Rae (Metuchen, NJ: Passion River, 2005), DVD.

## Coda

1. *Trudell*, directed by Heather Rae (Metuchen, NJ: Passion River, 2005), DVD.
2. www.ornettecoleman.com.
3. LaShonda Katrice Barnett, *I Got Thunder: Black Women Songwriters on Their Craft* (New York: Thunder's Mouth Press, 2007).

# Bibliography

## Books

Abu-Jamal, Mumia. *We Want Freedom: A Life in the Black Panther Party*. Cambridge, MA: South End Press, 2004.

Barnett, LaShonda, ed. *I Got Thunder: Black Women Songwriters on Their Craft*. New York: Thunder's Mouth Press, 2007.

Botkin, B. A., ed. *A Treasury of American Folklore: The Stories, Legends, Tall Tales, Traditions, Ballads, and Songs of the American People*. New York: Crown, 1944.

Brown, Elaine. *A Taste of Power: A Black Woman's Story*. New York: Pantheon, 1992.

Brown, James. *I Feel Good: A Memoir of a Life of Soul*. New York: New American Library, 2005.

Burdon, Eric. *Don't Let Me Be Misunderstood*. With J. Marshall Craig. New York: Thunder's Mouth Press, 2001.

Carawan, Guy, and Candie Carawan, eds. *Freedom Is a Constant Struggle: Songs of the Freedom Movement*. New York: Oak Publications, 1968.

Carmichael, Stokely, and Charles V. Hamilton. *Black Power: The Politics of Liberation in America*. New York: Vintage, 1967.

Carmichael, Stokely, and Ekwueme Michael Thelwell. *Ready for the Revolution: The Life and Struggles of Stokely Carmichael (Kwame Ture)*. New York: Scribner, 2003.

Carter, David. *Stonewall: The Riot That Sparked the Gay Revolution*. New York: St. Martin's, 2004.

Carter, Rubin. *The 16th Round: From Number 1 Contender to Number 45472*. New York: Viking, 1973.

Chambers, Jack. *Milestones: The Music and Times of Miles Davis*. New York: Da Capo, 1998.

Cleaver, Eldridge. *Eldridge Cleaver: Post-Prison Writings and Speeches*. Edited by Robert Scheer. New York: Ramparts, 1969.

Cohodas, Nadine. *Princess Noire: The Tumultuous Reign of Nina Simone*. New York: Pantheon, 2010.

Cone, James H. *A Black Theology of Liberation*. Maryknoll, NY: Orbis, 1994.

Cone, James H. *The Spirituals and the Blues: An Interpretation*. Maryknoll, NY: Orbis, 2008.

Cross, Charles R. *Room Full of Mirrors: A Biography of Jimi Hendrix*. New York: Hyperion, 2005.

Douglas, Mike. *I'll Be Right Back: Memories of TV's Greatest Talk Show*. With Thomas Kelly and Michael Heaton. New York: Simon & Schuster, 2000.

Duberman, Martin B. *Stonewall*. New York: Plume, 1994.

Dylan, Bob. *Chronicles: Volume One*. New York: Simon & Schuster, 2004.

Dyson, Michael Eric. *April 4, 1968: Martin Luther King Jr.'s Death and How It Changed America*. New York: Basic Civitas, 2008.

Gamson, Joshua. *The Fabulous Sylvester: The Legend, the Music, the Seventies in San Francisco*. New York: Picador, 2006.

George, Nelson. *Post-Soul Nation: The Explosive, Contradictory, Triumphant, and Tragic 1980s as Experienced by African Americans (Previously Known as Blacks and Before That Negroes)*. New York: Viking, 2004.

George, Nelson. *Thriller: The Musical Life of Michael Jackson*. Cambridge, MA: Da Capo, 2010.

Gillespie, Dizzy. *To Be, or Not . . . to Bop*. With Al Fraser. New York: Doubleday, 1979.

Ginsberg, Allen. *First Blues: Rags, Ballads, and Harmonium Songs 1971–74*. New York: Full Court Press, 1975.

Gottheimer, Josh, ed. *Ripples of Hope: Great American Civil Rights Speeches*. New York: Basic Civitas Books, 2003.

Guralnick, Peter. *Dream Boogie: The Triumph of Sam Cooke*. New York: Little, Brown, 2005.

Guralnick, Peter. *Sweet Soul Music: Rhythm and Blues and the Southern Dream of Freedom*. New York: HarperCollins, 1986.

Havens, Richie. *They Can't Hide Us Anymore*. With Steve Davidowitz. New York: Spike, 1999.

Hilliard, David, and Lewis Cole. *This Side of Glory: The Autobiography of David Hilliard and the Story of the Black Panther Party*. New York: Little, Brown, 1993.

Hughes, Langston. *Selected Poems*. New York: Vintage, 1974.

James, Etta, and David Ritz. *Rage to Survive: The Etta James Story*. New York: Villard, 1995.

Jolly, Kenneth S. *Black Liberation in the Midwest: The Struggle in St. Louis, Missouri, 1964–1970*. New York: Routledge, 2006.

Jones, LeRoi. *Blues People: Negro Music in White America*. New York: Morrow Quill Paperbacks, 1963.

Kaliss, Jeff. *I Want to Take You Higher: The Life and Times of Sly and the Family Stone*. San Francisco: Backbeat Books, 2008.

Kelley, Robin D. G. *Thelonious Monk: The Life and Times of an American Original*. New York: Free Press, 2009.

Lester, Julius. *Revolutionary Notes*. New York: Baron, 1969.

Letts, Don. *Culture Clash: Dread Meeets Punk Rockers*. London: SAF, 2007.

Lipscomb, Mance. *I Say Me for a Parable: The Oral Autobiography of Mance Lipscomb, Texas Bluesman*. Told to and compiled by Glen Alyn. New York: Da Capo, 1994.

Lomax, Alan. *The Folk Songs of North America*. New York: Doubleday, 1960.

Lomax, John A., and Alan Lomax. *American Ballads and Folk Songs*. New York: Dover, 1994.

Mahal, Taj. *Taj Mahal: Autobiography of a Bluesman*. With Stephen Foehr. London: Sanctuary 2001.

Mailer, Norman. *Miami and the Siege of Chicago*. New York: Plume, 1986.

Makeba, Miriam. *Makeba: My Story*. With James Hall. New York: Plume, 1989.

Mayfield, Curtis. *Poetic License: In Poem and Song*. Beverly Hills: Dove Books, 1996.

McCann, Ian. *Bob Marley: In His Own Words*. London: Omnibus Press, 1993.

Montague, Magnificent. *Burn, Baby! Burn! The Autobiography of Magnificent Montague*. With Bob Baker. Urbana and Chicago: University of Illinois Press, 2003.

Olaniyan, Tejumola. *Arrest the Music! Fela and His Rebel Art and Politics*. Bloomington, IN: Indiana University Press, 2004.

Otis, Johnny. *Upside Your Head! Rhythm and Blues on Central Avenue*. Middletown, CT: Wesleyan University Press, 1993.

Reagon, Bernice Johnson. "Women as Culture Carriers in the Civil Rights Movement: Fannie Lou Hamer." In *Freedom Is a Constant Struggle*, edited by Susie Erenich. Black Belt Press, 1999.

Ritz, David. *Divided Soul: The Life of Marvin Gaye*. New York: MacGraw Hill, 1985.

Robinson, Tiny, and John Reynolds, eds. *Lead Belly: A Life in Pictures*. London: Steidl, 2008.

Salewicz, Chris. *Bob Marley: The Untold Story*. New York: Faber and Faber, 2010.

Sanders, Ed. *1968: A History in Verse*. Boston: Black Sparrow Press, 1997.

Scott-Heron, Gil. *So Far, So Good*. Chicago: Third World Press, 1967.

Shelton, Robert. *No Direction Home: The Life and Music of Bob Dylan*. New York: Da Capo, 1997.

Shepard, Sam. *The Rolling Thunder Logbook*. New York: Viking, 1977.

Simone, Nina. *I Put a Spell on You: The Autobiography of Nina Simone*. With Stephen Cleary. New York: Da Capo, 2003.

Sloman, Larry. *On the Road with Bob Dylan*. New York: Three Rivers Press, 1978.

Smith, Suzanne. *Dancing in the Street: Motown and the Cultural Politics of Detroit*. Cambridge, MA: Harvard University Press, 2001.

Spellman, A. B. *Black Music: Four Lives*. New York: Schocken Books, 1970.

Szwed, John F. *Space Is the Place: The Lives and Times of Sun Ra*. New York: Da Capo, 1998.

Tate, Greg. *Midnight Lightning: Jimi Hendrix and the Black Experience*. Chicago: Lawrence Hill Books, 2003.

Tenaille, Frank. *Music Is the Weapon of the Future: Fifty Years of African Popular Music*. Chicago: Lawrence Hill Books, 2002.

Tyson, Timothy B. *Radio Free Dixie: Robert F. Williams and the Roots of Black Power*. Chapel Hill, NC: University of North Carolina Press, 2001.

Unterberger, Richie. *Turn! Turn! Turn! The '60s Folk-Rock Revolution*. San Francisco: Backbeat Books, 2002.

Van DeBurg, William L. *New Day in Babylon: The Black Power Movement and American Culture, 1965–1975*. Chicago: University of Chicago Press, 1992.

Van Ronk, Dave. *The Mayor of MacDougal Street: A Memoir*. With Elijah Wald. New York: Da Capo, 2005.

Vincent, Rickey. *Funk: The Music, the People, and the Rhythm of the One*. New York: St. Martin's Griffin, 1996.

Wexler, Jerry, and David Ritz. *Rhythm and the Blues: A Life in American Music*. New York: Knopf, 1993.

Wiener, Jon. *Come Together: John Lennon in His Time*. Urbana and Chicago: University of Illinois Press, 1984.

## Articles and Reviews

Frantz, Douglas, and Brent Pulley. "Harlem Church Is Outpost of Empire: House of Prayer Built Wide Holdings on Devotion to Sweet Daddy Grace." *New York Times*. December 17, 1995.

Hilburn, Robert. "Sand Runs Out on Ash Grove." *Los Angeles Times*. December 15, 1973.

Kruth, John. "Sound Advice: Ornette Coleman Finds the Eternal in Theory." *Wax Poetics*. April/May 2007.

Kuzins, Rebecca. "The Last Coffeehouse." *Los Angeles*. February 1985.

Poet, J. "Dirk Dirksen Godfather of SF Punk Scene, 1937–2006." *SF Weekly*. December 6, 2006.

Provenzano, Frank. "The Beat Moves On: John Sinclair." *Detroit Free Press*. October 26, 2004.

Rosenbaum, Ron. "The Playboy Interview: Bob Dylan." *Playboy*. March 1978.

Rubin, Mike. "This Band Was Punk Before Punk Was Punk." *New York Times*. March 12, 2009.

Wenner, Jann S. "A Conversation with Barack Obama." *Rolling Stone* no. 1056/1057. July 10, 2008.

Wood, Colette. "The Newsical Muse." *Hollywood Reporter*. July 20, 1970.

## Liner Notes

Beatnigs. *The Beatnigs*. Alternative Tentacles, 1988.

Chandler, Len. *The Lovin' People*. Columbia Reocrds, 1967. Liner notes by Robert Shelton.

Chandler, Len. *To Be a Man*. Columbia Records, 1967. Liner notes by Gordon Freisen and Len Chandler.

Havens, Richie. *Mixed Bag*. Verve/Forecast, 1967.

Hendrix, Jimi. *West Coast Seattle Boy: The Jimi Hendrix Anthology*. Sony Legacy, 2010. Liner notes by John McDermott.

Mayfield, Curtis. *His Early Years with the Impressions*. ABC Records, 1973.

Rollins, Sonny. *Freedom Now*. Riverside, 1958.

Sainte-Marie, Buffy. *Little Wheel Spin and Spin*. Vanguard Records, 1966. Liner notes by Nat Hentoff.

Scott-Heron, Gil. *Small Talk at 125th and Lenox*. Flying Dutchman, 1970. Liner notes by Nat Hentoff and Gil Scott-Heron.

Simone, Nina. *To Be Free: The Nina Simone Story*. RCA/Legacy, 2008. Liner notes by David Nathan.

## Internet Resources

"After Words with Mark Rudd." City Lights Bookstore, April 22, 2009. *C-Span Video Library*. www.c-span video.org/program/MarkR.

"Ash Grove Legend: The Story." *Ash Grove: Roots, Rock, and Revolution*. www.ashgrovefilm.com.

Associated Press. "Stars offer heartfelt performances in benefit: Aaron Neville, Harry Connick, Faith Hill sing to raise funds for victims." *Today Entertainment.* www.msnbc.msn.com/id/9146525/.

Ayers, Bill. "Weather Underground Redux." *Bill Ayers* blog post. April 20, 2006. http://billayers.word press.com/2006/04/20/weather-underground-redux.

*Black Rock Coalition* website. www.blackrockcoalition.org.

Buffy Sainte-Marie website. www.creative-native.com.

Cox, Tony. "Havens Relives 'Freedom': Ad-Libbed Performance Set Tone for Woodstock Festival." *NPR Music.* August 11, 2004. www.npr.org/templates/story/story.php?storyId=3845549.

D, Chuck. "Mr. James Brown; May God Rest His Funky Soul." *Public Enemy* website, December 25, 2006. www.publicenemy.com.

Federal Bureau of Investigation. *FBI Records: Freedom of Information/Privacy Act.* www.fbi.gov/foia/foia.

Franti, Michael. FrantiV: San Quentin. www.youtube.com/watch?v=0fMUMp8lhwU&feature=user.

Gross, Jason. "MC5-Wayne Kramer Interview, Part 2." *Perfect Sound Forever.* www.furious.com/PERFECT /mc5/waynekramer2.html.

"Katheleen Hanna: Three-Dimensional Role Model." *GritTV with Laura Flanders.* February 17, 2010. http://lauraflanders.firedoglake.com/2010/02/17/kathleen-hanna-three-dimensional-role-model/.

"Policing Protest: The NYPD's Republican National Convention Documents." *New York Civil Liberties Union* website. www.nyclu.org/rncdocs.

"Prince." *Tavis Smiley.* April 27, 2009. www.pbs.org/kcet/tavissmiley/archive/200904/20090427 _prince.html.

"Rolling Thunder Revue Concert." Madison Square Garden, New York, December 8, 1975. *Wolfgang's Vault.* www.wolfgangsvault.com/the-rolling-thunder-revue/concerts/madison-square-garden-december -08-1975-set-1.html.

Schwartz, Steve. "Archie Shepp: The Original Fire Music." *NPR Music.* June 3, 2008. www.npr.org /templates/story/story.php?storyId=91086057.

Staff of the Store Front Education Centers. "Preliminary Report on the Distrubances in Buffalo June 26– July 1, 1967." *Buffalonian.* www.buffalonian.com/history/articles/1951-now/1967riots/index.html.

Thomson, Katherine. "Alicia Keys Backtracks on Gangsta Rap Conspiracy Claims." *Huffington Post.* April 15, 2008. www.huffingtonpost.com/2008/04/15/alicia-keys-backtracks-on_n_96867.html.

*The United House of Prayer for All People* website. www.tuhopfap.org/index2.html.

Ware, Celestine. "Interview—Odetta." *Pacifica Radio Archives Preservation and Access Project.* May 27, 1971. www.pacificaradioarchives.org/pdf/transcripts/transcript_odetta.pdf.

Weiner, Jonah. "Alicia Keys Unlocked." *Blender.com.* March 13, 2008. www.blender.com/guide/61246 /aliciakeysunlocked.html?p=1.

Weiner, Tim. "The Last Word." *New York Times.* December 3, 2008. www.nytimes.com/packages /html/arts/20081203_odetta.html?hp.

Wittstock, Laura Waterman, and Elaine J. Salinas. "A Brief History of the American Indian Move-ment." *American Indian Movement* website. www.aimovement.org/ggc/history.html.

*Wondaland Arts Society* blog. www.wondaland.blogspot.com.

## Films

*Black Panthers.* Directed by Agnès Varda. Vanguard Cinema, 1995.

*Buffy Sainte-Marie: A Multi-media Life.* Directed by Joan Prowse. Cinefocus, 2006.

*Fela Kuti: Music Is the Weapon.* Directed by Jean Jacques Flori and Stephane Tchalgadjieff. Universal Import, 1982.

*FTA.* Directed by Francine Parker. Docurama, 1972

*Jimi Hendrix: Live at Woodstock.* Directed by Michael Wadleigh and Chris Hegedus. Experience Hendrix, 1999.

*Jimi Hendrix Voodoo Child.* Directed by Bob Smeaton. BIO Channel, 2010.

*The Murder of Fred Hampton.* Directed by Mike Gray and Howard Alk. Facets, 1971.

*The Night James Brown Saved Boston.* Directed by David Leaf. Shout! Factory, 2008.

*Sir, No Sir!* Directed by David Zeiger. Displaced Films, 2006.

*Soul Power.* Directed by Jeffrey Levy-Hinte. Antidote Films, 2008.

*Soul to Soul.* Directed by Denis Sanders. Rhino/Wea, 1971.

*Trudell.* Directed by Heather Ray. Passion River, 2005.

*The US vs. John Lennon.* Directed by David Leaf and John Scheinfeld. Lionsgate, 2006.

*The Weather Underground.* Directed by Sam Green and Bill Siegel. New Video Group, 2002

# Index